Joseph Mayer in his Egyptian Museum, 1856, by John Harris, Reproduced by courtesy of the
Williamson Museum and Art Gallery, Birkenhead

Joseph Mayer of Liverpool, 1803–1886

Edited by Margaret Gibson and Susan M. Wright

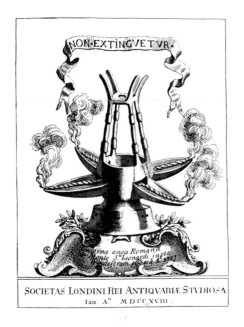

NON·EXTINGVETVR·

SOCIETAS LONDINI REI ANTIQVARIÆ STVDIOSA
Ian: A° MDCCXVIII.

Occasional Papers (New Series) XI

THE SOCIETY OF ANTIQUARIES OF LONDON
IN ASSOCIATION WITH
THE NATIONAL MUSEUMS AND GALLERIES ON MERSEYSIDE

Burlington House, Piccadilly, London W1V 0HS
1988

Distributed by Thames and Hudson Ltd.

British Library Cataloguing in Publication Data
Joseph Mayer of Liverpool, 1803–1886.—
  (Occasional papers. New series ; 12).
  1. Visual arts. Collecting. Mayer, Joseph,
1803–1886. Biographies
I. Gibson, Margaret Templeton   II. Wright,
Susan M.   III. Series
707′.5′0924

ISBN 0-85431-249-8
ISSN 0953-7163

Printed in Great Britain by
Henry Ling Ltd., at the Dorset Press, Dorchester, Dorset

Contents

IV   RENAISSANCE AND LATER

APPENDICES

Editorial Note

The Society is deeply grateful to the Trustees of the National Museums and Galleries on Merseyside, without whose generous financial assistance this book could not have been published so promptly, and to the Historic Society of Lancashire and Cheshire (of which Joseph Mayer was one of the founders) for a grant towards the publication of this volume.

May 1988   M.G.
                                                              S.M.W.

Illustrations

vii

viii

Preface

'He would look into Nature *for himself*, and consult and study her only.'
(*Early Exhibitions of Arts in Liverpool* (Liverpool, 1876), 98, italics mine.)

Joseph Mayer's judgement of Stubbs, here quoted, is as good a point of reference as I have been able to find for a man whose multifarious collections went far beyond his own modest scholarship. Rightly arranged and presented, the material itself will speak. He was at the other extreme from William Roscoe, who sat at home and wrote about Italy: Mayer had to see for himself. His family were burghers of Newcastle-under-Lyme — solid, provincial and remote from the world's debate. Although he spent most of his life in metropolitan Liverpool, travelled on the Continent and came to have good friends in London, he never quite lost the taste and sentiments of that pre-Victorian society. He withstood the religious and even to a great extent the medieval elements in high Victorian art. But he did in middle life begin to apprehend 'modern' archaeology. So he founded the Historic Society of Lancashire and Cheshire and bought the Faussett Collection. He enjoyed company. He revelled in 'outings' to historic sites, the long walk home and crumpets for tea.

The main purpose of the present volume is to review the Mayer Collection as it at present exists in Liverpool Museum, or as it can be reconstructed. With the exception of the small but quite important collection of Graeco-Roman sculpture, the major areas of strength all have their individual chapters. Much more could be said about the ceramics — not only the Wedgwood but the remarkable fund of Liverpool pottery from 'Herculaneum'. The smaller units are in some ways the most exciting for their very existence is scarcely known: the medieval enamels, the Burmese manuscripts that are neither roll nor codex, the splendid collection of Napoleonic memorabilia. We have tried to indicate the character and relative importance of these forgotten elements in the collection so that the specialist may decide whether or not to invest in a railway ticket. As to Mayer's stock-in-trade, in his shop in Lord Street — the silver, the jewellery, the clocks and watches — that must be the material of another enquiry.

We are immensely indebted to the curatorial staff in the Liverpool Museum, in their several departments: Lionel Burman and Pauline Rushton in Decorative Art, Edmund Southworth, Piotr Bienkowski and Fiona Paton in Antiquities, and David Flower and Jane A. Stafford in Photographic. For further photographic assistance we thank Rex Collins and Roger White. Sandra Mather and her colleagues in the Department of Geography, University of Liverpool, kindly drew figure 4. We have also received generous help from the Williamson Museum and Art Gallery, Birkenhead, the Public Library, Bebington, and both the Borough Museum and the Public Library, Newcastle-under-Lyme. Finally we should put on record the good will and exemplary patience of colleagues in the University of Liverpool, notably Peggy Rider, Suzanne Robinson and Pat Winker.

We are grateful to the following institutions for permission to reproduce material in their care: Bebington Public Library; the Master and Fellows of Corpus Christi College, Cambridge; Fitzwilliam Museum, Cambridge; J. Paul Getty Museum, Malibu; Liverpool City Record Office; Musée Cluny, Paris; National Museums and Galleries on Merseyside; Hofbibliothek, Aschaffenburg; Victoria and Albert Museum, London; Williamson Museum and Art Gallery, Birkenhead.

M.G.

Contributors

C. E. Bosworth, Department of Middle Eastern Studies, University of Manchester
Lionel Burman, Department of Decorative Art, Liverpool Museum
Irene Collins, Department of History, University of Liverpool
Richard Foster, F.S.A., Director, National Museums and Galleries on Merseyside
Margaret Gibson, F.S.A., Department of History, University of Liverpool
Sheila P. Girardon, Passmore Edwards Museum, London
Martin Henig, F.S.A., Institute of Archaeology, Oxford
Patricia Herbert, Oriental Collections, British Library
G. Lloyd-Morgan, F.S.A., Chester
A. R. Millard, F.S.A., Department of Oriental Studies, University of Liverpool
Nigel F. Palmer, Oriel College, Oxford
Fiona A. Paton, Department of Antiquities, Liverpool Museum
Michael Perkin, Special Collections, Sydney Jones Library, University of Liverpool
Pauline Rushton, Department of Decorative Art, Liverpool Museum
A. F. Shore, Department of Oriental Studies, University of Liverpool
E. C. Southworth, Department of Antiquities, Liverpool Museum
M. I. Waley, Oriental Collections, British Library
Roger H. White, Wroxeter
T. H. Wilson, Department of Medieval and Later Antiquities, British Museum
Eldon Worrall, Research Associate, Department of Antiquities, Liverpool Museum

Abbreviations

BL	British Library
BM	British Museum
DNB	*Dictionary of National Biography,* 21 vols. (London, 1885–)
Gatty, *Egyptian II*	C. T. Gatty, *Catalogue of the Mayer Collection,* i: *The Egyptian, Babylonian and Assyrian Antiquities,* 2nd edn. (London, 1879)
Gatty, *Mediaeval and Later*	C. T. Gatty, *Catalogue of Mediaeval and Later Antiquities contained in the Mayer Museum* (Liverpool, 1883)
Gore	*Gore's Directory for Liverpool and its Environs*
JBAA	*Journal of the British Archaeological Association*
JM	Joseph Mayer
JM, *Egyptian Museum*	*Catalogue of the Egyptian Museum, No. VIII Colquitt Street* (Liverpool, 1852)
Lugt	F. Lugt, *Répertoire des catalogues de ventes publiques intéressant l'art ou la curiosité 1600–1900,* 3 vols. (The Hague, 1938–64)
M	Mayer Collection, Liverpool Museum
Merseyside Painters	*Merseyside Painters, People and Places,* 2 vols. (text and plates) (Walker Art Gallery, Liverpool, 1978)
MPB	Mayer Papers, Bebington
MPL	Mayer Papers, Liverpool
MRT	*Medieval and Early Renaissance Treasures of the North West,* Exhibition Catalogue (Manchester, 1976)
Nicholson, *Prehistoric Metalwork*	S. M. Nicholson, *Catalogue of the Prehistoric Metalwork in the Merseyside County Museums,* Merseyside County Museums and the Department of Prehistoric Archaeology, University of Liverpool, Work Notes 2 (Liverpool, 1980)
Nicholson and Warhurst	S. M. Nicholson and M. Warhurst, *Joseph Mayer 1803–1886,* Merseyside County Museums Occasional Papers 2 (Liverpool, 1982)
NMGM	National Museums and Galleries on Merseyside
PSA	*Proceedings of the Society of Antiquaries of London*
Thieme and Becker	U. Thieme and F. Becker, *Allgemeines Lexikon der Bildenden Künstler von der Antike bis zur Gegenwart,* 37 vols. (Leipzig, 1907–50)

THSLC	*Transactions of the Historic Society of Lancashire and Cheshire*
VCH	The Victoria History of the Counties of England
WAG	Walker Art Gallery
WAG, *Foreign Catalogue*	Walker Art Gallery, Liverpool, *Foreign Catalogue*, 2 vols. (Liverpool, 1977) and suppl. (1984)

I. JOSEPH MAYER 1803–1886

Joseph Mayer

Margaret Gibson, F.S.A.

1803–22

Joseph Mayer was born on 23 February 1803 at Thistlebury House, Newcastle-under-Lyme (Staffs.).[1] The house itself is gone, but a local map of 1878 indicates that it stood in perhaps two acres of land on a ridge to the west of the borough, on the Chester (Keele) road. The few muddy photographs that survive show a three-storey house that could be Queen Anne, and a castellated Gothic summer-house surrounded by a moat.[2] The family itself had been in the district for generations: Mayer (Mare, Mair, Meyer, Meir, Mere, etc.) is a very common North Staffordshire name in the seventeenth and eighteenth centuries. Joseph's father, Samuel, was a tanner, having his business down by the river in what is now Queen Street and supplying straps, harness and leather goods to the potteries at Etruria, Longport and the 'six towns' as a whole.[3] He is said to have owned land in Newcastle,[4] and he was certainly a man of substance, being a hereditary burgess and eventually (1833) the first mayor to be elected by the burgesses as a whole rather than the inner cabal of office-holders. In retrospect at least, this was the vindication of a medieval grant that had been suspended in 1620, and a silver-mounted dressing-case marked Samuel's triumph.[5] On his mother's side Joseph Mayer was the grandson of John Pepper, the designer of several bridges on the Trent-Mersey canal and the builder (though not the architect) of major works at Trentham Park and Etruria.[6] He is remembered as the architect of the Theatre Royal, Newcastle-under-Lyme (1780), the local focus of good society; Josiah Wedgwood took shares in it, and Flaxman—doubtless at Wedgwood's request—provided the 3-ft. medallion of Shakespeare above the main entrance.[7] The family remained at much this social level well into the nineteenth century; never soaring into the creation or the acquisition of a country house, but always a significant force in the local oligarchy that ran the Potteries.

Joseph was the fifth surviving child and the third son. He was sent to the local grammar school, which, despite its later critics, may have been adequate enough for its day.[8] His drawings from the period, of buildings and canals, are plain and well observed, if wooden. He had no artistic genius, but he had an accurate eye.[9] At

1

the age of eight his collector's instinct was awakened by a small hoard of Roman coins and pottery turned up by the plough.[10] Four years later he had a brief taste of the great world as a drummer-boy in the 34th Regiment of Foot, which marched to Macclesfield (to release more seasoned men for France) in the weeks before Waterloo.[11] In 1819 he and five elder brothers and sisters were baptized by the vicar of St Giles, the parish church. Given that there is no record of Samuel Mayer's marriage (or baptism) in St Giles, it is possible that in Joseph's childhood the family had attended Nonconformist worship.[12]

A glance at the family tree (fig. 1) shows a well-ordered strategy of marriage and employment. Maria married well at home; Eliza settled in Liverpool, then the principal port for the Potteries via the Trent-Mersey canal; Samuel maintained the family business; Thomas took over the Dale Hall pottery at Longport.[13] It was for Joseph to move out. At the age of nineteen he came to Liverpool as an assistant to his sister Eliza's husband, James Wordley, a silversmith and jeweller.[14]

1822–48

How Mayer occupied himself for the next twelve years is a matter of pure inference and hypothesis. Liverpool in the 1820s was just balanced between the eighteenth-century port with no hinterland and the over-grown Victorian city. The picturesque charm of Lord Street—the main artery into town—could still be celebrated in water-colour. One such picture is indeed attributed to Mayer himself.[15] It is more than likely that Mayer belonged to, or associated with, the various clubs and societies for the promotion of the fine arts, which formed and reformed throughout nineteenth-century Liverpool. Half a century later he was to reprint several early catalogues as records of patronage and taste in Liverpool in the years 1774–87.[16] Again it is virtually certain that Mayer frequented the Royal Institution in Colquitt Street, the library, meeting rooms and art gallery established by William Roscoe in 1815.[17] Whereas the Liverpool clubs—the Athenaeum, the Lyceum and others—were gentlemen's clubs, with membership and predominantly daytime use, the Royal Institution was open to all, including those who had to work during the day. Through books and conversation Mayer could carry his education forward—up to a point. But he never ceased to feel the disadvantages of the autodidact, nor to try to make better and more systematic provision for others who might be in a similar position later on.[18] Relatively speaking, of course, Mayer was well-educated and socially secure; Roscoe, to whose vision the Royal Institution owed its being, had come from very much narrower circumstances.

By 1834 (the exact year is uncertain) Mayer was in partnership with his brother-in-law James Wordley at No. 62 Lord Street.[19] By 1837 (perhaps much sooner: the evidence is lacking either way) Mayer had set up house on his own, the Wordley children having grown to be teenagers. He lived for a year or so in Queen Street, Edge Hill, then moved to the not inconsiderable splendour of 20 Clarence Terrace, Everton Road.[20] That is the location of his first portrait (pl. I), done *c.* 1840.[21] Here is Mayer the connoisseur. He is seated in 'the Roscoe chair', contemplating a Wedgwood urn, carelessly fingering a learned pamphlet, the light falling on classical marbles, and on the table Greek and Etruscan antiquities. Etchings of the portrait were sent to his friends.[22] The portrait does show an enthusiast and a man of fashion, who may not quite have found his bearings as a collector. The Wedgwood

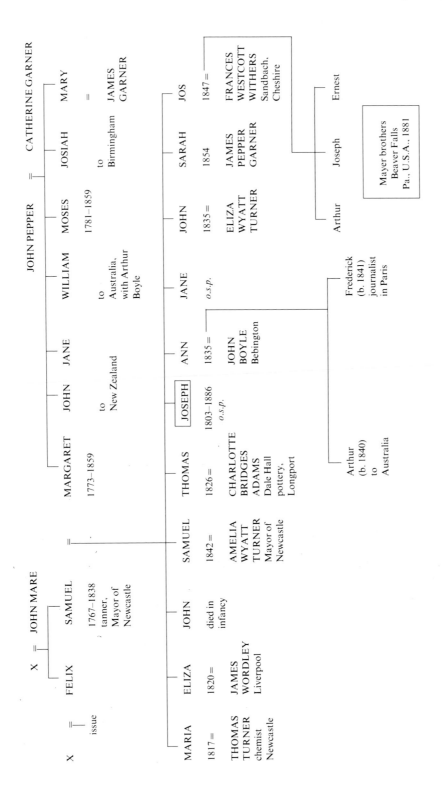

FIG. 1. Joseph Mayer's family

was a lifelong passion, the classical sculpture no doubt influenced by what was on display at the Royal Institution; there is strangely only a passing reference to Egypt. Had Mayer not yet acquired the Sams Collection, sold in 1839? Was there some forgotten third party, who bought from Sams and subsequently sold to Mayer? Certainly there is a random quality to the collection in the portrait of 1840 which has completely vanished in the definitive portrait of 1856 (frontispiece).

The few years in Clarence Terrace (1839–42) were the watershed in Mayer's life. He had a partnership, a spacious residence and on all the evidence sufficient funds. We should expect him to marry some suitable girl. The Mayers, the Peppers, the Turners and the rest all married within well-established families with whom they were fully acquainted; no doubt several anxious mothers were keeping Joseph Mayer in mind. He did stay in touch with Newcastle. In 1838 he offered to lend material to an exhibition at the Pottery Mechanics' Institute.[23] He slipped off with his youngest brother, Jos, to cockfights and bullbaiting.[24] He gave generous support to Isaac Cottrill, the local chief of police, in his provision of bread and circuses for the populace every spring. The christenings of the Princess Royal (1841) and of the Prince of Wales (1842), the marriage of the Duke of Sutherland's daughter at Trentham Park (1843), all these were the occasion of a sports day and dinner, with fireworks to conclude. Cottrill thoughtfully asked not only for a financial subvention but for actual fireworks, in the construction of which Mayer had such skill.[25] Cottrill's own status was enhanced by the gift of a cornelian seal for his official correspondence.[26]

But the lure of the Continent was strong. Mayer first went abroad as early as 1828, and he continued to travel regularly and extensively across Europe for the next thirty years.[27] In 1841 he and William Clements, the engraver, took a river steamer from Chalon right down the Saône and the Rhône to Arles, and presumably on to Marseilles. There had been disastrous flooding in the spring, and Clements paints a vivid picture of the devastation as far south as Vienne with its broken bridges and an entire silk factory reduced to ruins.[28] Mayer travelled on business, to observe trends and to buy stock;[29] but he was at the same time captivated by the art of the Middle Ages. It was when he was convalescing from fever at Dijon, and so had time to spend in the museum and picture gallery, that he had become (so he later maintained) himself a collector of antiquities.[30] A sharper anecdotal reminiscence by a friend is of Mayer at large in any foreign city: he knew every backstreet dealer and how to strike a bargain with him.[31] In the years at Clarence Terrace the choice still lay between the life of travel, acquiring *objets d'art* for the shop and antiquities for his own collection, and the responsibilities of a household. By 1843 the decision was made. Mayer gave up Clarence Terrace.

He was then still in partnership with James Wordley, now at No. 56 Lord Street. By 1844 he had set up on his own, at No. 68 (later Nos. 68–70), only a few doors further into town.[32] From then on he lived 'over the shop', having for the next decade no other residence. Many years later he said that he had wanted to be a manufacturing jeweller, designing and making his own work, whereas Wordley was content to act exclusively as a middleman.[33] Thus Mayer had practising metal-workers in his employ, Wordley merely shop assistants and clerks. Mayer's earliest trade card[34] makes the distinction plain:

JOSEPH MAYER

GOLDSMITH JEWELLER SILVERSMITH

DEALER IN PRECIOUS STONES CAMEOS INTAGLIOS

SHEFFIELD PLATE

PATENT LEVER WATCHES TIME PIECES

DESIGNER AND HERALDIC ENGRAVER

68 LORD STREET

LIVERPOOL

As soon as he had his own premises, Mayer invoked the great tradition of Renaissance goldsmiths. Benevenuto Cellini and George Heriot (pl. II) were being done in fresco on either side of the entrance even as the workmen finished the more mundane fittings and showcases. Here the subject matter and the artist—R. W. Buss—were familiar,[35] but the medium was new: the decor rated an approving page in the *Art Journal* of the following spring.[36] Two massive busts, male and female, were later set above the façade: these are known from a water-colour of 1855.[37] It is clear that Mayer wanted to 'create a mood' in the prospective customer. Here was Art in the context of History.

Mayer had a professional interest in antique jewellery: both in itself, to sell or retain for his own collection, and as a source of ideas for design. Even the dozen or so pieces now surviving show the development of types: one seventeenth-century love-token conveys little, but two together are a strong, if crude, reminder of the poems of John Donne.[38] How far Mayer's professional success depended on the sale of objects either antique in themselves or renewing a traditional design is another question. He did not deal primarily in antiques and it may be that in manufacturing he was not primarily a jeweller. What kept Mayer in the public eye was rather his facility in what may be called neo-Flaxman gold and silver plate. The design for his own bookplate (pl. IIIa) shows the ease with which he elaborated a theme that he had known from his youth upwards. It is presumably based on a Wedgwood design which is itself derived from a Greek pot.[39] He retailed the same formula in commemorative plate and private testimonials. The silver trowel with which Sir Philip de Malpas Grey Egerton, Baronet, M.P., laid the foundation stone of Birkenhead Docks was designed and made by Mayer (pl. IIIb); very similar figures appear on the gold snuff-box that was presented to the chaplain of the School for the Indigent Blind in 1851.[40] The same repertoire, on a grander scale, may be seen in the presentation silver that Mayer displayed at the Great Exhibition: the prize plate of the Royal Mersey Yacht Club showing Cleopatra sailing down the Cydnus, Queen Elizabeth on the Thames (visiting Sir Walter Raleigh) and Queen Victoria at Cowes; three Liver birds preside, and a Victory surmounts the whole.[41] By establishing himself as a supplier of yachting trophies and civic plate Mayer no doubt attracted further custom from a sector of Liverpool that was rapidly increasing in wealth and in social confidence.

Mayer's first years of independence coincided with the development of electroplate on a commercial basis.[42] Seeing its enormous potential—affordable silver for all—Mayer supported Thomas Spencer in his contributory experiments in electrotype;[43] but he was not himself the principal vendor of electroplate in Liverpool, initially at least. By 1848, however, he is writing the classic exploratory letter to Elkington's of Birmingham: 'thank you for the candelabra, I place an order for a tea service, I note the more favourable discount accorded to Messrs Hausburg [also of Liverpool], I shall be in your city in a few weeks' time . . .'.[44] By the mid-1850s Mayer was deeply committed to the new medium, and was even to be recognized as one of those who had promoted its development.[45]

It has seemed to twentieth-century observers that the man who amassed so great a collection as is reviewed in the present volume must have commanded enormous wealth. It was not inherited. Can it merely have been the discretionary income from a jeweller's shop, in however prosperous an era? Was Mayer perhaps fortunate in speculation? Did he deal in diamonds? No ledgers survive nor personal account books. Nevertheless I am inclined to think that Mayer's principal resource was indeed his shop, and that the income so generated would have been sufficient to support his lifestyle and finance his acquisitions as a collector. Mayer lived simply. Except for the years at Queen Street and Clarence Terrace (1837–42) he lived at the shop, Wordley's or his own, until he was fifty-four years of age (1857). He travelled abroad, which was cheaper than staying at home. As to the collection, some areas were more expensive than others: Romano-British and medieval antiquities came relatively cheap, classical sculpture was expensive, the Wedgwood Mayer—with his excellent local contacts—may well have acquired for a song. If we consider on the one hand what Mayer did not buy (these are some classical marbles and bronzes, but not many) and on the other that he was in the market in the two decades before the great price-rise of the 1850s,[46] it is easier to square his achievement with his income. In local terms he is the complete antithesis of Lord Leverhulme, who bought at the top of the market, pouring out infinite resources on what was fashionable.[47] Mayer collected what interested him, sometimes at no more cost than a civil word.

1848–51

On Christmas Eve 1848 the Revd Abraham Hume, Mr Henry Pigeon and Mr Joseph Mayer met at No. 68 Lord Street to finalize plans for the establishment of the Historic Society of Lancashire and Cheshire. It comes as no surprise that Mayer provided a seal for the Society[48] and a few years later a silver-mounted horn to commemorate this preparatory meeting.[49] Hume was the scholar in the enterprise. His study of the Roman and medieval metalwork and leather found in the sands of the Dee is still—with all the developments of scientific archaeology since—lucid, systematic and enlightening. He based his study on some 3,000 artefacts, about a third of which belonged to Mayer. Mr Mayer had been in the habit of walking out across the Wirral on a Sunday afternoon and falling into conversation with the inhabitants of Meols.[50] So the Society had a constituency, and a vivid sense of what might be learned from archaeology, particularly in Cheshire. Mayer's discovery of the archaeological side of history probably dates from the late 1840s when the potential of the Dee estuary was matched by that of the new railway cuttings; Mayer saved some notable Roman material when the LMS took the line up to Lancaster in 1850.[51] Rescue archaeology had come to the north-west.

Such issues were far more acute in London. The battle with the developers was in those days waged in person. Charles Roach Smith—and he was one of the few with both the knowledge and the commitment—would stand on the edge of an excavation bargaining with the navvies for objects that would today fetch thousands in a sale-room. There was no question of measuring the site, only of saving the major artefacts.[52] Then as now informed publicity was a good weapon. Roach Smith had been a Fellow of the Society of Antiquaries since 1836; and from 1843 he nursed the British Archaeological Association, planning and leading memorable expeditions to Canterbury (1844), Winchester (1845), Gloucester (1846), Warwick (1847), Worcester (1848) and in 1849 Chester.[53] These were affairs of three days and more, packed with visits, receptions, lectures, exhibitions and soirées. The railways made all things possible. For the Chester conference Roach Smith had the assistance of the newly-formed Historic Society of Lancashire and Cheshire. It is good to know that Mayer arranged a civic reception for over 1,500 people in the Town Hall at six days' notice. Nobody batted an eyelid—it was even easier than picking up the telephone.[54] The conference materially furthered Mayer's acquaintance with Roach Smith, which grew into a lasting friendship that was still vivid in the final years of Mayer's life. Roach Smith showed Mayer something of the light that archaeology could shed on ancient society, what use to make of the discoveries at Lancaster and Meols. Mayer wrote in 1882:

> I have sent by rail a small box containing a silver wine goblet and beg your acceptance of it in remembrance of the many years of pleasure your correspondence has given me, and the valuable education in allowing me to read the correspondence you carried on with other, Brother antiquaries from all parts of Europe, on all kinds of antiquarian subjects which gave an impetus to the study as corroborative help to written history.[55]

Within a few months of the Chester conference Mayer was finding his way among the antiquarians and collectors in London. On 10 January 1850 Mayer was elected a Fellow of the Society of Antiquaries.[56] This was the one title he never dropped—even in the bizarre form of 'Captain Joseph Mayer FSA' of the Cheshire Volunteers (1867).[57] Mayer soon joined the British Archaeological Association (1850), and over the next decade or so he accumulated memberships of an extraordinary range of learned societies across Europe: Abbeville, Copenhagen, Mainz, Zurich, etc., etc.[58] It was a new dimension to his familiar expeditions to the Continent. It was through the Antiquaries that Mayer came to know A. W. Franks, then establishing himself at the British Museum,[59] and the Anglo-Saxonist Thomas Wright.[60] It casts an odd light on the state of knowledge in 1850 that Mayer could contribute to Franks's 'Exhibition of Ancient and Mediaeval Art' at the Society of Arts a cameo brooch after Dürer, in which neither the stone nor the gold setting can possibly be early sixteenth-century.[61] For the Great Exhibition of 1851 Mayer was invited to exhibit 'works of ancient and medieval art';[62] but he in fact submitted specimens of his own work as a jeweller and silversmith. The cameo brooch was again exhibited, as 'Durer's portrait of his wife'. But the jury passed over everything, with the exception of two other items of jewellery (both lost) which received 'honourable mention'.[63]

In 1851 Mayer was in his prime. His business was prospering, and he could at last see his vocation as a collector and—though not himself deeply learned—the friend of scholars and the promoter of scholarship. This moment in his life is caught in Freizor's portrait (pl. IIIc).[64]

1852–67: the Egyptian Museum

Mayer was captivated by the wealth of the British Museum, and in particular the recently-opened (1846) Egyptian gallery,[65] which made a remote civilization freely and permanently available to all. Exhibitions passed, but museums remained. In May 1852, following a well-established local precedent,[66] Mayer opened his own 'Egyptian Museum' at No. VIII Colquitt Street, a few doors along from the Royal Institution. His purpose, as he explained in a prefatory note to the catalogue, was to give those of his fellow-citizens who were unable to get to London for themselves some idea of the glories of the past as these were displayed in the British Museum. Regretfully he had to charge for admission: one shilling for adults, sixpence for children.[67] This income would no doubt support the curator, who lived on the top floor: from 1857 this was probably Richard Harrison and from 1860 certainly Joseph Forrest.[68]

It is at this moment, and never again, that we have a clear view of Mayer's collection. He published drawings of the two principal rooms: the Mummy Room (pl. IV) and the Jewellery Room (pl. V). The contents there shown more or less correlate with the printed catalogue of 1852. Attention may be drawn to the colossal seated statue seen in profile at the left of the Jewellery Room and again, from below, in the Harris portrait of 1856 (frontispiece). Mayer continued to buy Egyptian material in the London sale-rooms: the Stobart Collection (1852), Valentia (1852) and Stürmer (1857).[69] But his museum displayed much else. The beach-combings from Meols were there, with further Roman and Anglo-Saxon material; and the library contained not only reference-books but western and oriental manuscripts. Another room was devoted to the history of pottery as such, and in particular Staffordshire ware including Wedgwood and the local Liverpool ware from Herculaneum (*c.* 1820). On the stairs were illustrations of the stages of engraving, a cartoon from the Divine Comedy and an oil-painting of the Flood (fig. 2).[70]

The Egyptian Museum then was not ruthlessly and consistently Egyptian. Indeed by 1862 the name had changed to 'Museum of Antiquities' and by 1867, grandly, to 'Museum of National and Foreign Antiquities'.[71] It provided for the proper display of Mayer's extensive and valuable Egyptian acquisitions, from the Sams Collection (1839) onwards. The Roman and Anglo-Saxon material correlated with the work of Roach Smith. The arms and armour section reflects an enthusiasm that got full rein in 1860 when Mayer became captain of the newly-formed Liverpool Volunteer Borough Guard. But the most revealing is the pottery, which was the history of a medium in which Mayer had a practical expertise that went beyond the working knowledge of Roach Smith or Franks. He was interested in experiments and techniques as much as in the shape of a pot or the subject-matter of a commemorative medallion. This concern with technique may explain the further reaches of his manuscript collection: the codex, the roll, the ivory or palm leaf manuscripts of Burma, the range of fine leather bindings on the Arabic and Persian manuscripts, the calligraphic annotation of equally calligraphic printing in the one Chinese book that has survived. The library in the Egyptian Museum, being perhaps not open to the public, is described only in general terms:

[It] contains the principal works which have been written on Egyptian History and Antiquities, among which is the Imperial Elephant edition of the result of

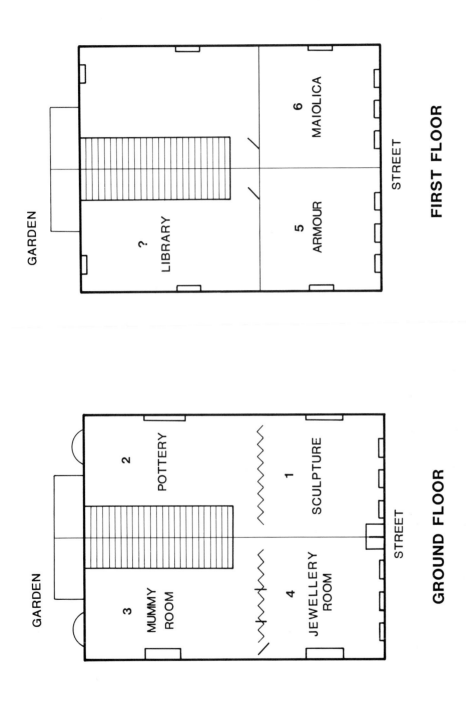

Fig. 2. The Egyptian Museum, No. VIII Colquitt Street, Liverpool

the expedition of the Savans sent out by Napoleon. Others are by Young, Champollion, Salt, Belzoni, Bonomi, Wilkinson, Rawlinson, Bunsen, etc. There are also works on antient Etruria, Pompeii, Herculaneum, together with many manuscripts in Hebrew, Sanscrit, Persian, Irish, etc. [72]

Thus it is not known specifically which manuscripts were in the collection by 1852: only that Mayer had already acquired examples of several different types of book in perhaps a dozen different languages. He could read none of them himself. The books are not textually significant: they are there as examples of 'the book in history and across the known world'. His most spectacular coup here was to go unrecognized: the deer-skin Mayan codex which had been acquired incidentally with the Fejérváry Collection in 1855.

By contrast Mayer has no place in the history of numismatics. He had some coins—as who has not?—but the tradition that the French government purchased his collection of Greek coins in 1844 is without foundation. [73] What he did collect were commemorative medals, particularly relating to Bonaparte; and these in turn may prove to have a direct bearing on the medals that he himself designed and struck.

The Egyptian Museum was impressive enough when it opened. Over the next few years it was augmented by three further collections—Faussett, Fejérváry and Rolfe—and briefly by a fourth, that of the London collector Bram Hertz. These are major, specialized collections which were acquired by private treaty, generally with the help of Mayer's acquaintance in London. Both Faussett and Fejérváry were the subject of controversy in the press: material of such outstanding importance ought to have been acquired for the nation. [74] The Trustees of the British Museum pleaded lack of funds, and Mayer consistently maintained that his objective was to prevent a coherent collection from being dispersed. Plainly in the case of Faussett this was a very strong argument indeed.

Faussett

The earliest expedition made by the British Archaeological Association had been to Canterbury in 1844. [75] Roach Smith had then taken the opportunity of organizing an excursion to Heppington to view the family collection of Mr Bryan Faussett. It was that initiative which brought the collection into public view and led to its ultimate purchase by Mayer. He brought it to Liverpool in 1854, in time for the visit of the British Association in September. The collection was put on view within the context of this learned scientific conference. Thomas Wright gave an expository lecture in the Philharmonic Hall, after which Mayer was presented with an Address in recognition of his services to scholarship (pl. XXXIII). [76] It is noteworthy that Mayer did not give the lecture himself; he invited a professional Anglo-Saxonist. The collection then went on display in the Egyptian Museum, [77] and Faussett's excavation notes were fully published at Mayer's expense—by Charles Roach Smith.

Fejérváry

The Fejérváry Collection as a whole descended by inheritance (1851) to Franz Pulszky, a Hungarian political exile living in London; it was dispersed only on Pulszky's departure from England in 1868. [78] But Pulszky, himself a passionate collector, was in need of funds. He first put the collection on display at the Archaeological Institute (1853), giving a series of expository lectures at seven guineas for a reserved seat throughout;[79] later he sold the maiolica to a French dealer who resold it in Paris.[80] The classical and medieval ivories, quite an extensive collection of Hungarian prehistoric metalwork and some Mexican items (pottery and the Codex Fejérváry-Mayer) were acquired by Mayer in 1855.[81] Recognizing the exceptional importance of the ivories Mayer commissioned a catalogue from Pulszky himself, which appeared in 1856.[82] It owes a good deal to the exhibition catalogue (1853) already prepared for the Archaeological Institute by another exile, Dr Emil Henszlmann. The Fejérváry items too went on display at No. VIII Colquitt Street.[83]

The Egyptian Museum is commemorated in a full-dress portrait—9 × 5 ft.—done by John Harris in 1856.[84] It is the frontispiece of the present volume. Mayer stands in the Mummy Room of the Museum itself, dwarfed by a colossal cast of one of the statues from Abu Simbel (top, right), and displaying on the table beside him the Asclepius–Hygieia diptych from the Fejérváry Collection, resting on a thirteenth-century German psalter in its medieval binding,[85] and the publication on the Faussett Collection, which stands open at the Kingston brooch. He makes a gesture of welcome as if to say, 'Come in!'

Hertz

It is in the light of the Harris portrait that we can understand Mayer's most ambitious, indeed grandiose, purchase: the Bram Hertz Collection of classical sculpture and engraved gems and cameos. Hertz's contribution to Franks's Exhibition of 1850 indicates the range and quality of the cameos; his own catalogue of the following year contains over 1,700 classical gems.[86] This kind of material was immeasurably more expensive than Anglo-Saxon antiquities or even the Fejérváry ivories. Mayer could afford it only as one of a consortium of Liverpool business men, who planned (it is said) 'to present the complete cabinet to their native city';[87] no doubt it was to be displayed in the Egyptian Museum. £12,000 was paid over, and the collection secured (1856); but by the spring of the following year part of the collection was back on the market. It was a relatively unimportant portion, that may indicate no more than rationalization. In February 1859, however, there was a two-week sale at Sotheby's of some 3,000 items, which fetched a total of £10,011. 2s. 6d. They were described as 'the collection formed by B. Hertz, now the property of Joseph Mayer Esq. F.S.A.'.[88] If the original figure of £12,000 is correct, Mayer may have balanced the books: the 1857 sale (for which we have no figure) could have made as much as £2,000. The remarkable thing is that he sold at all—classical bronzes and gems were precisely what was missing from a comprehensive display in the Egyptian Museum. The plainest inference is that the other members of the consortium had failed to pay their share.

1857–60: Rock Ferry

The late 1850s were a time of change, rather as the years in Clarence Terrace had been. Mayer took a house at Rock Ferry, the currently fashionable escarpment opposite Liverpool, on the Cheshire side of the Mersey.[89] We know nothing of Mayer's life there, and the house itself, Dacre Park, has long vanished. In September 1857 his mother was ill;[90] when she died two years later, Thistlebury House passed to the eldest son, Samuel, and in 1864 to Samuel's family.[91] That is not to say that Joseph received nothing from his mother's estate: Dacre Park may have been a temporary solution, pending his family inheritance.

Rolfe

The fourth and last major collection that Mayer acquired was that of W. H. Rolfe of Sandwich (1857).[92] These were local Anglo-Saxon antiquities assembled over a lifetime by a dedicated and solitary antiquarian of very modest means. Once more Mayer had the help of Roach Smith. He writes—rather heavy-handedly, it must be admitted—to Rolfe himself to open negotiations:

> No doubt Mr Smith told you my object in purchasing the collection of Anglo-Saxon and e. antiquities was that they may not be dispersed and as I intend to publish an account of all that we can find relating to the Saxons in England where of course as has been done in the Fassett volume your name would be for ever attached to your collection as the former owner of it. I shall soon be at liberty and then Mr Smith and I propose if you are at home to come down and I have no doubt we shall agree amicably about the price and I shall tell you what I intend to do to preserve them—for my own part I cannot bear the idea of breaking up and scattering a collection that must have been a source of pleasure to you to collect.[93]

In this case Mayer successfully made the purchase, but no volume followed. Certainly a simple register of the Rolfe Collection would have been of far more scientific use than 'all that we can find relating to the Saxons in England'.[94] This enterprise, like the yet more grandiose 'History of the Arts in England' to which Mayer was to devote his retirement, never came to fruition.

To sum up, the autumn of 1857 saw the high water mark of the Mayer Collection. Faussett, Fejérváry and Rolfe had all been secured, though Hertz was still in the balance. It is just at this moment, while a major part of the Hertz Collection is still in his hands, that Mayer appears as a major contributor to the Manchester Exhibition of 1857. He sent a number of the Fejérváry ivories, Anglo-Saxon antiquities (Faussett), medieval enamels and the collection of gems newly acquired from Bram Hertz.[95] But the strength and basis of Mayer's collection remained the Egyptian material: Sams, Stobart, Valentia (1854) and Stürmer. Critics will be swift to point out that its weakness was the Simonides papyri. At the same time all these high-profile acquisitions should be seen in the context of an uncounted multitude of lesser purchases, here and there in London and on the Continent, that Mayer made for the shop and for his own entertainment. For 'Joseph Mayer, dealer in Sheffield and electroplate . . . importer of Italian sculpture, alabaster, cameos . . . French clocks, bronzes and Bohemian glass'[96] there was no absolute distinction between the two.

1860–86: Bebington

Bebington lies a mile or so south of Rock Ferry. Mayer moved there in 1860, and in a short time established himself in a substantial brick-built dwelling called Pennant House. This was a home for his unmarried sister Jane (the genealogist of the family) and their niece Mary Wordley.[97] They were a few minutes' walk from another sister, Ann Boyle, of 'The Firs', Bebington, whose sons Frederick and Henry were on close terms with Mayer himself.[98] Thus ensconced Mayer entertained thoughts of marriage: a congratulatory note from an astonished but enthusiastic Joseph Clarke is dated August 1863.[99] But Joseph or the lady (in Kent) had second thoughts.

PLATE I

Joseph Mayer in Clarence Terrace, *c*. 1840, by William Daniels. Liverpool Museum (WAG 7355),
reproduced by courtesy of NMGM

PLATE II

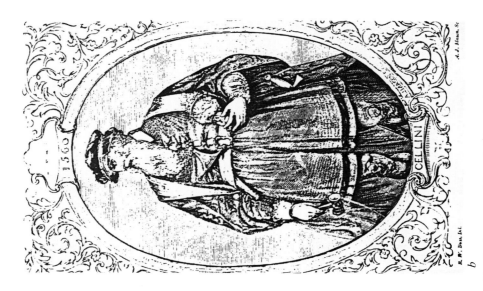

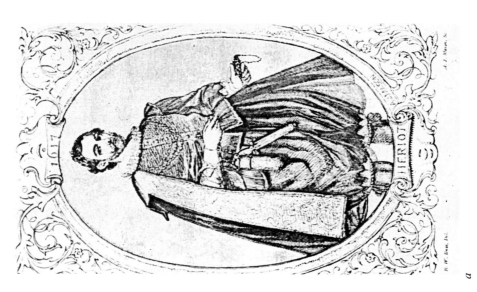

Frescoes of (*a*) George Heriot and (*b*) Benevenuto Cellini in the doorway of Joseph Mayer's shop, 1843, by R. W. Buss. MPL (original destroyed), reproduced by courtesy of Liverpool City Record Office

Photographs: Margaret Gibson

PLATE III

a. Joseph Mayer's bookplate.
In M 12080, on deposit in the
Sydney Jones Library, University
of Liverpool, reproduced by courtesy of NMGM

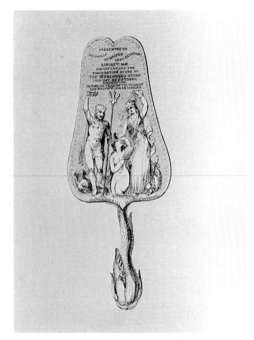

Photograph: Margaret Gibson

b. Ceremonial trowel, 1844. Drawing by JM, MPL, reproduced by
courtesy of Liverpool City Record
Office

c. Joseph Mayer in 1851, by G. Freizor. MPB,
reproduced by courtesy of Bebington Library

PLATE IV

Photograph: Roger White

Mummy Room in the Egyptian Museum, 1852, by Henry Summers. MPL, reproduced by courtesy of Liverpool City Record Office

PLATE V

Photograph: Roger White

Jewellery Room in the Egyptian Museum, 1852, by Henry Summers. MPL, reproduced by courtesy of Liverpool City Record Office

PLATE VI

JOSEPH MAYER,

68 & 70, LORD STREET, LIVERPOOL,

MODELLER, CHASER, ENGRAVER,

Gold and Silver Smith,

WHOLESALE AND RETAIL

Dealer in Precious Stones, Cameos, Intaglios, Sheffield Plate, Silver and Plated Cutlery, Gold and Silver Watches.

ELECTRO-PLATING

In all its various branches, comprising Tea and Coffee Sets, Breakfast and Dinner Services, Epergnes, Candelabra, Ice pails, Waiters, Baskets, Souffler Dishes, Spoons, Forks, Fish and Table Knives, and all other useful or Ornamental Articles to match Silver Services.

Watch and Clock Maker,

Timepieces in Gilt, Marble, Bronze, Alabaster, and Wood of various designs, suitable for the Drawing-room, Library, or Dining-room.

BRONZES

In Groups and Single Figures, being copies by the Glyptic Lathe, from the most celebrated Antiques, in the Townley, Florence, Vatican, Louvre, and other Galleries; also, some of the best modern productions, after Flaxman, Gibson, Bailey, Westmacot, Canova, and Thorwaldson.

SCULPTURED ALABASTER.

Groups and Figures executed solely for and under J. M.'s own direction.

Medallist, Heraldic Emblazoner, and Engraver of Seals, Gems, Dies, Consular Stamps, and Insignia of Public Companies,

Authenticated by Official Documents from the Herald's College.

ASSAYER OF GOLD AND SILVER ORES.

In consequence of there being no Hall in Liverpool for the Assaying of Precious Metals, J. M. has made arrangements with one of the first Assayers for the Goldsmiths' Hall, in London, and Assays, Values, and Purchases Gold Dust, Silver Ores, Diamonds, Pearls, Rubies, Emeralds, Topaz and other Gems.

From the great alterations in Form and Style of Silver Goods and Jewellery at the present time, J. M. takes in exchange all sorts of Old Fashioned Articles; and also has a great variety of all descriptions of Second-hand Silver Spoons, Forks, Cups, Urns, and other Goods.

The many applications for the loan of Silver for large parties, has induced J. M. to keep an entire service of Dishes, Covers, Tureens, Epergnes, Candelabra, Wine Coolers, Tea Urns, Coffee and Tea Sets, Waiters, Spoons, Forks, and Ladles, for hire, which he can supply in any quantity, at a short notice.

Joseph Mayer's trade advertisement, 1857. Gore's Directory, reproduced by courtesy of Liverpool City Record Office

PLATE VII

a. Fellow-tradesmen's address: detail showing Joseph Mayer's shop, 1873

b. Fellow-tradesmen's address: second page, showing Pennant House, *Victoria regia* lilies and items from the collection

MPL, reproduced by courtesy of Liverpool City Record Office

Photographs: Margaret Gibson

Pennant House contained what was virtually a second Mayer Collection, quite separate from the Egyptian Museum: some 20,000 prints and drawings, with autograph letters of English artists, which Mayer had gathered for his *magnum opus* on the history of the arts in the British Isles; the autographs, facsimile autographs and mementos of famous persons; documents relating to English history; some 200 engraved gems and rings;[100] and above all his papers and specimens relating to the history of pottery.[101] Mayer was here on home ground. His study of the Herculaneum ware from Liverpool is still definitive; it is suggested elsewhere in this volume that the early Chinese pottery caught Mayer's attention primarily for its technique—it solves some of the same problems of appliquéd ornament as recurred in the eighteenth century. The village of Bebington itself was transformed by Mayer's residence. He established a lending-library of 20,000 volumes (1866 and 1872),[102] public gardens (1871), a bowling-green and, finally, his Art Gallery (1878). On his death the contents of Pennant House were on his own instructions sold lock, stock and barrel to maintain these several foundations.[103] Thus the second Mayer Collection, which was in Pennant House in 1886, is scattered beyond recall: objects, documents, letters, ledgers. It stands to reason that some of this material related to the contents of the Egyptian Museum.

The Egyptian Museum itself passed to the town of Liverpool in 1867. Mayer proposed the gift in his usual halting style:

My proposal is that the Mayor and Town Council be the Conservators for the Public, that the Collection shall be kept together and be known as and called 'The Mayer Collection', but I have no doubt that all little detail would be easily managed.

I think I need hardly say that in my collecting I always had in view to make the Collection as much illustrative of the Arts of the different nations as I could, so as to connect Ancient and Modern Art.[104]

The value of the collection was reputed to be £75,000,[105] but of course that is not to say that it would have fetched so much on the open market or that a buyer would have taken it intact. It was exhibited in the William Brown Library and Museum, along with the Earl of Derby's natural history collection: both benefactors were honoured with statues in St George's Hall, the Earl in a toga and Mayer in modern dress (pl. x).[106] At the same time it is clear that, although Mayer gave the objects, he retained the records of purchase and provenance. The first Keeper of the Mayer Museum, Ecroyd Smith, imposed accession numbers according to fourteen categories: medieval ivories, for example, in Eight and manuscripts in Twelve.[107] Charles T. Gatty, his successor, published a quite admirable series of review catalogues and established slip-cards for each item. Together they reduced some 10,000 items to order with exemplary speed and clarity, advised—we are coming to see— by A. W. Franks of the British Museum.[108] Franks was on good terms with Mayer, three of whose medieval charters (from Pennant House) he exhibited on Mayer's behalf at the Society of Antiquaries in 1868.[109] But even he could be of no help in recovering the basic documentation of the Mayer Museum. It was stowed away— disordered and inaccessible—in Pennant House.

In November 1873, in his seventy-first year, Mayer retired from business. His fellow-tradesmen presented him with a fine illuminated address, set round the border with star items from the Mayer Museum and water-lilies from his already notable conservatory (pl. VII).[110] Three months later he had his employees to 'a sumptuous supper' at Pennant House to celebrate his birthday, and they too presented him with an illuminated address, not quite so well executed, signed by the eighteen 'workmen lately in [his] employ':[111] 'health and happiness,' they wrote, to 'a fine old English gentleman'. Mayer spent his retirement gardening, one suspects. The conservatories on each side of Pennant House (pl. VII*b*) held yucca plants and other exotica; the much sought after *Victoria regia* water-lily was cultivated in the open air.[112] The latter came from Kew in 1869, following an amicable meeting in Liverpool a few years earlier with Sir Joseph Hooker. Their other common passion was Wedgwood, Mayer having some rare items which Hooker, it seems, was hoping to obtain:

> a certain small circular medallion of Wedgwoods with a design of Flaxman? emblematic of Peace, Commerce and Plenty, and which was struck in commemoration of the colony of N. S. Wales ... It was made originally of clay brought I think by Sir Joseph Banks from Botany Bay.[113]

Throughout the 1870s Mayer was an active member of the Liverpool Art Club, an association of patrons rather than practitioners, whose annual exhibitions were in principle drawn from the private collections of the members.[114] We catch an occasional glimpse of the collection in Pennant House. Mayer contributed to the exhibitions of *Illuminated Manuscripts* (1876), *Wood Engravings* (1878), notably to the reconstruction of the Wedgwood catalogue (1879),[115] and finally to *Bookbindings* (1882), to which he sent several ivories and two impressive pieces of Limoges enamel. He was on the committees of *Oriental Art* (1872) and *Embroideries* (1875). Another lesser interest in these years seems to have been the Liverpool Academy of Art, to whose exhibition in 1876 he lent three paintings.[116] It was again in the 1870s that Mayer sold quite significant numbers of ceramics and *objets d'art* from the Pennant House collection.[117]

Having the leisure to arrange and rearrange the materials for his 'History of the Arts', Mayer was no nearer to writing it. Nor could he have written it—judging by the prose style of his surviving letters. So it was the more fortunate that one of Ann Boyle's sons was a professional journalist with the *Daily Telegraph*.[118] Frederick Boyle ghosted two books for his uncle in the 1870s: *Memoirs of Dodd, Upcott and Stubbs* and *Early Art in Liverpool with Notes on the Life of George Stubbs R. A.* The account of art in Liverpool is based on the exhibition catalogues of the day (1774–87). Mayer could 'read' a catalogue though he could not write a book. A similar enterprise, on a much grander scale, was Eliza Meteyard's two-volume life of Josiah Wedgwood, which was based on the major part of the early Wedgwood archive that Mayer had saved, by a happy accident, in 1848.[119]

Mayer was not a religious man—in the old phrase—and politically he was probably an independent.[120] One anchor was his sense of history: the specific history of Wedgwood or of Stubbs, not a merely romantic attachment to the past. Another was the family, which he honoured in his continued generosity towards Newcastle-under-Lyme,[121] and whose virtues are extolled in the 4-ft. memorial tablet in Carrara marble that commemorates Samuel and Margaret Mayer and both grandfathers: John Pepper, 'architect', and John Mare, '*armiger*'.[122] The coat of arms

FIG. 3.   Joseph Mayer's coat of arms: detail from title-page of his unwritten 'History of the Arts',
c. 1873. MPL, reproduced by courtesy of Liverpool City Record Office

(fig. 3), which is set proudly above the door of Pennant House, is presumably
Mayer's own creation. It appears on his presentation sword of 1860 and on the
silver-mounted horn celebrating Samuel Mayer's free election.[123] The design is
unknown to the College of Arms.[124] Yet it is happily chosen. The ships and the lions
passant, the *mer*maid and the rearing *mare* may stand here as the epitaph of a man
who had taken his own road through life, and with whose family motto (however
recently discovered) none of us would quarrel—'TYRANNY'S FOE'.

NOTES

[1] MPB, Jane Mayer's genealogical notes.

[2] The house stood at the junction of Deansgate and Seabridge Road: modern map in VCH, *Stafford,*
VIII (London, 1963), opp. 78; local map and poor twentieth-century postcards of house and
summer-house in the Public Library, Newcastle-under-Lyme.

[3] The Queen Street area was marshland until *c.* 1800; one of the houses then built (Nos. 6–8)
belonged to collaterals of the Mayers, who were veterinary surgeons: see V. M. Degg and M.
Hemmings, *Mayer House: the Building and its Inhabitants*, Staffordshire Historic Buildings Trust
(Stafford, 1984), not paginated.

[4] P. Lead, in *Newcastle-under-Lyme Times*, 3 Nov. 1971, no references given.

5 VCH, *op. cit.* (note 2), 24–7. The case was inscribed: 'To Samuel Mayer Esq. of Thistleberry. This box of instruments was presented on his accepting the office of mayor of Newcastle-under-Lyme [Being the first election by the voice of the burgesses for upwards of two hundred years] as a token of respect for his honest exertions in securing the rights of his brother freemen, October xxix, MDCCCXXXIII.' A silver-mounted horn—from the celebratory ox-roast—has a similar text: see below, note 123.

6 Degg and Hemmings, *op. cit.* (note 3). Pepper was already working for the Wedgwoods in 1782: Keele University Library, Wedgwood Papers (deposited by the Trustees of the Wedgwood Museum), 5036.31. In 1805–8 he was modernizing Maer Hall for Josiah Wedgwood II: *ibid.*, 5037.31–5043.31.

7 The Theatre Royal is now demolished; the Shakespeare medallion is in the Newcastle-under-Lyme Borough Museum.

8 VCH, *Stafford,* VI (London, 1979), 161–2.

9 Drawings done in 1818 include a rural scene with (poor) figures and two architectural views of Chester: MPL.

10 JM told the anecdote at his retirement dinner: *Liverpool Daily Post*, 14 Nov. 1873.

11 Nicholson and Warhurst, 1. The fear was that the textile workers would revolt.

12 Staffordshire Record Office, Deanery of Newcastle-under-Lyme unpublished parish registers: I am indebted for this reference to Mrs Phoebe Kemp. JM believed that in the 1790s his father 'was in politics an advanced Radical': *Liverpool Daily Post*, 20 Jan. 1886 (JM's obituary).

13 The original family pottery was E. Mayer and Son at Hanley; these are presumably Samuel's first or second cousins. John and Jos went into partnership with Thomas at Longport until the 1850s. John Boyle (Ann's husband) was a business associate of Wedgwood and Minton. But Mayer pottery had its real success in the next generation, when Joseph and Ernest Mayer (sons of Jos) bought the Economites Pottery Co. in Pennsylvania (1881). Within seven years they had a turnover of $100,000: *History of Beaver County, Pennsylvania* (Philadelphia and Chicago, 1888), 437–8. The Mayer China Co. (since 1984 a subsidiary of Syracuse China Corp.) still prospers in Beaver Falls.

14 1822: cf. JM's speech—'I was 51 years behind the counter' (*Liverpool Daily Post*, 14 Nov. 1873). JM had a written agreement with Wordley rather than a legal apprenticeship: MPL, Samuel Mayer to JM, 20 Oct. 1821.

15 Liverpool City Libraries, 423/16 [Lor] 8, 'Lord Street in 1827'.

16 See above, p. 21. There is no trace of JM in the Academy of Liverpool (which held six exhibitions in the 1820s), though he was eventually (1876) an honorary member. The Liverpool Society of Fine Arts included him amongst its many vice-presidents in 1859.

17 See G. Chandler, *William Roscoe of Liverpool 1753–1831* (Liverpool, 1953), for a useful account of Roscoe's collections, an edition of his minor poems and an engagingly cavalier treatment of his *Lives* of Lorenzo de' Medici and Leo X.

18 He is said to have been 'an instructor' at the Mechanics' Institution in Liverpool: *Liverpool Daily Post*, 8 Jan. 1872 (report of speech by JM).

19 Gore (1834), ad loc. He was not a partner in 1832.

20 Gore (1837 and 1839), ad loc. Both houses survive in water-colours by Worrall: MPL.

21 The portrait, which now hangs in Liverpool Museum, is signed and dated W. DANIELS 1843 along the edge of the table: *Merseyside Painters*, no. 7355. But a letter from the Secretary of the Royal Academy, dated 9 May 1840 (MPL), declines to explain the Academy's rejection of the portrait. Thus we infer the portrait's existence, perhaps in a form nearer the etching (see below, note 22), as early as 1840.

22 The etching (by R. W. Buss) shows Samuel Mayer seated at the table; in the painting he is represented by his portrait (WAG 7623) hanging on the back wall; cf. above, note 21.

23 MPB, Thomas Ryder to JM, 7 July 1838.

24 The cocking was at Wednesbury, where 'we beat the Earl of Derby's fowls', and the bullbaiting at Darlaston Wakes: Public Library, Newcastle-under-Lyme, MS note by JM in a scrap-book.

25 Cottrill's side of the correspondence (1841–6) is printed by R. Simms in the *Newcastle Guardian*, 28 April 1894, and 12 and 19 May 1894. Regrettably Cottrill himself was sacked for drunkenness and peculation in 1849: VCH, *op. cit.* (note 2), 42.

26 *Ibid.*, 38.

27 Nicholson and Warhurst, 2, with references.

28 MPB, Clements to his wife, 19–20 April 1841.

29 A passport to Belgium (1847) specifies that Mayer is travelling '*pour son plaisir et ses affaires*': MPL.

[30] Retirement address: *Liverpool Daily Post*, 14 Nov. 1873.

[31] JM's obituary: *Liverpool Daily Post*, 20 Jan. 1886.

[32] Mayer's design for a commemorative trowel to be used in Oct. 1844 to lay the foundation stone of Birkenhead docks is inscribed: 'JOSEPH MAYER DEL. // 68 Lord Street, Liverpool' (pl. IIIb and MPL). See also JM's obituary (above, note 31): 'in 1843 he separated from Mr Wordley'. By 1849 his address was Nos. 68–70: Gore (1849), ad loc.

[33] *Liverpool Daily Post*, 14 Nov. 1873. JM was registered at Chester as a manufacturing goldsmith and silversmith 1846–73; Wordley's name does not appear (C. J. Jackson, *English Goldsmiths and their Marks,* 2nd edn. (London, 1921), 399; cf. *ibid.,* 394, JM's 'maker's mark').

[34] MPL. Mayer is not yet dealing in electroplate: contrast note 96, below.

[35] Buss specialized in historical and allegorical subjects: Thieme and Becker, v, 290–1; cf. also above, note 22. Here Cellini is an obvious choice; Heriot was known from Sir Walter Scott's *The Fortunes of Nigel* (Edinburgh, 1823).

[36] *Art J.* (1845). Buss executed one of the historical frescoes in Westminster Hall (1845): Thieme and Becker, ad loc.

[37] By W. Herdman (Liverpool City Libraries, Herdman 384); cf. pl. VIIa.

[38] M 148 and 149.

[39] The original has not been identified. If it were in the round, the major infelicities would disappear, e.g. Mercury dousing the lamp. The owl at his feet is presumably JM's addition.

[40] For the trowel (pl. IIIb) cf. note 32, above. The snuff-box is Liverpool Museum 1966–105; cf. Sotheby's Exhibition Catalogue, *Chester Silver* (Chester, 1984), no. 215, wrongly identifying the School building as St George's Hall.

[41] *1851 Exhibition: Official Descriptive and Illustrated Catalogue* (London, 1851), 674, class 23, exhibitor 14, no 7.

[42] S. Bury, *Victorian Electroplate* (London, 1971). The principal Elkington patent was taken out in 1840.

[43] MPB, Thomas Spencer to JM, 1 Dec. 1862, citing *The Morning Post*, 28 Nov. 1862, with further references. Spencer, 'the discoverer of the art of electro-typing' (MPB: JM's will, p. 4), was commemorated in the 'Cellini' chalice (1849: now in Bebington) and in a Fontana medallion (now lost).

[44] Victoria and Albert Museum, Dept. of Metalwork, Elkington Papers, i, 233: JM to Elkington's, 26 Aug. 1848; cf. 215–29 (Hausburg, 1845) and 231 (Flower, 1846). Hausburg enjoyed a discount of 20 per cent.

[45] Science Museum Library, South Kensington, 'Prospectuses of Exhibitors', XV, xxiii–xxvi, Manufacturer's Catalogue (*c.* 1856), 31; JM's obituary in *The Times*, 21 Jan. 1886.

[46] J. B. Waring, *Art Treasures of the United Kingdom* (London, 1858), 10–12. JM's obituarist (see above, note 31) makes a similar observation.

[47] W. P. Jolly, *Lord Leverhulme: a Biography* (London, 1976), 143–4.

[48] *THSLC*, i (1848), 2. The seal itself was later accessioned to the Liverpool Free Public Museum as M 5645; it seems to have been a casualty of the fire in 1941.

[49] Williamson Museum and Art Gallery, Birkenhead, BIKGM 2868. JM was president of the Historic Society 1866–9.

[50] A. Hume, *Ancient Meols* (London, 1863), 50–1.

[51] JM, *Egyptian Museum*, 9.

[52] There is a vivid characterization by D. Kidd, 'Charles Roach Smith and his museum of London antiquities', *British Museum Yearbook*, ii (1977), 112–15. See further the forthcoming study by Michael Rhodes.

[53] *JBAA*, i (1846), sqq. (Winchester onwards), augmented with press-cuttings in the pasted-up volumes at the Society of Antiquaries of London.

[54] *JBAA*, v (1850), 283–336, with many further particulars in the pasted-up volume at the Society of Antiquaries of London; *THSLC*, ii (1849–50), 238–59. For the mayoral reception see Society of Antiquaries of London, pasted-up volume, as above, JM to C. Roach Smith, Sunday 29 July 1849: 'The Mayor yesterday gave us a carte blanche for a soirée at his expense at the Town Hall to invite all your society with about 1500 more'.

[55] MPL, 27 Jan. 1882. Roach Smith reciprocated by dedicating the first volume of his *Retrospections Social and Archaeological* (3 vols., London, 1883–91) to JM.

[56] *PSA*, ii (1850), 38. JM's membership paper was signed by Charles Roach Smith, Thomas Lott, Sand, Shepherd, T. J. Pettigrew, W. Chaffers Jr. and Fortunatus Dwarris. See also Society of

Antiquaries of London, pasted-up volume (as note 54, above), JM to C. Roach Smith, 18 Aug. 1849.

[57] Gore (1867), ad loc. Strictly the 4th (Bebington) Company of the 1st Cheshire Rifles, founded 1864.

[58] JM was a corresponding member of learned societies in Abbeville (1852), S. Omer (1853), Zurich (1854), Caen, Hanover and Copenhagen (all 1856), Société des antiquaires de Normandie and others (by 1856), Luxemburg (1857), Société des antiquaires de Picardie (by 1866). He also belonged to the Royal Asiatic Society, the Royal Society, the Royal Geographical Society and a number of local historical societies in the north of England: *THSLC*, viii (1855–6), xvii and MPL, *passim*.

[59] D. M. Wilson, *The Forgotten Collector: Augustus Wollaston Franks of the British Museum*, Walter Neurath Memorial Lectures 16 (London, 1985), 11–12.

[60] See below, p. 124.

[61] *Catalogue of Works of Antient and Mediaeval Art Exhibited at the House of the Society of Arts* (London, 1850), no. 286 (M 238). The stone is a female bust in profile, 'AD 1518', unknown to the most comprehensive catalogue of Dürer drawings: W. L. Strauss, *The Complete Drawings of Albrecht Dürer*, iii: *1510–1519* (New York, 1974).

[62] MPL, Edward Hawkins, Keeper of Antiquities in the British Museum, to JM, 11 Feb. 1850.

[63] *1851 Exhibition: Official Descriptive and Illustrated Catalogue, op. cit.* (note 41), 674–5: 15 items of plate and 18 items of jewellery, nos. 8 and 16 being commended (*Jury Reports*, III. 520, class xxiii). See further above, note 41.

[64] G. Freizor is presumably to be identified with G.-A. Freezor, active in London 1861/79 'English school': E. Bénézit, *Dictionnaire critique et documentaire des peintres, sculpteurs, dessinateurs et graveurs*, 2nd edn. (Paris, 1966), IV, 75.

[65] See M. Caygill, *The Story of the British Museum* (London, 1981), 35.

[66] William Bullock, jeweller and silversmith to the Duke of Gloucester, had a highly successful museum of ethnography and natural history in Church Street, Liverpool, *c.* 1800. By 1812 it had been removed to a purpose-built 'Egyptian Temple' in Piccadilly, just opposite Bond Street: see the *Companion* to Bullock's museum, 5th edn. (Liverpool, 1807), 12th edn. (London, 1812); and now E. P. Alexander, 'William Bullock: little-remembered museologist and showman', *The Curator*, xxviii (1985), 117–47. The XIVth Earl of Derby's natural history museum in Duke Street, Liverpool (1851), preserved some of the deceased inhabitants of his father's outstanding zoological collection at Knowsley.

[67] JM, *Egyptian Museum*, 2 (preface) and front cover (entrance charges).

[68] Gore (1860), ad loc. Richard Harrison was presumably 'Peggy's' husband: see below, p. 38.

[69] Lugt 21070 (Valentia). Stobart and Stürmer were not public sales.

[70] JM, *Egyptian Museum*, 47: by respectively Wagstaff, Gibson and Mosses.

[71] Gore (1867), ad loc.

[72] JM, *Egyptian Museum*, 39.

[73] M. Amandry of the Cabinet des Médailles kindly confirms that Mayer has left no trace in the records there. The tradition is quoted in *Men of the Times*, 23 Feb. 1874, and repeated by *The Times* obituarist, 21 Jan. 1886. We may note that JM resisted pressure to purchase the gold coins in the Rolfe Collection: MPL, Joseph Clarke to C. T. Gatty, 3 Feb. 1875.

[74] *Art J.*, new ser. i (1855), 276.

[75] A. J. Dunkin, *A Report of the Proceedings of the British Archaeological Association at the First General Meeting held at Canterbury in the Month of September 1844* (London, 1845), 187–9 and 362; many relevant letters are in the pasted-up volume at the Society of Antiquaries of London (cf. above, note 54).

[76] *THSLC*, vii (1854–5), 3*–6*. The banners seen in pl. XXXIII commemorate the annual meetings of the British Association since 1831; they were first displayed at the 1854 meeting (O. J. R. Howarth, *The British Association for the Advancement of Science: a Retrospect 1831–1921* (London, 1922), 111–12. See further below, pp. 118–20.

[77] J. Stonehouse, *Liverpool, its Highways, Byeways and Thoroughfares by Land and Water, being a Stranger's Guide through the Town*, 7th edn. (London, 1855), 34.

[78] F. Pulszky, *Meine Zeit, Mein Leben* (Pressburg, Leipzig, 1880), III, 187–9; the eventual Pulszky sale is Lugt 30536.

[79] E. Henszlmann, *Catalogue of the Collection of the Monuments of Art Formed by the Late Gabriel Fejérváry of Hungary Exhibited at the Museum of the Archaeological Institute of Great Britain and Ireland* (London, 1853). The lectures are advertised on p. [44].

[80] Pulszky, *op. cit.* (note 78), III, 189.

[81] Mayer paid 18,000 florins (under £1,500) for the ivories: *ibid.*, 189–90. For the metalwork, see Nicholson, *Prehistoric Metalwork*. The Mexican pottery has all but disappeared from view; the Codex Fejérváry-Mayer is reproduced in facsimile by C. A. Burland, *Codices Selecti*, XXVI (Graz, 1971).

[82] F. Pulszky, *Catalogue of the Fejérváry Ivories in the Museum of Joseph Mayer, Esq., F.S.A.* (Liverpool, 1856).

[83] At least, they passed with the rest of the Egyptian Museum to the town of Liverpool in 1867.

[84] Now in the Williamson Museum and Art Gallery, Slatey Road, Birkenhead: BIKGM 4566. For Harris himself see *Merseyside Painters*, 110–11, omitting the portrait of Mayer.

[85] M 12004: see below, pp. 139, 145–51.

[86] *Catalogue of Works of Antient and Mediaeval Art Exhibited at the House of the Society of Arts* (London, 1850), 12 (42 cameos); A. Michaelis, *Ancient Marbles in Great Britain* (Cambridge, 1882), 177–8.

[87] *Ibid.*, 178 and note 489; cf. MPL, Hertz to JM, 23 and 31 July, and 24 Oct. 1856.

[88] Lugt 23471 (24–6 Mar. 1857, Phillips); 24633 (7–24 Feb. 1859, Sotheby's). For the latter, see the marked-up Sotheby's catalogue in the British Library: S. C. Sotheby. (1).

[89] Gore (1857), ad loc.

[90] Society of Antiquaries of London, MS 857, no. 10, Mayer to Rolfe, 8 Sept. 1857.

[91] MPB, Jane Mayer's genealogical notes.

[92] For an informed and sympathetic notice of Rolfe, see C. Roach Smith, *Collectanea Antiqua*, V (London, 1861), 270–3.

[93] JM to Rolfe (as note 90, above); MPL, Rolfe to JM, 10 Sept. and 17 Nov. 1857.

[94] At the same time Roach Smith's *Antiquities of Richborough, Reculver and Lymne* (London, 1850) provided some record of the Rolfe Collection.

[95] *Catalogue of the Art Treasures of the United Kingdom Collected at Manchester in 1857*, 2nd edn. (Manchester, 1857), 152, 163 and 165.

[96] MPL, trade notepaper; cf. pl. VI. JM's earliest advertisement of electroplate is in Gore (1851).

[97] Liverpool County Record Office: census returns 1861, 1871 and 1881, ad loc.

[98] For Frederick see below. Henry supervised the conservatory (below, note 112) and is named as an executor in JM's will: MPB (see below, note 103).

[99] 'I am very happy to think that you have partially weaned yourself from things antique and turned your mind upon hot-blooded gems of coeval date, that you have distracted your attention from coats of mail and bent it upon crinoline, and I am in high glee at the pleasure of paying my most ardent yet humble respects to the Lord-Street Mayeress': MPL, Joseph Clarke of Saffron Walden to JM, 8 Aug. 1863. I owe this dramatic reference to Roger White.

[100] Catalogued by C. T. Gatty in 1879, who says (a) that the majority was *ex* Hertz and (b) that many other gems had been included in Mayer's gift to Liverpool in 1867.

[101] JM's obituarist (above, note 31) reckoned 'between four and five thousand original drawings, between fifteen and twenty thousand early engravings, and above fifty thousand autograph letters of English artists'. In principle all this material was sold by Sotheby's, 19–24 July 1887 (Lugt 46763, overlooks 19–20 July) or, if local, by Branch and Leete, 16 Dec. 1887.

[102] *Liverpool Mercury*, 8 Jan. 1872. See the printed catalogue of 1879. The books have since been dispersed or destroyed.

[103] MPB, JM's will; sales by Branch and Leete and Sotheby's (see above, note 101, and below, p. 227).

[104] Liverpool Museum, minutes of the Library, Museum and Education Committee, 14 Feb. 1867: JM to J. A. Picton, 4 Feb. 1867.

[105] The figure is notional. 'The collection, although said to have cost Mr. Mayer fully £50,000, is asserted to approximate more in value £75,000': *Black's Guide to Liverpool* (Liverpool, 1868), 17. By 1884 the figures had risen to £75,000 and £100,000: *ibid.* (Liverpool, 1884), 17.

[106] The statues still stand in St George's Hall, in a rather damaged state: WAG 7822 (JM by Fontana) and 7820 (Earl of Derby by Theed).

[107] Ecroyd Smith had a good working knowledge of British archaeology: cf. Hume, *op. cit.* (note 50), 50–1.

[108] Liverpool Museum Gatty papers, C. T. Gatty, 'Report upon the Mayer Collection Catalogue', 25 Nov. 1875.

[109] 12 Mar. and 7 May 1868: *PSA*, 2nd ser., IV (1868), 87–90, 115–16.

110 MPL, 13 Nov. 1873; text in *Liverpool Daily Post*, 14 Nov. 1873.

111 MPL, 23 Feb. 1874; text in *Liverpool Mercury*, 24 Feb. 1874. Note the size of the staff.

112 Contents of the conservatory and greenhouses are listed in the Branch and Leete sale catalogue, 8–10 July 1886, nos. 655–84. JM's water-lilies are featured in *The Field*, 26 Nov. 1870, 456 (article by Henry Boyle).

113 J. D. Hooker to JM, 13 April 1869; cf. 3 Jan. and 7 Feb. 1870, still harping on the same string. The original Sydney Cove medallion (designed by Henry Webber, 1789) is a great rarity, which there is no evidence that JM possessed. But he did have a later version: L. R. Smith, *The Sydney Cove Medallion*, Monographs in Wedgwood Studies 4 (The Buten Museum of Wedgwood, Pennsylvania, 1979), 16 and n., citing Meteyard.

114 The Liverpool Art Club ran from 1872–96. I rely here on a series of twenty-six exhibition catalogues in the Liverpool Athenaeum.

115 C. T. Gatty, *The Works of Josiah Wedgwood*, Exhibition Catalogue (Liverpool, 1879). See also the detailed review in the *Liverpool Mercury*, 4 Feb. 1879.

116 *Catalogue of the Collection of Works by Past and Present Members of the Liverpool Academy Exhibited at the Rooms of the Liverpool Art Club, Myrtle Street 1876* (Liverpool, 1876), nos. 16, 35, 72. JM was an honorary member of the Academy.

117 Sotheby's, 12–13 Feb. 1875, and 21 and 24 June 1878 (Lugt 35348 and 38537: annotated copies in the British Library).

118 MPB, JM's 'Book of Autographs', 95–7, 109–11 (entry by Frederick Boyle).

119 E. Meteyard, *A Group of Englishmen* (London, 1871), ix-xiii.

120 JM forbade any reference to religion or politics in the lectures he endowed and the further acquisition of books on these subjects for the Bebington Library: MPB, JM's will. He was buried in St Andrew's, Bebington, the tombstone commemorating his benefactions and bearing no scriptural text.

121 1851, a medallion for the mayor's chain; 1870–2, scholarships and books for the High School, a historical painting by R. W. Buss and a silver-mounted horn commemorating Samuel Mayer's free election; ?1873, a silver trowel for St Giles church (lost); 1882, over a hundred water-colours and topographical prints to the School of Art: VCH, *op. cit.* (note 2), 8; *Newcastle Guardian*, 15 Apr. 1882.

122 The tablet was intended for St Giles church. A faculty being refused, it was erected at the Bebington Library; in 1882 it was returned to Newcastle, where it is now outside the Borough Museum. The text is printed by J. Ingamells, *Newcastle-under-Lyme Directory*, 2nd edn. (Newcastle-under-Lyme, 1881), 33–4.

123 For the sword see below, pp. 28–9, note 2. The horn (now in the Civic Offices, Newcastle-under-Lyme) has a silver mount, not hall-marked, with a long inscription dated 1833; cf. above, note 5. The coat of arms is most unlikely to be so early.

124 JM has combined the arms of two families: Mere of Mere (the ship) and Delamare (the lions); the motto is his own. I am indebted here to Mr Michael Maclagan, F.S.A., Richmond Herald.

Philanthropy and Patronage

Richard Foster, F.S.A.

Joseph Mayer moved from Liverpool to the Wirral in 1857 when he took up residence at Dacre Park, Rock Ferry. The house no longer stands and we know little of his domestic life in the period 1857 to 1860, after which he decided to make his home in Bebington. The move to Bebington represented a watershed in Mayer's life at which point his interests and energies were devoted, in the main, to the improvement of the quality of life in the village. This chapter reviews Mayer's achievements in establishing the Free Library and Museum, and his association with the architect Edward Heffer and the sculptor Giovanni Fontana. Bebington is situated three miles south of Birkenhead on the east side of the Wirral Peninsula, about a mile and a half inland from the River Mersey. In response to the commercial prosperity of Liverpool and Birkenhead the community of Bebington grew substantially in the third quarter of the nineteenth century. Between 1841 and 1871 its population rose from 1,187 to 3,768. The construction of the railway between Birkenhead and Chester in 1840 and of the new Chester Road in 1844, and the introduction of steam ferryboats between New Ferry and Liverpool encouraged many professional people to reside in the village. To a contemporary observer the transformation from village to suburb was striking and had not a little to do with one of its residents.

> Without losing its rustic air the village has gained advantages such as many a town might envy in convenience and comfort. A very few years since the place was 'picturesque' and 'rural' to a degree. It had neither gas nor pavements, its younger population went barefooted and women fetched water from two miles distance. If all that be changed, and if Bebington may be held up as a model village in some respects the honour is chiefly due to Mr Joseph Mayer.[1]

One of the first recorded events connecting Joseph Mayer with Bebington throws some light upon the motivation for Mayer's remarkable series of philanthropic acts between 1864 and his death in 1886. In November 1860 Mayer was entertained to dinner by his neighbours at Bebington in his capacity as Captain of the Liverpool Borough Guard, which he had raised at his own expense. He was presented with a sword 'as a tribute of respect and esteem' for his services to the volunteer movement. In his response Mayer referred specifically to those two words 'respect and esteem', which he said were invaluable to him. 'It is that [respect] I want to possess. It is that [esteem] I wish to have from you.'[2] In spite of the gift of his Egyptian Museum to the town of Liverpool in 1867, Mayer must have realized that Liverpool could not offer him the personal involvement he so much enjoyed with those he sought to benefit. On moving to Bebington he therefore applied the experience gained in establishing the Egyptian Museum and his observations of the way in which the William Brown Library and Museum were created to enrich his newly-adopted home.

Bebington and Joseph Mayer took to each other with enthusiasm. This growing community provided the ideal context in which Mayer could live comfortably in retirement, surrounded by his collections. He was not a social revolutionary but he was to prove something of a social engineer. He saw the gifts of the library and art gallery as a way of creating a stronger community by giving people from different social backgrounds and educational attainments a focal point for their personal development.

Joseph Mayer moved to Bebington in 1860.[3] He acquired a medium-sized double-fronted farmhouse and outbuildings, which he renamed Pennant House after Thomas Pennant (1726–98), the traveller and naturalist, whose interests may have provided a model for Mayer's lifestyle in Bebington.[4] Photographs of the building in Bebington Library show it to be an early nineteenth-century farmhouse constructed of brick with a pitched roof and rounded dormer windows set above a low parapet (pl. VIIIa). Pennant House was intended as a repository for Mayer's private collection of 20,000 prints and drawings, including autograph letters, gems and rings, specimens and papers relating to the history of pottery and English artists, the source material for his intended 'History of the Rise and Progress of Art in England from 1550 until the Present Time'.[5]

Mayer opened his campaign for the hearts and minds of Bebington by strengthening his connection with the volunteer movement. In 1864 he raised and clothed at his own expense a company of the 4th Cheshire Rifles at Bebington, inaugurating the corps at Bebington School on 29 August 1864. Six months later, 104 men had enrolled and for nearly ten years Mayer served as their commander, camping at Hooton with the volunteers, supervising their welfare and tending to the administrative requirements of the force with great enthusiasm (pl. VIIIb).[6] He also became interested and involved in improving the public services in the fast-growing community of Bebington, which

... he quickly inspired ... with his own friendly and public spirit, and enriched ... with his gifts. Every movement for brightening life and enlarging the mind had his cordial concurrence ... While he was in the village a spirit of good fellowship prevailed, greater than ever before or since.[7]

He was a founder member of committees for bowling, cricket, quoiting and football clubs. He raised funds for a village hospital and a horticultural society and allotments were formed on his initiative. As Chairman of the Lower Bebington Local Board, for which he devised a seal, he was instrumental in introducing (1863) gas and water into the area.[8]

Mayer, no doubt impressed by Sir William Brown's achievement in creating a Free Library and Museum in Liverpool, decided in the early 1860s to establish a free library in Bebington. There is slight evidence that he may have been influenced in this decision by Miles Pilling Elsby, a schoolmaster in the village.[9] Mayer evidently felt strongly on the need for informal education; he stated that he would sooner invest in a library than a school.[10] He later articulated his reasons for providing the library—'He who reads lives in a larger world and has a knowledge and grasp of possibilities far wider than he who is without the art, and even prospers when the latter would succumb.'[11] To accommodate the library Mayer rented the house which had formerly been occupied by an eccentric stone mason and contractor called Thomas Francis (1762–1850). Francis had enjoyed a number of bizarre enthusiasms. During the Napoleonic Wars he had built a kind of Martello tower in his garden overlooking the road from Birkenhead, causing Nathaniel Hawthorne, the American Consul in Liverpool from 1853–7 (and resident at Rock Ferry), to comment on the curious nature of the house. Francis's particular obsession concerned his own funeral arrangements. He is reputed to have made wooden coffins for himself and his wife, and for both to have celebrated their anniversaries by sitting in their coffins for the day. He was also the author of the number of Gilbertian puzzles inscribed in stone walls, fragments of which remain today in the walls of Mayer Park, adjacent to the Free Library.[12]

From 1866 until 1870 Francis's house provided premises for the free library. Mayer invited several of his ready helpers on other public matters to meet him and make arrangements for issuing the books. The first honorary librarian was the schoolmaster, Miles Pilling Elsby. The library opened on 1 January 1866 and was a huge success, so much so that an extra room had to be provided almost immediately. Within three years it was clear that the demand for the library would overwhelm the accommodation in Francis's house and in 1869 Mayer purchased a plot of land in Townfield Lane for which he developed plans for a permanent library, reading room and public hall. At the same time (1869) a farmhouse, barn and other buildings adjoining Pennant House and standing in about five acres of orchard and meadow were offered for sale. Mayer seized this opportunity for adding what was to become a public park to his intended gift of a library and hall and the whole estate was quickly secured.[13] The first objective was to lay out the garden and walks at the rear of the farmhouse which was shortly to become the Free Library. The old orchard was removed and by April 1869 the grounds were practically complete. On 10 April 1869 the last tree in the Avenue was planted and the park opened to the public. The avenue of chestnut trees was called Dickens Avenue to mark the visit of the novelist to Liverpool on the same day, an event which Mayer was instrumental in arranging. Mayer sat opposite Dickens at the banquet given in his honour in St George's Hall. Dickens Avenue, or Library Walks as it was known, became a favourite resort for the villagers and each year a flower show was held at which Mayer was an extensive exhibitor of flowers, plants and fruit.[14]

Shortly afterwards what was to be the first phase of the conversion of the farmhouse for the new library was begun. The roof of the farmhouse was raised to form a central reading room, 29 ft. long by 21 ft. wide, the walls of which were shelved all around. Fixed desks were provided in the central area for readers. Around the room ran a gallery with an iron balustrade interspersed at regular intervals by pedestals on which were placed busts of eminent figures in literature and history. From the centre of the ceiling hung a large gasalier with supplementary lighting provided by six gas burners attached to the pillars supporting the gallery.[15] A diminutive Gothic clock tower was added to the front, with a datestone of 1716 belonging to the original

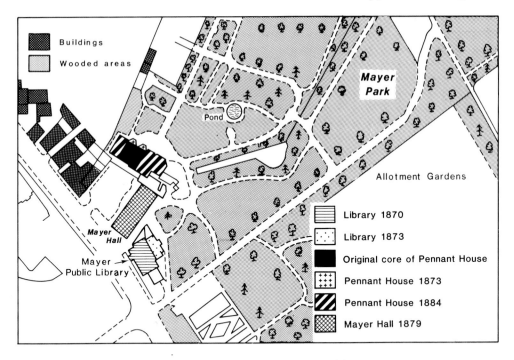

FIG. 4.   Mayer buildings in Lower Bebington

farmhouse relocated in a lozenge on the front of the tower (pl. IX*a*). The clock tower contained three bells which sounded first on Mayer's sixty-seventh birthday, 23 February 1870. Earlier, on 18 January when the library was officially opened, Mayer was entertained to dinner at the Wellington Hotel by a grateful community to mark the event.[16]

The library was open on Monday and Friday evenings between 6.30 and 8.30 and on Wednesday afternoons from 3.00 to 4.00. Mr Elsby had the support of twelve volunteer helpers with occasional help from Joseph Mayer himself, who enjoyed meeting the readers. Library tickets were issued on receipt of an application endorsed by two householders. The tickets were of strong pasteboard and were marked with the borrower's name and address and registered number. The Free Library was not entirely free, a charge of one penny being made for the issue of the ticket. The ticket had to be presented each time a book was borrowed. The ticket (retained by the reader) was marked with the title of the book borrowed and a slip bearing the name of the borrower was put in place of the book. Remarkably few books were lost, the average being about five a year. A third of the library's volumes (in 1878) were novels, the remainder being travel, poetry, history, biography, natural sciences, geology, general science and art.[17] A contemporary observer (1878) felt the Bebington Free Library demonstrated that:

> . . . a free library on a large scale can be worked without risk or serious trouble with incalculable advantage in a country district . . . The population of the neighbour-hood is mixed, partly agricultural and partly mercantile with many families

extremely poor within it and some extremely rich, a vast majority standing between the two. All classes meet at the library, farmer's boys in corduroy and heiresses in sable, clergy of the church and little girls of their Sunday School, servants and masters. Most notable is the proportion of young people ... A motely assemblage may be beheld any Monday or Friday night, one to make our forefathers stare with distrust. The bulk of the readers dwell ... in villages at a radius of two and a half miles or so around Bebington, but a large number come from a distance much more inconvenient, these mostly farmers, their wives and children. Each night of 'the library' a crowd assembles around the door as if it were a theatre waiting with patience until Mr Elsby and his helpers are prepared to receive them.[18]

Mayer next turned his attention to the barn, acquired in 1869, which stood between the Free Library and Pennant House. This he converted into a single-storey public hall, known as the Free Library Hall, for exhibitions and lectures.[19] In September 1871 a substantial art exhibition was held in the Hall in the presence of Eliza Meteyard, the biographer of Josiah Wedgwood, who provided an introduction to the catalogue. The proceeds of the exhibition were to go towards the building of a village hospital. The show was originally intended to last one week but it was so successful that it was extended for a further two weeks. Mayer in his speech said the exhibition was to raise funds and 'to encourage a taste for education and fine arts in the district'.[20]

It is not entirely clear whether Joseph Mayer had employed an architect to design the first phase of the conversion of the farmhouse. However, the clock tower bears some resemblance to the work of Edward Heffer, a Liverpool architect whom Mayer commissioned to undertake further work on the Free Library in Bebington.[21] The first recorded involvement of Edward Heffer in Joseph Mayer's building works is in August 1872. Heffer noted that he 'with JM took dimensions of the Free Public Library Mr M. desiring to make additions thereto'. This second phase of the works to the library consisted of the addition of two rooms on each side of the garden front, including a crenellated tower bearing a panel containing the Mayer monogram and supporters from his armorial bearings. Heffer designed and supervised the work, which was completed in less than six months. Heffer recalls Mayer's consistent kindness to those who worked for him and his taste for holding commemorative dinners. On 3 January 1873 Mayer gave such a dinner for the building workers who had constructed the library.[22] The library held over 10,000 volumes, one of the new rooms providing an area for newspapers, periodicals, chess and draughts, while the other was reserved for study and a place of deposit for Mayer's personal library of 2,000 volumes.[23]

Mayer was increasingly short of space in Pennant House to accommodate his large collection. Heffer records that about the middle of 1873 Mayer commissioned him to prepare plans for enlarging Pennant House. An illustration from the illuminated address presented to Joseph Mayer by his employees on his retirement in 1873 at the age of seventy-one reveals Heffer's first modifications to the house (pl. vii*b*).[24] This took the form of a double-fronted, two-storey bay with a parapet on the garden front with a central, recessed porch, supported by classical columns. The illustration also shows two glasshouses adjoining the house which held yucca plants and other horticultural exotica. In 1870, under the guidance of Henry Boyle, Mayer had successfully cultivated and brought to flower in the open air the rare and giant *Victoria regia* water-lily acquired from Kew Gardens.[25] In the autumn of 1873 Heffer was further instructed by Joseph Mayer to prepare plans for a substantial enlargement of Pennant House. Heffer described his approach to the problem:

> On 10 September I measured Pennant House for further additions and drew out a design for a new wing with a tower to form a central feature in the whole of the garden front. As the proposed new rooms are somewhat loftier than the old ones and as it was desirable to harmonize the whole as much as possible some care was necessary to attain this result.[26]

Heffer's scheme added a plain brick wing to the west of the original farmhouse and a lofty tower and a substantial wing to the east (pl. IXa). The tower reflects Heffer's liking for soaring height but is out of scale with the house and whether viewed from the north or the south hardly achieves his intention of 'harmonizing the whole'. Nevertheless, Joseph Mayer was pleased with the result.

Our knowledge of Heffer's life is based largely on the autograph describing his career which in 1879 Joseph Mayer had asked him to prepare. He was born in London in 1836. After leaving school in May 1850 he entered the Government School of Design at Somerset House remaining there as a student until July 1852. Even as a student Heffer revealed an instinct for the vigorous promotion of his work. Having completed a sketch of Nelson's tomb in the crypt of St Paul's, he took it to both the *Builder* and *The Illustrated News*, but neither journal would publish it. As his career developed, however, the *Builder* was frequently to publish short, illustrated reviews of his buildings.[27] In 1853 Heffer entered the studio of John Thomas, sculptor and architect, then of Old Church Street, Paddington. He was kept occupied preparing drawings for tombstones and mausolea as well as the Musical Instrument Court at the Crystal Palace and the decorative masonry at Buckingham Palace. Towards the end of this period he was engaged in the work of rebuilding the New Palace of Westminster, working on the designs for the sculptured decorations.[28] In July 1857, after four years with Thomas, he left London for Liverpool where, until November of that year, he was an assistant at Ward and Hay, a firm of architects in Cable Street. It was not long before he decided that he could attract enough work to set up on his own in Mount Pleasant. By 1862, 'with business improving', he had moved to 46 Church Street where his entry in the directory reads 'professor of drawing & painting, artist, designer & architectural draughtsman'.[29]

Edward Heffer first met Joseph Mayer on 23 February 1858, when he was introduced to him by a Mr Greenwood at Mayer's premises in Lord Street. Heffer acknowledges the pleasure and significance of this meeting which 'led in the course of time to valuable connexions and began an intimacy that exists unimpaired at the time I write these lines' (September 1879).[30] Shortly after that first meeting Heffer provided Mayer with 'a specimen of emblazoning', following which he received an order 'to do one coat of arms on vellum' (subjects not known). At this time Joseph Mayer was on the point of moving to Bebington and Heffer was putting his experience gained with Thomas to good effect in winning competitions for the Barnston Memorial at Farndon, Cheshire, which he persuaded the *Builder* to publish (1859).[31] Heffer collaborated with Edwin Stirling of Liverpool, a sculptor and stone mason, (as earlier at Barnston) on a clock tower in memory of Prince Albert in Wellington Square, Hastings (1863).[32]

Heffer was trying hard to establish his practice and was anxious not to turn work away. He undertook several private commissions including a memorial cross to the Revd C. Cooke in front of the Catholic Church in Aigburth, a tomb for Mr Molyneux at Childwall, a drawing of the pediment of Liverpool Town Hall, and a sketch for a clock case commissioned by Joseph Mayer.[33] Heffer's reflections on these years in Liverpool indicate the resilience needed by an aspiring architect anxious to establish a reputation. In all, by 1879 Heffer had entered fifty-six competitions but had been successful in only three. He commented ruefully on the plight of the struggling designer:

> For some years an enthusiastic candidate for honours in public competitions for Buildings I entered the lists with more valour than discretion and reaped but few Victories. After twenty five years experience I am now by no means such an ardent admirer of this road to fame but there is no doubt the high position that some leading architects have attained to has been due to their talent in being made known by this means.[34]

In the mid-1860s Heffer was occupied with a number of minor schemes in Liverpool and one major commission which represents the high point of his career. His scheme for St Bridget's, Wavertree, is of the Italian Romanesque style, exceptional for its date, of real basilica form with a disproportionately high campanile.[35] In Heffer's words this church was 'an attempt to introduce the simple form of the very early Christian churches to the use of the present age'. The Renaissance Revival influenced the design for a new Liverpool Cathedral which he presented to the Historic Society of Lancashire and Cheshire in January 1875. While acceptable in secular surroundings, Heffer's scheme was not welcomed for an ecclesiastical project and was 'condemned as pagan'. Heffer records it met with 'the usual opposition' and, turning his back on Liverpool, he sought a new practice in Kilburn, London, in 1876.[36]

Edward Heffer retained his friendship and professional association with Joseph Mayer following his return to London. In 1878 Mayer began the last element in the group of buildings on which he had laboured for so long for the community in Bebington. Throughout the 1870s the nearby barn situated between the library and Pennant House had been used for occasional lectures and art exhibitions.[37] Mayer's own collection now required more space than his house could provide, in spite of the extensions which Heffer had provided in the early 1870s. In 1878 Mayer decided to pull down the barn and create a purpose-built lecture hall and picture gallery and Edward Heffer was asked to prepare the designs. Mayer Hall—some 61 ft. long and 28 ft. wide—is on two levels with a principal entrance from the main village street. A porch on the eastern elevation links it to 'Library Walks' in Mayer Park. The office for the curator or keeper is on the ground floor to the left of the entrance and residential accommodation for the curator is provided in the other ground-floor room and immediately above on the first floor. A massive pitch-pine staircase links the two levels. A lift to the first floor provided access to the exhibition gallery for Mayer's collection of pictures and sculptures (pl. ixb). The main ground floor hall was to be used for lectures and concerts.[38] The elevation to the street reveals Heffer's choice of domestic revival style for the entrance to Mayer Hall. The now familiar black and white applied half-timbering, plain mullion windows, oriel window and

PLATE VIII

a. Pennant House, Joseph Mayer seated foreground, 1865

b. Cheshire Rifle Volunteers at Hooton, Joseph Mayer seventh from left, *c*. 1870
MPB, reproduced by courtesy of Bebington Library

PLATE IX

Photograph: Jim Foster

a. Pennant House (left), Mayer Hall (centre) and the Mayer Library (right), 1986

b. The museum in Mayer Hall, Bebington, 1901. MPB, reproduced by courtesy of Bebington Library

PLATE X

Joseph Mayer as donor of 'the Mayer Museum', 1869, by Giovanni Fontana. St George's Hall (WAG 7822), reproduced by courtesy of NMGM

elaborate Tudor chimneys are featured here some ten years before Douglas and Lockwood brought the 'black and white' revival to Chester.

Mayer's collaboration with Heffer was paralleled by his patronage of Giovanni Fontana, a sculptor born in Carrara in 1821. Fontana studied at the Royal Academy of Carrara and was awarded a prize which permitted him to continue his studies in Rome. After the French invaded Rome he fought for the republican cause, but following its defeat he left Italy, initially for Paris and then London, where he was employed by Thomas Campbell and engaged in the modelling of the statue of Lord George Bentinck.[39] It seems likely that Fontana was introduced to Joseph Mayer by their mutual acquaintance, Charles Roach Smith, who visited Fontana at his studio in London. Fontana's work represents that of a sculptor working at the end of the classical tradition. Most of his commissions called for monumental statuary or portrait busts and reliefs. He seems to have undertaken commissions for Mayer from as early as September 1852 when he made a relief in memory of Mayer's friend Thomas Dodd and May 1855 when he received £100 for the completion of a statue in marble entitled the 'Genius of Commerce'.[40] It was clearly not an easy time for Fontana who, having set up his own studio at 22 Newman Street, London, was experiencing cash flow problems. He wrote to Mayer in August 1855 asking for his help in finding a purchaser for two sculptures and requesting an advance for the 'Prisoner of Love' which he had almost completed for his patron.[41] It seems that the 'Genius of Commerce' and the 'Prisoner of Love' had been left unsold for twenty-four years when in 1879, together with six other sculptures, they were sold by Fontana to the government of New South Wales. Fontana used his acquaintance with Roach Smith on more than one occasion in attempts to persuade Mayer to recommend him for important commissions. In May 1861 he asked him to use his influence with Mayer to gain a recommendation for the Wellington Monument in Liverpool. Fontana was unlucky on this occasion.[42] In March 1867 he wrote to Roach Smith asking him to suggest to Dr Hume that he be chosen to make the sculpture of Joseph Mayer which Liverpool Town Council were to commission for St George's Hall in acknowledgement of Mayer's gift to Liverpool of his collection of antiquities.[43] In the event, Mayer himself was consulted and he did select Fontana, who was to be paid £1,000 for the work.[44] The statue (pl. x) was unveiled on 28 September 1869, and shows Joseph Mayer holding the deed of gift by which the town of Liverpool received his collection.[45]

Mayer's patronage of Fontana is best illustrated by his commissioning from the sculptor, between about 1855 and 1881, a series of marble busts and reliefs initially intended for display in Pennant House. During this period Fontana produced over twenty marble reliefs and busts of Mayer's close friends and relations, and of literary and other heroes from the past. Where possible these were modelled from life, but Fontana also worked from photographic shots of face and profile. It was character-istic of Mayer that he should declare his affection and admiration by constructing a visible 'Gallery of Friends.'[46] He never married, but one of the earliest reliefs (1856) is that of 'Peggy' or Margaret Harrison, his much-admired travelling-companion on overseas tours.[47] Another early relief is that of Charles Roach Smith, through whom Mayer acquired the Faussett Collection in 1854. A number of busts of Josiah Wedgwood were commissioned, of which the earliest (present location not known) was made in 1858,[48] and another in 1864, modelled perhaps on Flaxman's relief of 1803 on the Wedgwood monument in Stoke-on-Trent.[49] Mayer's admiration for

Charles Dickens and his visit to Liverpool in 1869 caused him to commission a number of busts of Dickens of which the version of 1872 was placed in Mayer Hall.[50] Other reliefs and busts from the 'Gallery of Friends' include Jane Mayer, Eliza Meteyard, Joseph Clarke the antiquarian and naturalist, Thomas Reay, a Liverpool cutler, Thomas Dodd, auctioneer and printseller, William Upcott, collector of manuscripts, and the Revd Thomas Redhead, Vicar of St Peter's, Rock Ferry, a friend and neighbour for nearly twenty years.[51]

Examples of Fontana's work can still be seen in Bebington, albeit in a weathered condition, on the exterior of the Free Library. In 1878 he produced two reliefs, one for each side of the entrance to the Library. The one on the left represents a man teaching a youth and the one on the right a mother instructing small children. The accompanying texts are an apt expression of Mayer's sentiments towards the people of Bebington:

> Wisdom is the principal thing, therefore, get wisdom and with all thy getting get understanding . . . Take fast hold of instruction, let her not go; keep her, for she is thy life.[52]

Giovanni Fontana enjoyed a close and affectionate relationship with Joseph Mayer; although working from his studio in London, he occasionally stayed with Mayer at Pennant House. One such visit took place in August 1880 on Fontana's return from Sydney, Australia, where he had attended the International Exhibition in 1879.[53] Fontana had received a commission from Sir Henry Parkes, Premier of New South Wales, for three statues in marble of Queen Victoria, the Prince of Wales and an allegorical figure of New South Wales, all to be 6 ft. 6 in. high for installation in the foyer of the Colonial Secretary's building in Macquarie Street, Sydney, where they remain today. Fontana discussed sketches for this commission with Mayer in 1880, made the plasters in the following year, and left for Florence to carve the sculptures in Carrara marble. After exhibiting the completed works at his studio at 217 King's Road, Chelsea, in October 1883, Fontana shipped the sculptures to Sydney, arriving early in 1884 to supervise their erection. He was paid £3,000 for the commission. Fontana also executed an over-life-size bronze statue of Sir John Dunmore Lang in Wynyard Square, Sydney.[54]

The upkeep of the library, hall and gardens had been borne entirely by Joseph Mayer, no charges falling on the community. In 1878 Mayer, looking to the future, established the Mayer Trust to look after the property and invited four close friends to manage its affairs.[55] After Mayer's death on 19 January 1886 the Trust managed to keep going until 1894 when its resources proved inadequate to maintain an efficient library service. From that date until 1930 the library was assisted by an annual grant from the Urban District Council, the Council thereafter assuming full responsibility for it.[56] In 1965 it was decided to replace the Mayer Library and in 1971 a new building on the opposite side of the road was opened. Mayer Hall continued to be used for village events, but the museum collections have long since been removed and both buildings now face an uncertain future. The establishment of a new civic complex removed the centre of community affairs from the ambience of Joseph Mayer's library and art gallery.

There was a great sense of loss in the community when Joseph Mayer died. Today Pennant House, the Free Library, Mayer Hall and Park survive, but they stand in need of repair and new uses. Indeed, in his centenary year (1986), there were calls to demolish Mayer Hall, a sad reflection on those who might have used the occasion to honour the memory of a remarkable man by restoring the buildings which sustained the community for almost a century.

NOTES

[1] Bebington [Beb.] Library [Lib.], Local [Loc.] History [Hist.] Collections [Coll.], 'A Free Village Library' (Bebington, 1878), reprinted from *The Standard*, 11–12.

[2] W. Lowndes, *The Story of Bebington* (Bebington, 1953), 41–2. The sword is now in the Williamson Art Gallery, Birkenhead, BIKGM 4518.

[3] *Ibid.*, 15; see above, p. 12.

[4] Lowndes, *op. cit.* (note 2), 29; cf. *DNB, sub* Pennant. Mayer clearly admired Pennant's combination of scholarly, military and squirearchical interests, which may have provided a model for his own lifestyle at Bebington. See also photographs of the garden front and gardens of Pennant House taken in the 1860s: Beb. Lib., Loc. Hist. Coll., cat. nos. 48, 347, 532, 539, 541, 546, 550, 562, 566, 570, 571, 575.

[5] C. Roach Smith, *Retrospections Social and Archaeological*, 3 vols. (London, 1883–91), II, 75, where Roach Smith describes Pennant House briefly: '. . . in which is also a spacious library of manuscripts, illustrated works, drawings, paintings and choice works of art; and here Mr Mayer receives such of his friends as are happily situated near enough to avail themselves of the privilege of paying him a weekly visit.' See also Eliza Meteyard, *Catalogue of the Fine Art Exhibition held in the Free Library Hall Bebington September 1871* and Beb. Lib., Loc. Hist. Coll., photographs cat. nos. 531, 567.

[6] Lowndes, *op. cit.* (note 2), 41.

[7] W. Lewin, *Clarke Aspinall: a Biography* (London, 1893), 90–1.

[8] Lowndes, *op. cit.* (note 2), 30; Lewin, *op. cit.* (note 7), 90–1.

[9] P. Sulley, *The Hundred of Wirral* (Birkenhead, 1889), 303.

[10] Beb. Lib., Loc. Hist. Coll., A. Robinson, 'Captain Joseph Mayer and his Free Library', unpublished monograph (1977), 12.

[11] *Staffordshire Weekly Times*, 5 Mar. 1870 (report on JM's speech at a dinner given in his honour after the opening of the Free Library in Feb. 1870).

[12] Lowndes, *op. cit.* (note 2), 21–5; Lewin, *op. cit.* (note 7), 80–6; Beb. Lib., Loc. Hist. Coll., photograph cat. no. 56, shows Francis's house and Martello tower.

[13] Beb. Lib., Loc. Hist. Coll., J. Harding, 'Joseph Mayer and Bebington', unpublished manuscript (*c.* 1900), 46.

[14] *Ibid.*, 48. See also unidentified press cutting (1871) describing the Bebington Floral and Horticultural Exhibition, Sept. 1871: Beb. Lib., Loc. Hist. Coll.

[15] 'A Free Village Library', *op. cit.* (note 1), 16; cf. Lowndes, *op. cit.* (note 2), 34.

[16] *Liverpool Mercury*, 18 Jan. 1870. This article describes the Library and mentions that the busts were of Herodotus, Homer, Virgil, Bede, Lorenzo de' Medici, Shakespeare, Milton, Scott, Byron and Dickens. It also describes the tower and the arrangement of the bells.

[17] 'A Free Village Library', *op. cit.* (note 1), 16–17.

[18] *Ibid.*, 18–19.

[19] MPL, unidentified press cutting, 20 Dec. 1873. A press notice of a dinner given for the Cheshire Rifle Volunteers refers *inter alia* to the 'Free Library Hall, a place which formerly served the purpose of a barn . . . now having been rebuilt and adorned with pictures, engravings, busts and works of art'. See also Harding, *op. cit.* (note 13), 51, and Meteyard, *op. cit.* (note 5), *passim.*

[20] *Ibid.* Mayer exhibited several original drawings collected to illustrate his projected 'History'. He also exhibited a collection of bronzes, gemstones, ceramics, two gold cups and Roman mosaics: see further unidentified press cuttings reviewing the exhibition in Beb. Lib., Loc. Hist. Coll. In her introduction to the catalogue, Eliza Meteyard stated that the object of the exhibition was 'the encouragement of sympathy between all classes.' The exhibition brought together works of art from many private houses in the Bebington area. In Meteyard's words, 'The impassable barrier between class and class is thus bridged over by a method as wise as it is humane and though the tendency

seems to be for all art treasures to gravitate towards public collections, the increasing taste for art amongst the general public will neutralize this tendency and serve to keep objects of vertu in private hands.'

[21] The *Builder*, 7 Mar. 1863, 170 (description of the Prince Consort Memorial, Hastings (illustrated)). It was a Gothic memorial, 65-ft. high, in the perpendicular style with a tall shaft surmounted by a clock chamber and louvred bell turret. Heffer collaborated with Edwin Stirling on the sculpture for Prince Albert and the remainder of the decorative scheme.

[22] Beb. Lib., Loc. Hist. Coll., file CWB 920, Heffer, autograph letter (1879). A number of JM's close associates were invited to write an account of their lives and work. These included Edward Heffer, Eliza Meteyard and Giovanni Fontana.

[23] Lowndes, *op. cit.* (note 2), 34.

[24] MPL, illuminated address, 23 Feb. 1874. See also above, note 4, for comparison with earlier views of Pennant House and gardens.

[25] Branch and Leete sale catalogue, 8–10 July 1886, lists contents of the conservatory. See also H. Boyle in *The Field*, 26 Nov. 1870, 456; MPL, T. F. Redhead to JM, 1863, on the growth of fruits.

[26] Heffer, *op. cit.* (note 22). The overwhelming effect of the tall thin tower in relation to the rest of the building may be compared to the campanile and basilica of St Bridget's, Wavertree, by Heffer (1868–71); cf. below, note 35.

[27] *Ibid.* Heffer mentions that while he was at the Government School of Design he worked on the designs for the Duke of Wellington's hearse and baldachino.

[28] *Ibid.* While at Thomas's, Heffer worked on designs for Somerleyton Hall, Suffolk; Preston Hall, Kent; Fish Market, Hotel and Railway Station, Lowestoft; and designs for furniture for Sultan Abdul Mejid.

[29] Gore (1862), ad loc.

[30] Heffer, *op. cit.* (note 22).

[31] The *Builder*, 19 Nov. 1859, 760; N. Pevsner, *The Buildings of England: Cheshire* (Harmondsworth, 1971), 218.

[32] The *Builder*, *op. cit.* (note 21). Here again Heffer won the competition for the design.

[33] Heffer, *op. cit.* (note 22).

[34] *Ibid.*

[35] The *Builder*, 15 July 1871, 544–7: cf. Pevsner, *op. cit.* (note 31), 254–5; see further Heffer, *op. cit.* (note 22).

[36] For references to Heffer's work in London after 1876 see The *Builder*, 12 July 1879, 785 (Anchor Coffee Tavern), 30 Oct. 1880, 541 (Queens Park Hall Mission), and 30 May 1885, 760 (letter suggesting new treatment of the west side of Westminster Hall, illustrated). See also A. G. Temple, *Descriptive and Biographical Catalogue of the Works of Art belonging to the Corporation of London* (London, 1910), 175–6, and cat. nos. 477–82 for water-colours by Heffer presented by him to the Corporation of London. See further A. Graves, *The Royal Academy of Arts, Complete Dictionary of Contributors 1769–1904*, 8 vols. (London, 1905–6), IV, 61–2 for designs exhibited by E. A. Heffer, 1862 (871), 1872 (1224 and 1238), 1873 (1135), 1874 (1186), 1875 (1038), 1878 (1122), 1885 (1804).

[37] MPL, programmes, invitations, etc., illustrating the kind of events held in Mayer Hall.

[38] The *Builder*, 1 Jan. 1881, 10. A description of the building is illustrated with plans and an engraving of the main elevation. See further pl. ix*b* for interior view of gallery in 1901, showing Robert Burns' chair in foreground, Fontana's 'Gallery of Friends' and portrait of Mayer by John Harris, now in Williamson Art Gallery. See also *Liverpool Courier*, 27 Jan. 1886, obituary for list of objects left by Mayer in his will to Bebington Free Library and Museum.

[39] Beb. Lib., Loc. Hist. Coll., file CWB 920, G. Fontana, autograph letter (1876).

[40] *Ibid.* Note by Fontana recording the making of a relief in memory of Thomas Dodd. MPL, receipt from JM to Fontana, 9 May 1855. See also MPL, sketches of 'Genius of Commerce', 'Industry', 'Innocence' and 'Genius of Art'. See further Fontana, *op. cit.* (note 39), where Fontana states that nine sculptures including 'Genius of Commerce' and 'Industry' were sold to the government of New South Wales in 1879. Only one sculpture, 'La Sonnambula', is known to survive in the Art Gallery of New South Wales (cat. no. 1163).

[41] MPL, G. Fontana to JM, 21 Aug. 1855: Fontana asks JM to help him in finding a purchaser for a 'David' and an 'Industrious Girl' (possibly Industry referred to above, note 40), mentioning that the 'Prisoner of Love' is almost complete but that he (Fontana) may need an advance to continue working.

[42] MPL, G. Fontana to C. Roach Smith, 13 May 1861, and G. Fontana to JM, 14 Oct. 1861.

[43] MPL, G. Fontana to C. Roach Smith, 30 Mar. 1867.

[44] MPL, G. Fontana to C. Roach Smith, 17 Apr. 1867.

[45] WAG, *Foreign Catalogue*, no. 7822.

[46] Roach Smith, *op. cit.* (note 5), II, 75. In this tribute to JM, Roach Smith describes Pennant House and mentions that 'the other rooms of the mansion are also stored with choice works of art, not the least interesting of which are the marble busts and profiles of friends by Signor Fontana, one of the most able sculptors of the day.' See also Meteyard, *op. cit.* (note 5), 23, cat. no. 30. Three marble busts by Fontana (indicated as owner) were shown at the exhibition. These were 'Religion', 'Modesty' and 'England's Flower' (location not known). See further Liverpool City Libraries, Hf 920 MAY, 'Portraits of Joseph Mayer and his friends'. The Walker Art Gallery has sixteen of these sculptures in its collection: see WAG, *Foreign Catalogue*, 306 no. 7640. A selection of busts and reliefs from the Gallery of Friends is on display in the new sculpture court in the Walker Art Gallery.

[47] WAG, *Foreign Catalogue*, no. 7640, a marble relief of Peggy, of whom there is also a bust, no. 7610, the sitter presumed to be Margaret Harrison. No. 7610 is inscribed 'An offering to the memory of Peggy whose elegant manners cultivated taste and affectionate friendship made her a delightful companion in my pilgrimages to shrines of art and antiquities in many lands by Joseph Mayer FSA.' The sculpture was exhibited at the Royal Academy Summer Exhibition in 1866. See also MPL, G. Fontana to JM, 4 Mar. 1856: work on a female bust (relief?) is almost completed; suggests that he will bring the bust and his tools to Liverpool in case it needs altering. Could this be a reference to WAG 7640?

[48] MPL, G. Fontana to JM, 7 Sept. 1858: Fontana thanks JM for supporting his attempts to get his work shown at the Royal Academy; mentions that a bust of Wedgwood is far advanced and that he will bring it to Liverpool shortly.

[49] WAG, *Foreign Catalogue*, no. 7611. Eliza Meteyard used a version of the 1864 bust in her *Life of Josiah Wedgwood* (London, 1866), II, 615.

[50] WAG, *Foreign Catalogue*, no. 7601.

[51] Liverpool City Libraries, Hf 920 MAY, 'Portraits of Joseph Mayer and his friends'. See also WAG, *Foreign Catalogue,* no. 7640, for a list of the busts and reliefs of this Gallery which are now in the Walker Art Gallery's collection.

[52] Prov. 4:7 and 13 (both theologically neutral).

[53] Beb. Lib., Loc. Hist. Coll., G. Fontana, 'Autograph Book'. There is an account of the work undertaken on the commission by Fontana, and sketches and a photograph of the sculpture entitled 'New South Wales'. The sketches are annotated by JM.

[54] MPL, G. Fontana to JM, 24 Jan. 1881: the modelling of the statues is nearly completed, as is the relief of the Revd Thomas Redhead (WAG, *Foreign Catalogue*, no. 7619). See further information on this commission in NMGM correspondence, 28 Jan. 1987, between Deborah Edwards, Art Gallery of New South Wales, and Richard Foster.

[55] *Liverpool Mercury*, 27 Jan. 1886: the obituary details the main provisions of the will and in particular the conditions of the 1878 trust. The first managers were Joseph Mayer, A. T. Squarey, Clarke Aspinall, R. L. Wilson and Dr Main.

[56] Robinson, *op. cit.* (note 10), 24–8.

II. ANTIQUITIES

Introduction

Mayer's Egyptian Museum (1852–67) was provided with a complete catalogue when it opened. Over the next five years it received the Faussett Collection of Anglo-Saxon antiquities (1854), the Fejérváry ivories and prehistoric metalwork (1855), the Hertz Collection of gems, with perhaps also some antique bronzes (1856), and, finally, W. H. Rolfe's extensive collection of Anglo-Saxon antiquities, excluding the coins (1857). The Faussett Collection was published as *Inventorium Sepulchrale* and the Fejérváry ivories in Pulszky's catalogue, but there was no second edition of the general catalogue of the Eygptian Museum to take account of the four new collections and the multifarious individual items that had been acquired since 1852. Some material may have been withdrawn when Mayer moved to more spacious private accommodation at Rock Ferry (1857) and Bebington (1860); we do not know. The essential problem is that the organization of the Egyptian Museum was at the level of putting like objects in the same room: there is no such thing as a Mayer accession number. The four major collections were probably kept intact;[1] even so, in 1867 'the Mayer Museum' was a munificent gift trembling on the verge of chaos.

Ecroyd Smith and C. T. Gatty, the first two curators, established four- and five-digit accession numbers in fifteen categories. For example, Medieval was 8, Greek, Roman and Etruscan 10, manuscripts 12, Egyptian 13, Assyrian 14. Thus, a late Roman ivory diptych might be M 10044, a medieval ivory M 8020, a manuscript M 12004 or M 12061. The diptych is the forty-fourth in its class, the medieval ivory the twentieth, the manuscripts respectively fourth and sixty-first. Crude but workable, the Ecroyd Smith–Gatty system extends across the entire Mayer collection: manuscripts, printed books, Etruscan jewellery, Roman ivories. Material that was already in the Liverpool Free Public Museum has year-based accession numbers (e.g. 11.8.62.5), as have Mayer donations subsequent to 1867.

Gatty in particular was indebted to A. W. Franks, both for advice on the cataloguing system and for informed guidance on Mayer's extensive holdings in ethnology.[2] His achievement may be seen in the four catalogues of 1876–83,[3] and in the exhibition of prehistoric antiquities and ethnography that he mounted in the Walker Art Gallery in 1880.[4] The prehistoric metalwork has recently been carefully described by Susan Nicholson.[5] It has not been feasible to include in the present volume a discussion of the ethnological material.

MARGARET GIBSON

43

NOTES

[1] For the sale and partial repurchase of the Hertz Collection see below, pp. 94–6.
[2] See D. M. Wilson, *Augustus Wollaston Franks: the Forgotten Collector*, Walter Neurath Memorial Lecture 16 (London, 1984), 31–6.
[3] See below, p. 228.
[4] C. T. Gatty, *Catalogue of the Loan Exhibition of Prehistoric Antiquities and Ethnography held at the Walker Art Gallery, Liverpool, May 1880* (London, 1880).
[5] Nicholson, *Prehistoric Metalwork.*

The Egyptian Collection

A. F. Shore

In the spring of 1887 Miss Amelia B. Edwards, novelist and tireless promoter of Egyptology in this country, visited the docks at Liverpool to arrange the onward passage to the U.S.A. of some antiquities recently arrived from Egypt. These had come from excavations in the Delta undertaken by the Egypt Exploration Fund (now the Egypt Exploration Society), newly founded for the purpose of encouraging the study of ancient Egypt, notably by excavations and epigraphic surveys. Miss Edwards seems to have taken the opportunity to visit the Liverpool Museum, for in a brief paper on the British provincial and private collections of Egyptian antiquities published in the following year she wrote, 'Next to the contents of the Egyptian galleries in the British Museum, the most important collection of Egyptian antiquities in England is that of the late Mr Joseph Mayer presented by him in 1867 to the Liverpool Museum ... To give a detailed description of the contents of this large gallery would carry me far beyond the limits placed at my disposal by Professor Maspero; I therefore propose from time to time to submit to readers of the *Recueil de Travaux* a selection of the more interesting inscriptions, and some account of the more important objects, in the Mayer Collection.'[1] She proceeds to describe eleven objects, all but one inscribed, without reference to the catalogue published by order of the Committee of the Liverpool Free Public Library, Museum and Gallery of Art. This catalogue was compiled by Charles T. Gatty, who acknowledges his debt to Samuel Birch, at that time Keeper of Oriental Antiquities at the British Museum. Birch had examined the collections in March 1877; from his work, Gatty writes, 'he has drawn so freely and without whose personal help he would not have accomplished this task'.[2] To comprehend the quality and scientific value of Mayer's collection it is necessary to see his aims and achievement against nineteenth-century concepts of collecting in general and against the awakening interest in ancient Egypt at popular and scholarly levels. To his contemporaries Mayer would have been seen as an antiquary with a partiality for things Egyptian. The statue of him by Fontana in St George's Hall, Liverpool, incorporated in the background a stela inscribed with a hymn to the sun god, supported by Nebamun kneeling in the attitude of a worshipper (M 13503: cf. pl. x).[3] It had been acquired from Joseph Sams. In Harris's portrait (1856), showing Mayer standing under the arch leading to the Mummy Room in the Museum at Colquitt Street, his figure is dwarfed by the artist's licence in enlarging the two, seated granite figures of the lioness-headed goddess Sekhmet (M 11809–10). Acquired from the Valentia sale of 1852, the pair had originally come from the temple of Mut, at Karnak. These standing and seated figures of the goddess, also at the time commonly identified as Bast or Bastet, were favourite pieces for early collectors. To use the overworked word of the nineteenth-century travellers, the temple was picturesque: 'I dare not say', wrote Amelia Edwards of her visit to Thebes, 'how many small outlying temples we saw in the course of that rapid survey. In one place we came upon an undulating tract of coarse halfa grass, in the midst of which, battered, defaced, forlorn, sat a weird company of green granite Sphinxes and lioness-head Basts.'[4]

A century earlier Mayer would have been called a 'curioso', a collector of objects valued not for their aesthetic appeal but for their age, rarity or novelty, or for romantic associations with famous and infamous people and events of the past. Callers at the Egyptian Museum were doubtless as fascinated by the 'large wheel-lock Gun, used at the execution of Mary Queen of Scots' as by 'Obelisk—a portion of the great one at Karnac, containing a cartouche, being the prenomen of the Pharoah [*sic!*] supposed to have erected this wonderful monument' (M 13513). The gun was to be seen in the room described as the Armoury where there was to be found a 'cocoa-nut Cup, set in silver, formerly belonging to Oliver Cromwell' (M 4312). The room boasted also 'a pair of leather boots, time of the Commonwealth', said to have been Cromwell's, as well as another curious item of footwear, 'Pair of Shoes, worn by her present Majesty, on the night of her marriage to Prince Albert'. Though his background was very different, Mayer emulated those gentlemen of education and means who had emerged in the late seventeenth and eighteenth centuries, their interests embracing specimens of natural history and geology, ethnographical material, pieces of antiquity, coins and medals. Some of these notable private collections were to form the nucleus of national and civic museums as we now know them: Elias Ashmole, whose gift to Oxford University in 1677 was the foundation of the university museum which bears his name; Sir Hans Sloane, physician by profession, whose immense collections were the impetus for the founding of the British Museum; the architect, Sir John Soane, whose collections assembled in his house in Lincoln's Inn Fields were bequeathed to the nation in 1833. If collections such as these contained little Egyptian material, it was because it was not at that time readily available.[5]

There had been only a trickle of Egyptian objects to Europe in the eighteenth century and earlier. Travellers who braved the difficulties and dangers of a journey south of Cairo brought back the occasional memento of their visits, the nature of which gives an insight into their tastes, if not their characters. The Revd Robert Huntington, scholar and divine, chaplain to the Levant Company at Aleppo 1671–81, assiduously collected manuscripts and the occasional antiquity. In 1683 he presented to the University of Oxford the limestone cornice for a false door in a mastaba tomb of Fourth-Dynasty date (*c.* 2700 B.C.) at Saqqara.[6] The Honourable Edmund Wortley Montagu, that wayward son of the most famous of English woman letter-writers, Lady Mary Wortley, sent back to his brother-in-law, the 3rd Earl of Bute, a finely painted wooden coffin made for a certain Iti-neb, with a mummy, which may not be the original occupant of the coffin. The Earl thought it a suitable gift for George III who in turn presented it in 1766 to the newly-created British Museum.[7] A morbid interest in Egyptian mummies was encouraged by the irrational belief that powdered mummy had medicinal properties, particularly efficacious in the case of wounds and impotence. Samuel Pepys recorded in his diary for May 1668 how, in the course of an evening party in which the company had been 'mighty merry', the highlight of the evening's entertainment had been a visit to a merchant's warehouse to see a mummy: 'all the middles of the man or woman's body, black and hard. I never saw any before, and therefore pleased me much, though an ill sight; and he did give me a little bit, and a bone of an arme, I suppose: and so home and there to bed.'[8] A century later mummies were the stock-in-trade of the political cartoonist and satirist.

Not, however, until the beginning of the nineteenth century was there deliberate and determined amassing of collections of Egyptian antiquities running into tens of thousands of items. The opportunity arose with the opening up of the country following Napoleon Bonaparte's occupation of Egypt and the subsequent rise to power of the Albanian Mohammed Ali, nominally as viceroy of the Ottoman Sublime Porte, *de facto*, after his slaughter of the Mamluk Beys in 1811, an independent ruler intent upon modernizing Egypt and opening it to European entrepreneurs.

The standing monuments in Egypt provided distinctive architectural elements, reliefs and stelae in stone, and sculpture, often parts of colossal statues of a size and weight requiring practical skills to transport them. In spite of the long tradition of tomb robbery in Egypt, it is clear that in the Theban area at least there was still a substantial amount of material to be recovered in the early nineteenth century, mainly from the tombs on the west bank at Thebes. The particular climatic and topographical features of the Nile valley ensured the survival of the most fragile and perishable material, at times in almost pristine condition. No other ancient people have in fact left so striking a legacy of their taste in the decorative and applied arts, and in such diversity of material.

The men who collected this material in Egypt were from a variety of backgrounds. Some were consular representatives of European powers, often employing agents of colourful or roguish character. One of the most successful and energetic was the British Consul-General, Henry Salt (1780–1827), a friend of Elgin's secretary William Hamilton whose lively intervention had secured the inclusion of the Rosetta Stone, the key to our understanding of the Egyptian hieroglyphs, among the antiquities surrendered by the French under the terms of the Treaty of Alexandria in 1802.[9] Salt employed as his principal agents Giovanni Battista Belzoni, a Paduan by birth, and Giovanni d'Athanasi, a Greek. Mainly through what was then considered to be excavation on their part, Salt built up no less than three great collections. The first was acquired by the Trustees of the British Museum in a series of transactions of increasing acerbity. The second was purchased by the King of France on the encouragement of Champollion. The third was auctioned posthumously at Sotheby's over nine days in 1835 and dispersed in public and private collections; it consisted of 1,053 lots. Other collectors had aristocratic backgrounds. George Annesley, Viscount Valentia, who had travelled extensively in the Near and Far East from 1802–6, with Salt as his secretary and draughtsman, until he succeeded as 2nd Earl of Mountmorris, amassed a collection at Arley Castle, Staffordshire, mainly through Salt, in the years 1817–20. Joseph Sams (1784–1860) was a bookseller of eccentric character settled at Darlington who visited Egypt and Palestine in 1822–3. He brought back an extensive collection of antiquities, particularly rich in papyri and stelae, many acquired by the British Museum through a Parliamentary grant in 1824. Sams continued to purchase and to deal in Egyptian antiquities. Henry Stobart was an English clergyman who visited Egypt in 1854–5.

The stimulus provided by the discovery of the Rosetta stone in 1799 and the expectation of fresh information which texts could provide led to scientific expeditions to record the standing monuments. Though essentially epigraphic in purpose, these expeditions also collected antiquities for national museums. The most notable was the great Prussian expedition of 1842–5 under the patronage of the King of Prussia. It was led by Karl Richard Lepsius (1810–84) who sent back to Berlin 15,000 Egyptian antiquities and plaster casts as well as innumerable paper squeezes of inscriptions. 'We made,' wrote Lepsius, 'our selection of the monuments not for ourselves, but commissioned by our government for the Royal Museum in Berlin, therefore for the benefit of science and a public eager after knowledge.'[10]

The manner in which antiquities were collected for this public 'eager after knowledge', or (as others might put it) for the satisfaction of an uninstructed public curiosity, destroyed (as one can now see) almost as much evidence as it recovered. In the passage in which Lepsius defends his collecting of antiquities against his critics, he writes, 'We have been chiefly accused of a thirst for destruction, which under the given circumstances, would presuppose a peculiarly barbarous feeling to have existed in our party; for as we did not, like many of our rivals, excavate and transport the monuments, the greater part of which had previously been invisible, hurriedly and by night and with bribed assistance, but leisurely, and with open aid from the authorities, and before the eyes of numerous travellers, all disregard in our treatment of the remaining monuments, of which perhaps they formed a part, would have certainly been the more blameable, since it was so easy to avoid it.'[11] The hallmark of excavation was violence; and even after greater government control was exercised by the foundation of the Egyptian Antiquities Service in 1858, under the directorship of Auguste Mariette, there was lack of understanding of the scope of archaeology, the techniques of excavation, and the value of all antiquities, no matter how common or how small, for advancement of knowledge. In Mayer's day the study of objects was pursued in isolation in a museum. The notion, now commonplace, that the recovery of the objects and the study of them must be integrated into a single process in the field itself was not yet formulated. In Egypt the first tentative steps to the development of such practice was taken by Alexander Henry Rhind (1833–63), who excavated among the Theban tombs in 1855–7, his own collection of antiquities forming the nucleus of the Egyptological collections of the Royal Museum of Scotland.

No sooner had these great private collections been built up in the first half of the nineteenth century than they were promptly dispersed, in part by private sale, in part by public auction. It is difficult to avoid the conclusion that personal profit was one motive in their formation. In the 1830s, in addition to the disposal of the Salt Collections and the private sale of Sams's material to the British Museum, there were no less than five major sales at Sotheby's: Barker (Salt's successor in Egypt) in 1833, Burton in 1836, Giovanni Anastasi in 1839, and d'Athanasi (Salt's agent) in 1836 and again in 1837; the latter was over seven days, with the residue of the collection being sold in 1845.

Joseph Mayer's collecting instincts seem to have been attracted to Egyptian material about the middle of the century. The earliest portrait of Mayer as connoisseur, painted *c.* 1840, shows no Egyptian material (pl. I). When he opened his

Egyptian Museum in 1852 he already possessed a large collection, the most important single source being purchases from the collection retained by Sams after the sale to the British Museum. It had been enriched by discerning purchases from the Salt sale and from other sources. The collection was shown in both London and Darlington, and a note on it in the *Gentleman's Magazine* for April 1833 speaks of 'upwards of two thousand two hundred' items. Sams issued a catalogue in 1839 under the title *Objects of Antiquity Forming Part of the Extensive and Rich Collections from Ancient Egypt brought to England by, and now in the Possession of J. Sams.*

Mayer's collections were enhanced by notable acquisitions from three other sources. Substantial purchases were made at Sotheby's Valentia sale of 1852, including some large stone objects typical of Egypt in popular imagination, the two Sekhmet figures (M 11809 and 11810: cf. frontispiece) and the great granite sarcophagus of Bakenkhonsu (M 13864) from his tomb on the west bank at Thebes at Dra' Abu el-Naga' (Tomb 35).[12] A statue taken from the tomb at about the same time by the Italian Drovetti, now in the Glyptothek, Munich, contains an account of his career. Only the most high-ranking of officials enjoyed a stone sarcophagus in the New Kingdom; Bakenkhonsu held the office of First Prophet of Amun at Thebes for twenty-seven years under Ramesses II (*c.* 1279–1213 B.C.). Mayer continued to make substantial purchases of Egyptian material for about five years after the opening of his Egyptian Museum, after which his interests seem to have been directed elsewhere, as the changes in the name of the museum imply.[13] Some of the most important material in the collection, particularly of papyri, came from the private purchase of the collection of the Revd H. Stobart, acquired in Egypt in 1854–5.[14] Stobart was one of the increasing numbers of visitors to Egypt from the middle of the century, sufficient to attract the attention of the publishers John Murray of London, who produced a *Handbook for Travellers in Egypt* in 1847. Three years earlier William Thackeray had visited Egypt under the auspices of the Peninsular and Orient Steam Navigation Company. His *Notes of a Journey from Cornhill to Cairo* (London) appeared in 1846; in it he writes of the Hotel d'Orient, accommodating travellers to and from India, as 'England in Egypt'.[15] Two events were to further the development of tourism and so popular interest in ancient Egypt: the visit of the Prince of Wales (the future Edward VII) and his young bride, the Princess Alexandra, in 1868–9 and the opening of the Suez Canal in November 1869. Mayer's changing interests may account for his apparent indifference to seeing the country whose antiquities he had assiduously been collecting, as he says in the preface to the 1852 Catalogue 'at a great outlay of time and money'. The collection of another traveller, T. J. Bourne, who apparently also visited Nubia, is briefly mentioned as being acquired in a note at the end of the 1852 Catalogue. The last major purchase of Egyptian material by Mayer was in 1857, the collection of Bram Hertz (*c.* 1839–65), a catalogue of which had appeared in 1851 under the title *The Collections of Assyrian, Babylonian, Egyptian, Greek, Roman, Indian and Mexican Antiquities formed by B. Hertz* (London).[16]

The mummy room

Within the various categories into which the public and private collections may be conveniently divided, an obvious group is formed by bandaged mummies and objects associated with burial and embalment—painted coffins, canopic jars used as receptacles for the organs removed in the course of mummification, amulets, *ushabti*-figures and boxes. From the beginning of the display of Egyptian objects a 'mummy room' was an expected feature. These physical remains continued to exercise the same fascination for ambitious collectors as they had for earlier travellers. That the mummified remains included bandaged animals, birds, even fish and reptiles, added a further macabre interest to the group.

In the Egyptian Museum seven mummies, together with the coffins with which they were associated, provided the dominant interest of Room 3, called in the 1852 Catalogue 'The Mummy Room' (pl. IV). They were exhibited prone in standard island cases; on the tops were placed Greek vases. Two other mummies and cases were to be found in the Sculpture Room. The mummies all came from the Sams Collection; the coffins are of the Late Period (after 1000 B.C.), when it was customary to keep coffins and mummies above ground, stacked in old tomb chapels or temple rooms, and so readily accessible. Descriptions of these caches of mummies are a commonplace of the early travellers. Though these coffins have mostly suffered from damage at the time of the Second World War, their surfaces were originally richly decorated, divided into several registers with brightly painted representations of strange deities, part human, part animal, and scenes of a ritual and mythological character. In the best preserved the colours remained brilliantly fresh due to the mineral nature of the pigments used. Of the coffins none is out of the ordinary. In early days one (M 13994) attracted a certain interest for having on it in three places the cartouche with the prenomen of Amenophis I, a king of the Eighteenth Dynasty (*c.* 1525–1504 B.C.). The interior was drawn for the 1839 Sams Catalogue.[17] It was supposed that the coffin must be contemporary with the king, though in fact it is some six or seven hundred years later, that king being worshipped as patron of the necropolis on the west bank. In Gatty's catalogue of 1877 the name of the owner of the coffin was read as 'Nasamen' (Nesamun), a priest of Amonre; in the only place at which names have survived, on the right-hand side of the exterior of the coffin chest, the intended recipient of funerary offerings seems to be a chantress-priestess of Amun called Djedkhonsu-iuesankh.[18] The coffin is, therefore, likely to belong to the large cache of coffins of priests and priestesses of Amun in the great temple of Deir el-Bahari, on the west bank at Thebes, subsequently found and cleared in 1891.[19] Another coffin of interest for the rich gilding and contrast of black hieroglyphs on yellow background, dating to the Ptolemaic period (*c.* 200 B.C.), is inscribed for a certain Horwennefer (M 13996). In the 1839 Sams Catalogue it is described as 'probably one of the finest and best preserved of the kind in existence'. The text goes on with the enigmatic statement, 'When it was first discovered in Egypt the sum of Five Hundred dollars were offered in that country for it, but refused.'[20] Of interest too was the possession of three cases enclosing the mummy of a door-keeper of the temple of Amun, Peteamun, wrapped in an outer shroud of linen dyed red; the innermost is composed of cartonnage (layers of linen and glue, covered by a layer of stucco) and the other two of wood, the inner in anthropoid form, the outer rectangular in shape and incorporating the familiar scene of the weighing of the heart of the deceased (M 14003).

There is reason to suppose that the mummies associated with these coffins did not originally belong with them, the coffins either being reused in later times or the mummies being placed in any convenient coffin by the native dealers. Two other mummies show marked similarities with examples acquired by the British Museum and by the Leiden Museum of Antiquities. The mummy from the coffin of the woman Tamutheru of Twenty-First-Dynasty date (M 14047), that of a young adult female, is exceptional for the careful way in which the body has been prepared. The head has been modelled with resin and carefully swathed to fill out the shrunken contours. The features are painted on the surface of the outer covering in a manner reminiscent of Old Kingdom practice. The limbs are wrapped tightly and separately, and some attempt has been made to reproduce the rounded contour of a living person.[21] A second mummy (M 13997), that of a woman acquired with the coffin of the chantress-priestess of Amun, called Ese, is similarly treated.[22] An example of the same kind in the British Museum was acquired in the Salt sale of 1835.[23] Three mummies prepared in the same manner in Leiden are from Anastasi.[24] An unusual feature on one of the Mayer examples (M 13997) is its frame of palm fibre bound with linen threads, suspended like a collar about the neck, on which are strung small wooden amulets originally gilded, of standard funerary type.[25] A similar frame, or wicker-work, lies across the chest of one of the Leiden mummies and it is possible that all in this group were similarly accoutred.[26] One other example is known, on a mummy of an adult man acquired by the British Museum in 1839 from the Anastasi Collection. It is wrapped in more standard style, with an outer shroud on which there is a painted representation of Osiris in the style of the Roman period.[27] It is to this date, the second or third century A.D., that the group as a whole must belong.

The human mummies remained wrapped. Mayer does not seem to have been interested in that destructive form of investigation not unpopular in the Victorian period, a publicly staged unwrapping of a mummy ostensibly in the interests of science. The appearance of desiccated flesh, 'black and hard' as Pepys observed, could, however, be seen in a fragment of a mummified body (M 11438). It consisted of the left hand, identified as female, thickly coated with bitumen, with remnants of gilding, having rings shaped like obelisks on the first and second fingers, the shafts of lapis lazuli with apex and base of gold.[28] It formed part of the collection of the Revd Stobart and was said to come from Saqqara, the necropolis of ancient Memphis, some twenty miles south of Cairo. There are two other gold rings on the hand, one plain, the other set with a scarab of lapis lazuli.

Papyri

Papyrus, the name given to a sedge-like plant once natural in Egypt and to the form of paper manufactured from slices of the interior pith, is as familiar as are mummies in the popular concept of Egypt. Though there had been some interest in the acquisition of Coptic (Christian) vellum and paper codices, early visitors to Egypt do not seem to have been aware of, or familiar with, papyrus rolls. The imagination of contemporaries had been stirred by the recovery of 800 papyrus rolls in 1752 at Herculaneum, buried under volcanic ash during the eruption of Vesuvius in A.D. 79. It is, however, not until 1778 that there is the first recorded interest in papyrus in Egypt itself when a commercial traveller was offered some rolls by native peasants. One of those purchased eventually found its way as a gift to Cardinal Stefano Borgia. The banal nature of its contents, a list of villagers in the Faiyum liable for compulsory labour on the local dykes and canals—not some lost masterpiece of Greek literature—acted perhaps as a discouragement to collectors. So far as papyri written in Egyptian are concerned, there seems to have been no interest in them, partly perhaps because of lack of availability, partly because the texts could not be understood and the hieratic and demotic scripts employed on papyrus did not have the same fascination as the monumental hieroglyphs carved on stone. An interest in the illustrated copies of the *Book of the Dead* might have been expected, but it is not until the collectors of the early nineteenth century that there is an urge to acquire ancient papyri, spurred on by an unconscious expectation that they would contain secret and lost wisdom. The great sales of the first half of the nineteenth century contained considerable numbers of papyri, the names for instance of Salt, Sams, Cureton, Barker, Anastasi, to mention only some, being still associated with individual papyri of literary, documentary or religious character.

The demand for papyri was such that native dealers were encouraged to make up forged rolls by gumming very small fragments to a core, tying them with strips of linen and impressing on them mud sealings, to simulate a genuine roll. One is surprised that so many have found their way into collections. Mayer seems to have acquired some, for the description of item 246 in the 1852 Catalogue, 'Papyrus Roll, bound round with inscribed linen bands, which are sealed with clay', certainly suggests a made-up roll of this kind. Some pieces, presumably from Sams, were however genuine: item 217 of the Catalogue, 'A Roll of Papyrus, in the demotic character, with parts of it written in red colour. Along the top are figures', is probably to be identified with item 187 in the Gatty Catalogue, where it is described as containing eleven pages of the 'Ritual of the Dead' in large hieratic writing for Peterharptah, son of Tatekhensu (M 11161). There were also some fragments of earlier *Books of the Dead*, though none as complete or as fine as that given to the Liverpool Royal Institution in about 1828.[29] It was not until the purchase of the Stobart Collection in 1854–5 that Mayer acquired a papyrus of outstanding importance, a secular document of major juridical interest, still known as Papyrus Mayer A (M 11162). Associated with it is a second fragmentary piece known as Papyrus Mayer B. These two texts belong to a series of well-preserved papyri, written in hieratic script, which record the arrest and examination of ordinary Egyptians, men and women, accused of robbery of royal tombs and sacred places of the west bank of Thebes in a period of civil disorder towards the end of the New Kingdom period (c. 1100–1050 B.C.).[30] No other series is so informative for the light shed on state legal procedures in ancient Egypt and the lives and conditions of the poorer classes of the population, or for allusions to the confused historical events of the time and references to buildings and monuments which still stand to this day.

Nothing is known for certain of the circumstances of discovery but it may be plausibly conjectured that the appearance of a number of texts of the same age and character over a short period of time is the result of a single find, usually fortuitous, in this case an archive of documents preserved perhaps in the temple of Medinet Habu, discovered about 1854–5 (their condition would suggest in jars), and sold separately to a number of private collectors and travellers by whose names some are still commonly known. One papyrus of the series was broken by its finders into two halves, the lower portion being acquired by Lord Amherst of Hackney who visited Egypt in 1860, the upper portion coming to light on examination by Capart of antiquities brought from Egypt by the Duke of Brabant, the future Leopold II of Belgium, who visited Egypt in 1854 and 1862–3.[31]

Pap. Mayer A bears entries for Year 1 and Year 2 of 'The Repeating of Births', a name chosen to initiate a new era when order was finally restored in Thebes and attempts made to restore the damage done and to recover stolen material. The date corresponds to Years 19 and 20 of Ramesses XI, the last of the New Kingdom pharaohs, *c.* 1069 B.C. The papyrus consists of a series of short reports into the examination of the accused in two separate series of thefts, one from certain gilded portable shrines, the other from various tombs in the royal necropolis. Earlier stages of the investigation into the robberies in the necropolis, held before the same judges, are given in a papyrus in the British Museum (Pap. BM 10052) written in the same hand and style, one of three papyri belonging to the series bought in 1870 from Miss Selina Harris, whose father, a merchant resident for several years in Alexandria, had secured a magnificent collection of major texts of historical and literary importance. The investigation into the thefts from the portable chests connects Pap. Mayer A with another papyrus in the British Museum (Pap. BM 10403), bought from an Italian Egyptologist, Luigi Vasalli, in 1856. A third papyrus in the British Museum (Pap. BM 10221), concerned with an earlier investigation, contains on the verso two lists of names, one of thieves from a portable shrine, the other of thieves from tombs in the necropolis. Both include names associated with the thefts investigated in Pap. Mayer A. It was bought in 1857 from Dr Henry Abbott, a former medical orderly in the British Navy; a fascimile edition appeared in 1860.[32] Pap. Mayer B is a fragment containing confessions to the robberies in the tomb of Ramesses VI. It cannot at the moment be brought into historical connection with other papyri in the tomb robbery series.

The Revd Henry Stobart had acquired his Greek and Egyptian papyri at Thebes on his visit to Egypt in 1854. Among his acquisitions was a papyrus containing the lost funerary panegyric by the Attic orator Hyperides over the dead of the Samian War. It came from the same dealer as other fragments of Hyperides, acquired slightly earlier, proving to be one of the earliest major finds of lost Greek literary works.[33] These Hyperides papyri were purchased by the British Museum. There seems, however, to have been some delay or indifference to the remainder of Stobart's collection which resulted in their being offered to Mayer.

The papyri lay unexamined at Liverpool until the notorious forger of texts, Constantine Simonides, called on Mayer in February 1860 in the company of James Smith, seeking permission to see the Egyptian Museum.[34] At this time the reputation of Simonides was already compromised: two years earlier he had returned to London after dubious transactions in Germany leading at one point to his arrest at the instigation of Lepsius. Like all rogues he seems to have possessed a certain plausible charm; he succeeded in ingratiating himself into Mayer's confidence and deceiving him by the audacity of his own claims to knowledge of ancient Egyptian writings. He dedicated to Mayer his brief, imaginative explanation of four antiquities in the Museum, published in Greek and English in 1860.[35] On 9 May 1861, he read a paper to the Historic Society of Lancashire and Cheshire on the subject of a gold plate, allegedly 1 ft. 10 in. (560 mm.) long by 7 in. (178 mm.) wide, of the thickness of a sheet of cardboard, with embossed hieroglyphs. 'We must warmly congratulate Mr Mayer, the lover of antiquity, on his possession of this treasure, from which we have elicited some important matters hitherto unknown.'[36] The interpretation of the text by Simonides is so wild that it gives no clue to what the object may be to which he is referring. Simonides was allowed to unroll papyri under the watchful eye of Mayer and his curator, John Eliot Hodgkin. He describes the papyri as being 'for the most part, so torn and damaged, lying pell-mell together, and offering neither connection nor continuity'; later he writes of his own 'finds' as being 'discovered in the Collection of the accomplished Mr Stobart, and all the rest in the Egyptian Collection of Mr J. Sams, now in the possession of Mr Mayer.'[37] Subsequently he was allowed to work on the papyri at his address in Liverpool and while so doing claimed to have found with them fragments of a Greek text of the Gospel of Matthew, purporting to have been written by Nicolaus the Deacon at the dictation of the Evangelist in the fifteenth year after the Ascension. There rapidly followed announcements in a series of letters to the press of the discovery of fragments of the epistles of James and Jude and lost works of Greek antiquity, including the fanciful claim of the ten commandments written in Greek and Egyptian Demotic characters, in parallel columns, 'belonging also to the first century before Christ'. The claims excited interest among the public and scepticism among scholars. The matter of their authenticity was the subject of an investigation by the Royal Society of Literature at whose premises in London they were exhibited, together with 'two hieratic rolls', doubtless Pap. Mayer A (M 11162) and the other fragment of the same character and date, mounted on linen by Simonides, known as Papyrus Mayer B (M 11186). The initial and name of Simonides appears written in Greek on the bottom right-hand corner of the papyrus, followed by the Greek word ἀνακάλυψις, doubtless a reference to the unrolling. Though there is no direct reference to the source of the fragment, it must also have been part of the Stobart purchase.

The merit of recognizing the character and importance of the two papyri, Mayer A and B, belongs to Charles Wycliffe Goodwin who had been an influential voice in the exposure of the Greek forgeries of Simonides.[38] Goodwin was one of the great pioneers in the decipherment of the hieratic script and a notable example of how the scientific knowledge of ancient Egypt was advanced by polymath scholars before there were established academic posts. A graduate from Cambridge in classics and mathematics, he subsequently read for the bar at Lincoln's Inn and was called in 1842. Finding the practice of the law uncongenial, he returned to Cambridge to a fellowship at his old college, St Catherine's, resigning it to return to London to practice as a barrister. In 1865 he was appointed Assistant Judge for the Supreme Court for China and Japan, married and removed to Shanghai. In a note to the second edition of the Catalogue, Gatty records his death there: 'Mr C. W. Goodwin, the eminent Egyptologist, whose services are acknowledged in the Preface, died at Shanghai early in the year 1878.'

One other text acquired by Mayer from Stobart proved of particular interest: it is written in demotic script upon the whitened surfaces of four flat pieces of wood, pierced to allow them to be tied by cords. Such writing tablets comprising several leaves, of a size conveniently held in the closed hand, were widely used in the Graeco-Roman world for letters, accounts, school exercises and memoranda of all kinds. The Stobart tablets record the dates of entry of the planets and the moon into the zodiacal signs covering the period A.D. 63–140; originally there must have been at least eleven such tablets.[39] Such compilations of planetary tablets were used for the casting of horoscopes; the basis of computation is uncertain. They provided for any specific day the zodiacal sign within which each planet was located. This practice does not go back to Egyptian thought of the pharaonic period; it derives from the influence of Babylonian astrology in the Graeco-Roman world. So thoroughly, however, was it absorbed into Egyptian culture that Egypt rather than Babylonia was widely believed to be the repository of this secret knowledge.

Stelae

A third major category of objects readily available and of appeal to the early nineteenth-century visitors to Egypt was fragments of relief from temples and tombs and the inscribed stone funerary tablets known as stelae.[40] These were commonly placed against or embodied in the tomb chapel, marking the place at which offerings were made to the deceased. The stelae would normally have a representation of the deceased, seated before an offering table or worshipping Osiris and other deities; commonly he was accompanied by his wife, with other members of the family also depicted. Texts in the hieroglyphic script give the name and titles of the deceased, sometimes some biographical information, more usually spells of a ritual nature to ensure the provision of the necessary offerings. This category was well represented in Mayer's Museum with examples ranging in date from the Old Kingdom to the Graeco-Roman period. Sams is the principal source. In the 1852 Catalogue the first room is called the 'Egyptian Stele and Monumental Room', but tablets were also to be found in the Third Room, that is the Mummy Room.

The frontispiece in the 1852 Catalogue is a drawing of a limestone stela of a man, Tuthmose also called Pasnebnefer, described as a 'doctor', dating to the Nineteenth Dynasty, *c.* 1200 B.C. (M 13851: pl. xi*a*). It is unusual in having a pointed top representing a pyramidion above the rounded upper edge and is inscribed also on the back and the sides with standard formulae. The front of the stela is divided into three registers. The upper shows Tuthmose accompanied by his wife offering incense to Osiris with the two goddesses Isis and Nephthys behind. In the middle register is a representation of the ceremony of the 'opening of the mouth' performed on the mummy of Tuthmose to ensure the deceased the use of his limbs and organs. The formula of the spell is read by his eldest son, dressed in a leopard skin in the role of the *sem*-priest, and behind is a group of mourning women. In the lower register are eight relations, male and female. The entries in Mayer's catalogue of 1852 are very summary, and seldom informative; it is uncertain which item in the catalogue refers to the frontispiece unless it was one of those exhibited in the Mummy Room (because of its middle register?) described simply as '44a to 60a Stele, with figures and inscriptions'. In the catalogue prepared by Gatty there are more detailed descriptions, giving names and titles and the character of the text, provided by Samuel Birch who visited the collections in March 1877. Two selected for particular comment by Llewellyn Jewitt in the *Art Journal* of 1870, to show of this class of object 'their high antiquity, their great interest and their beauty', are M 13860 and M 13850, both of which have survived the Second World War.[41] The former is sculptured from a substantial block of red granite from the Aswan region, some $27\frac{1}{4}$ in. (692 mm.) high, 15 in. (381 mm.) wide and $1\frac{1}{4}$ in. (31·7 mm.) thick. It dates to the Twelfth Dynasty, *c.* 1800 B.C. Mayer in his catalogue described it as being of Hyksos date 'anterior to the time of the Israelites, and considered to be of historical importance', displaying that interest which Egyptian objects had for their early admirers, for their possible biblical associations. The Hyksos, 'the shepherd kings', were known from Manetho and Josephus.[42] The stela is exceptionally well cut and polished, and it is inscribed for Chnumu, who is shown seated with two other members of his family. The second stela (M 13850), described by Mayer as being 'in hard Egyptian marble, called by the Italians travertine', and correctly dated to the Fourth Dynasty (*c*. 2700 B.C.), is a well-carved panel from a limestone false door at Saqqara; it is 8 in. (203 mm.) thick, showing a certain Nyankhtet seated before an offering table with, to the right, a standard list of linen cloths.[43]

Both these pieces are described in Amelia Edwards's paper in the *Recueil de Travaux* for 1888.[44] A third piece which she describes (M 11015: pl. xi*b*) is of particular current interest. It is a black granite pyramidion which must originally have capped a small pyramid, perhaps of brick, such as are a feature of the free-standing tomb chapels (with their shaft tombs) in the New Kingdom cemetery south of the ancient causeway connecting the valley temple with the pyramid of Unas. It is inscribed for a vizier Neferronpet. Two viziers of this name are known. Neferronpet I was in office in the latter part of the reign of Ramesses II (*c* 1230 B.C.) and he held also priestly titles distinctive of the cult of Ptah, principal god of Memphis. Neferronpet II held office under Ramesses IV (*c*.1150 B.C.), whose cartouche is carved on a kneeling figure of a Neferronpet supporting a shrine containing an image of Osiris (now in Leiden). Since this statue bears the same priestly titles as those held by Neferronpet I, either the statue was originally made for Neferronpet I and usurped by Neferronpet II (perhaps a grandson) by the expedient of adding the cartouche of his reigning sovereign, or Neferronpet II was appointed also to the same priestly offices as Neferronpet I. The Mayer pyramidion is the only monument associated with either Neferronpet which gives information on family relationships. Whether it is Neferronpet I or II who is named on the pyramidion may well be resolved in light of the recent excavations by Professor Tawfiq (of Cairo University) in the area of the New Kingdom cemetery at Saqqara, the ancient necropolis of Memphis. He has succeeded in relocating the tomb chapel of a vizier Neferronpet, with two burial shafts, each containing an imposing stone sarcophagus. It is doubtless from this tomb that the Mayer pyramidion, formerly in the Sams Collection, originally came.[45]

Statuary

Altogether thirty-three stone funerary stelae from the Mayer Collection are listed in Gatty's catalogue, in addition to five in wood. Mayer was no less successful in obtaining representative examples of Egyptian stone sculpture in the round; in the section of Gatty's catalogue devoted to 'Figures of Individuals' there are seventeen statues, mainly of limestone, between 1 and 2 ft. in height, most of which were exhibited in the wall cases of the First Room at Colquitt Street. Statues of this kind were either placed in tombs or set up in temples for votive purposes, the dedicator from the time of the New Kingdom frequently being shown in the attitude of a worshipper of the gods, holding a shrine with an image of a god or a stela with hymns inscribed upon it. Those acquired by Mayer date from the Middle to New Kingdoms, with a number coming from the last great period of Egyptian sculpture, from 700 B.C. down to the Graeco-Roman period. They may be said to be good examples of their categories.

There were no royal statues in Mayer's Egyptian Museum except for the lower part of a statue measuring just under 2 ft., described in the Gatty Catalogue as being of black granite; the figure (M 13933, lost in 1941) is represented kneeling and identified from the hieroglyphic inscription on the plinth as Alexander the Great (332–323 B.C.) or his son by Roxane, Alexander IV (316–304 B.C.); the epithet 'beloved of Banebdjed, the Great God living in Re' following the name is one associated with the Delta city of Mendes and its neighbourhood. The fragment had formerly been in the collection of Lord Valentia and the circumstances of its acquisition are recorded in his account of his travels to the Near and Far East, published in 1811. 'A Kamsin, or hot wind set in,' he writes 'and drove us to our tents, but in the evening we ventured out, and at one extremity of Medinet Timac discovered the ruins of a temple, the columns of which had been thrown down and broken: they were of granite, together with their capitals and bases. A little boy carried us to a spot, where we saw the lower part of a statue in basalt, of very fine workmanship; this I bought from him for a dollar, and hired an ass from the Schech of the town to carry it to Mansoura. Whoever discovers an antique, has a right to dispose of it; they say it is God's property, and he gives it to whom he pleases.'[46]

Also lost is the base for a royal statue (M 13510) of historical interest. It was reproduced in the 1839 Sams Catalogue, with 1837 as the date of its acquisition, and recognized as a statue base.[47] It was exhibited in the Stele and Monumental Room, and is of interest for the erasure of the name in two of the six cartouches: it corroborated the historic account of the names of offending kings being often erased, as a mark of disgrace. Of limestone, measuring 3 ft. 5 in. (1041 mm.) in length and 2 ft. 2 in. (660 mm.) in width, some 8 in. (203 mm.) thick, it was hollowed out to receive the statue of a king from the confused period of troubled succession and short reigns following the death of the pharaoh Merneptah, the successor of Ramesses II, *c.* 1200 B.C. Three of the cartouches contained the name of Amenmesses, two had his prenomen erased, three others gave the name of Sethos II, suggesting that he usurped the statue of Amenmesses, as he did other monuments of that king.

In Mayer's time Egyptian sculpture was little appreciated except as curiosities from a time before the attainment of the perfect beauty portrayed in the sculptures of ancient Greece. In contrast with them it was thought to lack anatomical detail in its parts and to be wanting in the grace of motion. 'Their figures', Sir James Barry taught at the Royal Academy Schools, 'appear neither to act nor think, and have more the resemblance of dead than of animated nature.'[48] The technical accomplishment in the carving of the harder ornamental stones, such as granite and basalt, was recognized. The colossal scale of some royal sculpture impressed itself upon the Victorian imagination and came to be a popular association of the ancient civilization of Egypt. Except for the two Sekhmet statues Mayer lacked the large-scale sculpture which is characteristic of the early collection of Egyptian sculpture in the British Museum, mainly from the Salt Collections. Such material was, however, represented at Colquitt Street in the form of the cast of a colossal royal head wearing the double crown which is depicted to the left of the general view of the Jewellery Room (pl. v). The cast cannot be identified in the 1852 Catalogue. Gatty refers to a cast of the upper part of a colossal statue of Amenophis III (M 13811), stating that the original is in the British Museum, but the drawing does not correspond to any of the colossal heads acquired by the British Museum from the area of the mortuary temple of Amenophis III on the west bank at Thebes, destroyed except for the monumental statues of quartzite blocks known as the Colossi of Memnon. Either the draughtsman has drawn the head partly from imagination (a more distant prospect of it, as seen from the Mummy Room (pl. IV), is scarcely recognizable as being

Egyptian) or some other statue is represented. The double crown suggests a head which was recovered with a colossal arm by Belzoni in 1817 from 'Karnak', long regarded as a head of Tuthmosis III (British Museum no. 15), but more recently identified as coming in fact from a statue of Amenophis III, at the temple of Mut.[49]

More attractive to the modern eye than the standard stone statues which Mayer acquired are some of the smaller wooden figures of officials and priests which served the same purpose as their stone counterparts. In pose and style they follow in general the conventions of stone sculpture, but the material allows a delicacy of carving and lively alert expression. From the New Kingdom they frequently have with the adoption of contemporary costume a more naturalistic appearance. Notable for their state of preservation and refinement of the modelling of the head and torso are the two statues of Nebreshy and Amenhetep, carved in dark wood, from the earlier part of the New Kingdom, *c.* 1600 B.C., represented in a kilt with upper part of the body bare, in the normal standing attitude, left leg advanced. The arms hang stiffly at the side, carved in one piece with the figures unlike the majority of these figures in wood (M 13505–6). The figures are set in rectangular wooden bases which are inscribed in hieroglyphs with the conventional text for funerary offerings: of unusual interest is the information that Nebreshy and Amemhetep are full brothers, the sons of Nefer and Sankhrenef.[50]

The finest of the wood figures acquired by Mayer (M 13519) served a different purpose: carved in ebony, $8\frac{1}{2}$ in. (216 mm.) in height, it belongs to a very small group of servant figures carrying large jars, dating from the late Eighteenth Dynasty, *c.*1350 B.C. In some cases traces of the original contents of the jars of this type have been retained, wax or grease forming a base for some cosmetic preparation intended for medicinal or magical use by the deceased from whose tomb the figures have come. The statuette is in the form of an elderly male servant, the features suggesting a Nubian, dressed in a long pleated skirt, bent double under the weight of the pot carried on his shoulders (pl. XII).[51] Depiction of any form of action or movement in sculpture is rare, but the ancient craftsman has captured the natural pose of someone carrying a heavy load and in the fineness of his carving has produced a genuine masterpiece. The provenance of the object—its quality would suggest that it came from the tomb of a high official—is not known. Mayer acquired it from Sams who had himself acquired it from a Belgian, Charles Bogaert.[52] Sams included a drawing of it in his 1839 Catalogue describing the figure as 'a Nubian female slave bearing a vase of water, the whole elegantly carved, and the Nubian countenance strikingly depicted'.[53] At the time, for its quality of workmanship, imaginative depiction and state of preservation, it could be matched only by a similar posed figure of a Nubian servant girl from the Anastasi Collection at Leiden[54] and another Nubian servant girl carrying the jar at her hip, formerly in the collections of Alnwick Castle assembled by the 4th Duke of Northumberland, who travelled in Egypt in 1826.[55] The latter is said to have come from the tomb at Thebes of Meryptah, chancellor and chief priest of Amun under Amenophis III.

Objects of daily life

This fine wooden figure belongs to the class of antiquities usually described as objects of daily life. Though coming from tombs, this class comprises a wide range of objects which would also be used in daily life: furniture, the apparatus of the toilet, jewellery, musical instruments, tools and weapons, scribal equipment, and other household effects.[56] Illustrations of these objects and reproductions of the scenes in which they appear in the tomb chapels provided the source material for one of the most popular works on ancient Egypt, John Gardiner Wilkinson's *Manners and Customs of the Ancient Egyptians including their Private Life, Government, Laws, Arts, Manufactures, Religion, Agriculture and Early History, derived from a Comparison of the Paintings, Sculptures, and Monuments still existing with the Accounts of Ancient Authors.* First published in three volumes in 1837, it went through many reprints and abridgements until its final revision by Samuel Birch in 1878. The eye does not need to be tutored to see at a glance the delicacy of form, the skill of the craftsman working in wood, ivory, faience, glass, metal, and semi-precious stones, or the novelty and range of its secular decorative themes drawn from the formerly rich and exotic flora and fauna of the Nile Valley. They have immediate sensual appeal. Any judgement of the aesthetic tastes and abilities of the ancient Egyptians which is based solely on their monumental sculpture, relief and painting must necessarily be founded on evidence which is far from complete.

The New Kingdom (*c.* 1550–1069 B.C.) may be described as the golden period for the decorative arts, and local villagers of Gourna, the village sprawling out over the Theban tombs on the west bank of the Nile, as the principal source for the early collectors. Three of the eleven objects noted by Miss Amelia Edwards in her paper of 1888 belong to the class of toilet objects, two inscribed with their owner's name and titles.[57] One, in wood, is unusually divided into five cylindrical compartments inscribed for a priest of Amun called Nefer (height 3 in. (76 mm.): M 11187).[58] Another in the form of a palm-capital is inscribed for a royal scribe called Heko (height 7 in. (178 mm.): M 11762).[59]

The variety of themes is seen in particular in the so-called cosmetic-spoons, which it is now suggested may represent some form of New Year gift. An unusual and fine example was acquired by Mayer from Sams in whose catalogue it is illustrated and described as 'a sacrificial spoon, elegantly carved in hard acacia. The bowl is a leaf and the handle a leopard.' (length $8\frac{7}{8}$ in. (226 mm.): M 13516; pl. XIII*a*).[60]

In contrast with these wooden cosmetic containers and spoons, some as fine as anything in their classes, Mayer's collection lacked pieces of jewellery of distinction, surprisingly in view of his own profession. The necklaces described as being in Drawer 2, in Room 4, 'Egyptian Jewellery, Vase and Idol Room', seem in general to have belonged to the class of made-up strings, mainly of genuine elements of different dates. One piece, however, attracted particular attention, perhaps because it was thought to have belonged to the king whose name it bore, mistakenly identified as the pharaoh who appointed Joseph as governor. It was described by Mayer in the 1852 Catalogue as a 'signet of solid gold, weighing nearly an ounce and a half, hung on a swivel, bearing in a cartouche the Royal name of Amenophis the 1st and an inscription on each side' (M 11437). It is correctly assigned in Gatty's catalogue to Amenophis II. Finger-rings with a rectangular plaque bezel on a swivel or rigid with the shank came into fashion at the beginning of the Eighteenth Dynasty and are not uncommon with the names of Tuthmosis III and his successor Amenophis II. They were probably given as gifts from the king to individuals. On one side the hieroglyphic text reads 'the one who fights hundred thousands, son of the Sun-god, Amenhotep, the god the ruler of Heliopolis' (pl. XIII*b*). On the other side are the further titles 'the good god, son of Amun, lord of might' (pl. XIII*c*). The ring had been acquired by Sams from the Salt Collection, and is mentioned by the contributor to the *Gentleman's Magazine* for April 1833.[61]

In the same drawer in the Jewellery Room were to be seen a pair of gold earrings (M 11440) from the Salt Collection, 'taken by him from the ears of a mummy'. According to Mayer they each weighed 'just half a shekel', thereby corroborating the faithfulness of the rendering of Genesis 24:22, 'a gold ring of half a shekel weight'. Earrings did not become fashionable until the New Kingdom when they were worn by men and women. The example is typical of the early part of the Eighteenth Dynasty, a wide-ribbed hoop composed of triangular tubes. The most eye-catching object in the drawer was, however, a 'diadem of gold. It is about 7 inches [178 mm.] in diameter, about $\frac{7}{8}$ of an inch [22 mm.] wide, and $\frac{1}{8}$ of an inch [3 mm.] in thickness.' In the centre a pyramid bears spurious cartouches: the band is embossed with signs of the zodiac. The object is said to have been taken from a mummy. Its source is not known, but it is not ancient, and is not included in Gatty's catalogue. Omitted too from Gatty's catalogue as spurious are two silver figures (M 11510 and M 11511) which were also to be seen in the same drawer, one a figure of Bes, the other a statuette; Mayer records their weights at 4 oz. 13 dwt. each. It is an early date for elaborate forgeries of this kind to have been made, if that is what they are. Possibly they belong to the class of esoteric mock-Egyptian objects without pretence to antiquity, which had a certain vogue in the early part of the nineteenth century, though one would have expected Mayer to have recognized them for what they were.

It is not possible to indicate all items within this category of objects of daily use of interest for the quality of the work, unusual design or association with named persons. A few more may be mentioned to give an idea of the range of material collected by Mayer. There is a finely executed small faience playing-piece in the form of a bound Asiatic figure (height 1 in. (26 mm.): M 11942). Two other wooden objects of note are a cubit rod inscribed with a prayer to Amenre, Ptah and Thoth for Nakhy, a workman from the village of Deir el Medineh (length $28\frac{5}{8}$ in. (727 mm.): M 13825),[62] and part of a walking stick inscribed for Ipuy, from the cemetery of the village (length 2 ft. 10 in. (863 mm.): M 13821).[63] An alabaster vessel is of interest for having on it the name of Cheops, builder of the great pyramid at Giza (height 9 in. (228 mm.): M 13628).[64] A remarkable textile is the so-called girdle of Ramesses III (M 11156), some 17 ft. in length, the antiquity of which has been doubted on the grounds of the technique of weaving.[65]

Deities

The final category into which the Egyptian collection was readily divided is the representation of deities in wood, faience, metal or stone, uncompromisingly described as 'idols' and 'idolets' in the 1852 Catalogue, terms repeated in the Gatty Catalogue. Into this same group of religious and cult objects came also the great variety of amulets, scarabs and those common figures intended to answer for the deceased in the next world, called in the early catalogues 'sepulchral figures', that is *shabtis* or *ushabtis*.

Bronze figures of gods and goddesses, sacred animals and emblems, are a particularly common category.[66] Most surviving examples have not been found in the course of scientific excavation. From time to time a cache of such figures is brought to light and the probability is that most are votive offerings made at the temple or shrine from which they were cleared, as occasion required, and disposed of by burial within the sacred precincts. Several in the Mayer Collection are of interest for the quality of their workmanship and condition, for the comparative rarity of the type or for the presence of a dedicatory inscription in heiroglyphs in which the deity of the image is invoked with life wishes for the dedicator. They date for the most part to the second half of the first millennium B.C., from the Twenty-sixth Dynasty to the Roman period.

There is a good example of a small figure of a cat in the usual seated attitude with tail curving to the right, ears pierced for gold earrings, on a pedestal bearing the name of its dedicator, a certain Hanmut (M 11493). A seated figure of a goddess in human form may be identified from the fish on top of her head as Hatmehyt, whose chief cult centre was the Delta town of Mendes. The goddess, whose name means literally 'she who is in front of the fishes', may be entirely represented as the lepidotus fish and is the most prominent example of the rare adoption of fish in the iconography of ancient Egypt (M 11431: pl. xiv*a*).[67] She is shown suckling the child Horus, the role normally associated with Isis. A standing figure of Osiris in the conventional mummified form with hands protruding, is distinguished by the presence of a hieroglyphic text giving the name of the dedicator, a woman Tetebast-iuesankh, daughter of Petekhons and Harbast (M 11396). A more unusual example of Osiris shows him seated with lunar disc (M 11574: Osiris-Iah). Two different forms of Khons are represented, both inscribed. One shows him walking, falcon-headed, surmounted by the sun and lunar discs, dedicated on behalf of Harsiesis (M 11592). In the other, Khons is in the form of a young god with the side lock of youth and lunar disc, dedicated by Herba son of Petenakht (M 11611). Mention should also be made of a fine figure of Neferhotep, dedicated by Pertum son of Haper (M 11702). Neferhotep was first used as an epithet applied to certain deities, particularly Khons, but later acquired an individual personification.

At the time of the publication of Gatty's catalogue, another bronze could rightly be called unique.[68] It was exhibited in Room No. 4 in Colquitt Street and is described in the 1852 Catalogue as 'A Statue, in bronze, of the Egyptian Hercules, in a walking position, with his club' (M 11594: pl. xiv*b*). The statue is in the form of a male striding figure, left leg advanced in the normal Egyptian convention, brandishing in his right hand a sword or knife, with a grotesque head, with the mane and ears of a lion. Two similar figures, not however identical in detail, have subsequently come to light: one, now in the Cairo Museum, was bought in 1885.[69] The second was acquired in 1902 in Egypt by F. G. Hilton Price, Director of the Society of Antiquaries of London from 1894 until his death in 1909.[70] The Mayer example bears a dedicatory text by Nesptah, son of Unemuamen and Paneter, and the deity is identified as a form of Amun-Re, the same identification being found also on the Hilton Price example. The Cairo bronze identifies the figure as Amun-Min. The Mayer bronze was originally dated in the Gatty Catalogue to *c.* 900 B.C. It is, however, more likely on the basis of the syncretic form in which the god appears that the figure is to be dated later, possibly to the Ptolemaic or early Roman period. The head is that associated with the popular household deity known as Bes and the conical reed cap, originally perhaps surmounted by a sun's disc (the *atef*-crown), may be worn by Amun amongst other gods. With the exception of Bes, gods are seldom equipped with human weapons, and it might be supposed that the attitude of this

PLATE XI

b. Pyramidion of black granite inscribed for a Vizier Neferronpet, *c.* 1230 or 1150 B.C. (M 11015)

Reproduced by courtesy of NMGM

a. Limestone stela of Tuthmose. *c.* 1200 B.C. (M 13851)

PLATE XII

Wooden figure of Nubian carrying a jar, *c.* 1200 B.C. (M 13519). Reproduced by courtesy of NMGM

PLATE XIII

a. Spoon in the form of a leopard and leaf, *c.* 1200 B.C. (M 13516)

b, c. Signet ring with the name of Amenophis II, *c.* 1450 B.C. (✝) (M 11437)

Reproduced by courtesy of NMGM

a

b

c

PLATE XIV

b. Rare syncretic figure identified as Amun-Re,
c. 100 B.C. (M 11594)

Reproduced by courtesy of NMGM

a. Seated bronze figure of the goddess Hatmehyt suckling Horus
c. 600 B.C. (M 11431)

curious syncretic figure is apotropaic, warding off malignant forces which might threaten the safety and security of the dedicator.

Conclusion

As some of the examples of jewellery indicate, Mayer is perhaps better described as an assiduous rather than a discriminating collector. That his collections contained such important material from the scholarly and artistic point of view was because the time was opportune for acquiring quantities of Egyptian antiquities, of a variety, character and condition which will not present itself again. For a brief period of about ten years following the opening of the Museum in 1852, there were substantial additions made from Valentia, Hertz and Stobart, before Mayer's curiosity was attracted to other fields. We get, however, a very clear idea of Mayer's motivation and ambitions in opening his collections to the public. There was a conviction that the material, whatever its kind or character, by its visual display must lead the mind of the viewer to a desire to appreciate, as he put it in the preface to his catalogue, 'the highest branches of cultivation the human mind is capable of—the history of mankind'. The opportunity of examining the contents of his museum was, so he hoped, to be a 'string, by which some of our townsmen may be led to a study of the high state of civilization which the Egyptians had attained'. The very diversity of the material collected becomes part of its *raison d'être*. It is important to have examples of the ordinary, familiar types of familiar categories. Behind the opening of the museum is ultimately the simple belief that to a man who shaves daily with lather and cut-throat, an ancient Egyptian razor will excite the same degree of interest, if not of wonder, as fine sculpture or fine painting. His curiosity aroused, the viewer will wish to learn more.

It is this fundamental belief in the value of visual display as a stimulant to the imagination, leading to a desire for knowledge, that prompted Mayer to open his collection to the public. The style of display, as preserved for us in two contemporary drawings, one of the Mummy Room (pl. IV), the other of the Jewellery Room (pl. V), is reminiscent of the British Museum before 1939, with the same sort of island cases for mummies, cabinets for small objects, and wall cases with rows of shelving on which objects were placed in only a loose ordering into categories and with little sense of design. For a modern museum officer it would be more storage than exhibition, and he would be encouraged to thin down the display, to be so selective in his choice as to forget the virtues of the visitor being allowed to browse.

A didactic element was provided by the catalogue. If Mayer's catalogue of 1852 seems little more than a check-list with the occasional historical note, of little value, the hope was expressed in the preface to offer the visitors very shortly 'a catalogue which he is preparing with a view to instruction'. The reader is warned, however, that the research requisite for such work must necessarily occupy a long time 'especially when it is borne in mind that in Liverpool there is no public library to consult such subjects, and those researches can only be made in the hours of rest from a business that requires the constant attention of the writer'. It is interesting to note in this respect that the Egyptian Museum contained also a 'Library' which, the catalogue proudly pointed out, contained 'the principal Works which have been written on Egyptian History and Antiquities'. It specifically mentions the *Description de l'Égypte* (24 vols., Paris, 1809–28), 'the imperial Elephant edition of the result of the expedition of the Savans sent out by Napoleon'. Others scholars named are Young, Champollion, Salt, Belzoni, Bonomi, Wilkinson, Rawlinson and Bunsen. The last scholar was responsible for an encyclopaedic work in German, translated into English in five volumes as *Egypt's Place in Universal History* (London, 1854–7); the last volume was almost entirely written by Samuel Birch. Here, too, in the library was to be found Mayer's collection of early manuscripts in Hebrew, Sanskrit, Persian and Irish.

In the preface to his catalogue Mayer expressed the hope that Liverpool would build a museum worthy of her great name. Private collecting by individual and learned societies and the philanthropy which led men like Mayer to open their collections to the public at large encouraged the formation of municipal museums and galleries as we now understand them. Between 1845 and 1885 six acts were passed granting town councils the power to fund and maintain them.[71] The 'Liverpool Free Library and Museum' was opened in 1859 and eight years later in 1867 Mayer gave his collection of over 14,000 items to the town of Liverpool. In spite of the losses of 1941, the Egyptian collection of the Liverpool Museum remains one of the major representative collections in this country. Its nucleus, the Mayer Collection, has been enlarged by the gift of material from excavations in Egypt and the Sudan by John Garstang from the former Institute of Archaeology of the University of Liverpool and by the Egypt Exploration Society, among whose distinguished field directors was Walter Bryan Emery born in Liverpool on 2 July 1903. 'When about 13 years of age', writes his successor to the Petrie Chair of Egyptology at University College London, 'he started reading the romances of Rider Haggard to which he always attributed his initial passion for Egyptology. Fortunately for him, Liverpool was at that time second only to London as a centre of Egyptological studies in Great Britain. Emery was able as a boy to hear the public lectures of Professor John Garstang on his discoveries in Egypt, the Sudan and the Near East, and to see the exhibitions of his finds; to visit the Institute of Archaeology, and listen to Professors P. E. Newberry and T. Eric Peet; and to browse in the rapidly accumulating Egyptian collections of the City of Liverpool Museum.'[72] It is particularly appropriate that in the centenary year of Mayer's death the museum which owes the nucleus of its Egyptian collection to his generosity should have acquired national status.

NOTES

[1] A. Edwards, 'The provincial and private collections of Egyptian antiquities in Great Britain', *Recueil de Travaux*, x (1888), 129. Its editor, Gaston Maspero, was at this time the Director of the Egyptian Antiquities Service. In a letter to Miss Edwards dated 29 April 1888 he complains of the lack of subscribers, hardly any of whom are Egyptologists, about seventy being amateurs interested in ancient Egypt, lawyers, clergymen and retired army officers: W. Dawson, *J. Egyptian Arch.*, xxxiii (1947), 85–6. On Amelia Edwards's role in the creation of the Egyptian Exploration Fund, see M. S. Drower, 'The early years', in T. G. H. James (ed.), *Excavating in Egypt: The Egypt Exploration Society 1882–1982* (London, 1982), 9–36; *id.*, 'Gaston Maspero and the Egypt Exploration Fund', *J. Egyptian Arch.*, lxviii (1982), 299–317. For an account of Miss Edwards as novelist and of her literary method, see R. R. Bowker in *Harper's New Monthly Mag.*, lxxvii (no. 457) (June 1888), 23–4: the article, the second on 'London as a literary centre', gives her a place beside (among others) Thomas Hardy, R. L. Stevenson, Rider Haggard, Ann Thackeray, Mrs Oliphant and Charlotte M. Yonge.

[2] C. T. Gatty, *Catalogue of the Mayer Collection*, i: *The Egyptian, Babylonian and Assyrian Antiquities*, 2nd edn. (London, 1879), iv. The first edition was published in 1877 with illustrations drawn earlier for Mayer by Llewellyn Jewitt, F.S.A. The second edition incorporates these drawings with the

exception of a Graeco-Roman funerary stela (M 13652) and an Old Kingdom panel (M 13850). There are several additional woodcuts by 'Mr Lewin of London' and ninety-seven plates. A short description of the Babylonian and Assyrian antiquities is also added.

[3] WAG, *Foreign Catalogue*, 308–9. The statue (M 13503), destroyed in the Second World War, is illustrated in J. Sams, *Objects of Antiquity* (London, 1839), pl. 27.

[4] A. Edwards, *A Thousand Miles Up the Nile* (London, 1877; re-issued London, 1982), 154.

[5] On these cabinets of curiosities in sixteenth- and seventeenth-century Europe, see O. Impey and A. MacGregor (eds.), *The Origins of Museums* (Oxford, 1985).

[6] P. R. S. Moorey, *Ancient Egypt* (Oxford, 1970), 2 and pl. 2.

[7] BM 6694. W. Dawson and P. H. K. Gray, *Catalogue of Egyptian Antiquities in the British Museum*, i: *Mummies and Human Remains* (London, 1968), 23 no. 43 and pl. xiia. For the history of the Egyptian collections of the British Museum, see T. G. H. James, *The British Museum and Ancient Egypt* (London, 1981); I. E. S. Edwards, 'Notable acquisitions of Egyptian antiquities in the years 1753–1853', *Brit. Mus. Quarterly*, xviii (1953), 14–16.

[8] R. Latham and W. Matthews (eds.), *The Diary of Samuel Pepys*, ix (London, 1976), 197.

[9] For Salt and other names associated with the early days of Egyptology see W. R. Dawson and E. P. Uphill, *Who was Who in Egyptology*, Egypt Exploration Society, 2nd edn. (London, 1972).

[10] R. Lepsius, *Letters from Egypt, Ethiopia and the Peninsula of Sinai*, transl. L. and J. B. Horner, Bohn edn. (London, 1853), 41.

[11] *Ibid.*

[12] B. Porter and R. L. B. Moss, *Topographical Bibliography of Ancient Egyptian Hieroglyphic Texts, Reliefs and Paintings* (Oxford, 1927–), ad loc.

[13] See above, p. 8.

[14] *Egyptian Antiquities Collected on a Voyage made in Upper Egypt in the Years 1854 & 1855 and Published by Revd. H. Stobart, M.A., Queen's College Oxford.* The work, issued by publishers in Paris and Berlin in 1855, consists of five plates with captions. At the bottom of each plate is printed 'Berlin, Värsch and Happe, lithogr. fac-sim. under the direction of Dr. H. Brugsch'. On the papyri see below, pp. 52–4.

[15] See below, pp. 53–4.

[16] For the history of the Hertz Collection see below, pp. 94–6.

[17] Sams, *op. cit.* (note 3), pls. 3–4.

[18] Noted by Dr Colin Walters in his manuscript catalogue of the coffins in the collections. Nesamun might well be the father or husband of Djedkhonsu-iuesankh. Cf. the similarly decorated coffin of the chantress-priestess Nesmut, BM 36211: Brit. Mus., *A Handbook to the Egyptian Mummies and Coffins Exhibited in the British Museum* (London, 1938), 39, pl. xiii; Brit. Mus., *A Guide to the First, Second and Third Egyptian Rooms*, 3rd edn. (London, 1924), 81–2, pl. 12 (the owner identified as a priest Nes-Khensu).

[19] Porter and Moss, *op. cit.* (note 12), I² ii (1964), 630.

[20] Sams, *op. cit.* (note 3), pl. 31. Contrast d'Athanasi's story of Salt's acquisition of the finely decorated coffin of Soter (BM 6705). Mummy and coffin had been originally purchased for an undisclosed sum by Sir Frederick Henniker in the course of a visit to Egypt in 1820. He happened to be present on the west bank at Thebes when 'the resurrection men' found a family tomb dating to the time of the Emperor Hadrian. The haul (which was to turn out to comprise fourteen painted coffins) was apparently on offer, unopened, for four guineas: F. Henniker, *Notes during a Visit to Egypt, Nubia, The Oasis, Mount Sinai and Jerusalem* (London, 1823), 136–7. Henniker is discreetly referred to as an 'English Traveller' by d'Athanasi: 'having taken it into his head, whilst on the road to Cairo, that there might be some gold coins in this mummy, he caused it to be opened, and not finding any thing in it of the nature that he sought, he threw it into the Nile, and gave the case belonging to it to Mr Salt' (d'Athanasi, *A Brief Account of the Researches and Discoveries in Upper Egypt* (London, 1836), 51).

[21] P. H. K. Gray and D. Slow, 'Egyptian mummies in the City of Liverpool Museums', *Liverpool Bull.*, Museums No., xv (1968), 6–10.

[22] *Ibid.*, 10–16.

[23] Salt sale of 1835, lot 590: BM 6704; Dawson and Gray, *op. cit.* (note 7), 33 no. 64. C. Andrews, *Egyptian Mummies* (London, 1984), fig. 26.

[24] P. H. K. Gray, 'Radiological aspects of the mummies of ancient Egypt in the Rijksmuseum van Oudheden, Leiden', *Oudheidkundige mededelingen uit het Rijksmuseum van Oudheden*, xlvii (1966), nos. 7, 15, 16.

[25] Gray and Slow, *op. cit.* (note 21), 10 and pls. 7 and 11.

[26] Gray, *op cit.* (note 24), no. 16.

[27] BM 6714: Dawson and Gray, *op. cit.* (note 7), 34 no. 65; Andrews, *op. cit.* (note 23), fig. 40.

[28] Gray and Slow, *op. cit.* (note 21) , 66–9 no. 20. The object was exhibited to the Historic Society of Lancashire and Cheshire: *THSLC*, x (1857–8), 343.

[29] Now in the collections of the School of Archaeology and Oriental Studies, E. 506, damaged in 1941; H. A. Ormerod, *The Liverpool Royal Institution: a Record and a Retrospect* (Liverpool, 1953), 25 note 3.

[30] T. E. Peet, *The Mayer Papyri A and B* (London, 1920). With the exception of Pap. Leopold-Amherst, the other papyri in the series are edited with translations in T. E. Peet, *The Great Tomb-Robberies of the Twentieth Egyptian Dynasty* (Oxford, 1930). For Pap. Leopold-Amherst see J. Capart, A. H. Gardiner and B. van de Walle, 'New light on the Ramesside tomb-robberies', *J. Egyptian Arch.*, xxii (1936), 69–93. On the historical background see C. Aldred, 'More light on the Ramesside tomb robberies', in J. Ruffle, G. A. Gaballa and K. A. Kitchen (eds.), *Glimpses of Ancient Egypt: Studies in Honour of H. W. Fairman* (Warminster, 1979), 92 –9.

[31] See above, note 30.

[32] *Select Papyri in the Hieratic Character from the Collection of the British Museum*, part II (London, 1860), pls. I-VIII.

[33] R. A. Pack, *The Greek and Latin Literary Texts from Graeco-Roman Egypt*, 2nd edn. (Ann Arbor, Michigan, 1965), no. 233.

[34] On Simonides see Dawson and Uphill, *op. cit.* (note 9), 271–2; J. A. Farrer, *Literary Forgeries* (London, 1907), 39–66; A. N. L. Munby, *Phillipps Stud.*, iv (1956), 114–31.

[35] C. Simonides, *Brief Dissertation on Hieroglyphic Letters* (London, 1860).

[36] *THSLC*, xiii (1861), 309. The author is described as 'Ph. Dr.'. I owe this reference to Roger White.

[37] C. Simonides, *Fac-similes of Certain Portions of the Gospel of St. Matthew* (London, 1861), 5 and 9.

[38] C. W. Goodwin, 'Notes on the Mayer Papyri', *Zeitschrift für ägyptische Sprache und Altertumskunde*, xii (1874), 61–5. For Goodwin see W. Dawson, *Charles Wycliffe Goodwin, 1817–1878. A Pioneer in Egyptology* (Oxford, 1934).

[39] Most recently studied by O. Neugebauer and R. A. Parker, *Egyptian Astronomical Texts*, iii: *Decans, Planets, Constellations and Zodiacs*, Brown Egyptological Stud. 6 (Providence, Rhode Island, 1969), 225–8, 232–5. For previous publications see O. Neugebauer, *Trans. Amer. Philos. Soc.*, cvi (1962), 383–91.

[40] For concise accounts of Egyptian stelae see J. Baines and J. Malek, *Atlas of Ancient Egypt* (Oxford, 1980), 62–3; J. Vandier, *Manuel d'archéologie égyptienne* (Paris, 1952 and 1955), I, 724–44, and II, 389–522; K. Martin in *Lexikon der Ägyptologie*, VI(1), ed. W. Helck and W. Westendorf (Wiesbaden, 1985), cols. 1–6.

[41] *Art J.* (1870), 59.

[42] W. G. Waddell, *Manetho, with an English Translation* (London and Cambridge, Mass., 1940), 78–83.

[43] Porter and Moss, *op. cit.* (note 12), III^2 (1979), 741–2.

[44] Edwards, *op. cit.* (note 1), 130.

[45] Sams, *op. cit.* (note 3), pl. 2; Porter and Moss, *op. cit.* (note 12), III^2 (1979), 706. For Neferronpet I and II see W. Helck, *Zur Verwaltung des Mittleren und Neuen Reichs*, Probleme der Ägyptologie 3 (Leiden, 1958), 451 (27), 463 (41). I am grateful to my colleague Dr K. A. Kitchen for kindly drawing my attention to the problems of identity of Neferronpet I and II. The excavations are very briefly noted in J. Leclant and G. Clerc, 'Fouilles et travaux en Égypte et au Soudan: 1983–84', *Orientalia*, liv (1985), 354.

[46] Lord Valentia, *Voyages and Travels to India, Ceylon, the Red Sea, Abyssinia and Egypt, in the Years 1802, 1803, 1804, 1805, and 1806*, III (London, 1811), 421–2. The passage is quoted in H. de Meulenaere and P. MacKay, *Mendes II*, ed. E. S. Hall and B. V. Bothmer (Warminster, 1976), 55–6.

[47] Sams, *op. cit.* (note 3), pl. 9. For text and bibliography see K. A. Kitchen, *Ramesside Inscriptions*, IV (Oxford, 1982), 203.

[48] *The Works of James Barry*, I (London, 1809), 345.

[49] T. G. H. James and W. V. Davies, *Egyptian Sculpture* (London, 1983), 30–1 and pl. 36.

[50] Liverpool Mus., *Handbook and Guide to the Egyptian Collection on Exhibition in the Public Museums Liverpool*, 4th edn. (Liverpool, 1932), pl. 9.

[51] *Ibid.*, pl. 2. The piece has been frequently published.

[52] Nicholson and Warhurst, 4.

[53] Sams, *op. cit.* (note 3), pl. 22.

[54] Museum of Fine Arts, Boston, Exhibition Catalogue, *Egypt's Golden Age: The Art of Living in the New Kingdom 1558–1085 B.C.* (Boston, 1982), 204, no. 238.

[55] Most recently published by J. R. Harris, 'Some well known Egyptian pieces reconsidered', *Arts of Asia*, xiii (6) (Nov.–Dec. 1983), 79 and pl. 23.

[56] For a survey of the material see Museum of Fine Arts, Boston, *op. cit.* (note 54).

[57] See above, note 1.

[58] Museum of Fine Arts, Boston, *op. cit.* (note 54), 223, no. 279.

[59] Edwards, *op. cit.* (note 1), 131.

[60] Sams, *op. cit.* (note 3), pl. 13; Museum of Fine Arts, Boston, *op. cit.* (note 54), 210, no. 249 with bibliography. The purpose of these spoons is discussed by R. E. Freed, *ibid.*, 207.

[61] *Gentleman's Mag.* (Apr. 1833), 312.

[62] B. Bruyère, *Rapport sur les fouilles de Deir el Médineh 1928* (Cairo, 1929), 18; Porter and Moss, *op. cit.* (note 12), I² ii (1964), 748.

[63] *Ibid.* The stick and the cubit rod both belonged to royal workmen from the village of Deir el-Medina. For an account of the community, responsible for the construction and decoration of the tombs in the Valley of the Kings, see M. Bierbrier, *The Tomb-builders of the Pharaohs* (London, 1982).

[64] Liverpool Mus., *op. cit.* (note 50), pl. 11.

[65] Porter and Moss, *op. cit.* (note 12), I² ii (1964), 845. On the history of the piece see T. E. Peet, 'The so-called Ramesses Girdle', *J. Egyptian Arch.*, xix (1933), 143–9; cf. R. Hall, *Egyptian Textiles* (Aylesbury, 1986), 46–7.

[66] On bronzes, see G. Daressy, *Statues de Divinités*, Catalogue général du Musée du Caire, 2 vols. (Cairo, 1905–6); G. Roeder, 'Ägyptische Bronzewerke', *Pelizaeus-Museum zu Hildesheim Wissenschaftliche Veröffentlichung*, iii (1937); *id.*, 'Ägyptische Bronzefiguren', *Staatliche Museen zu Berlin Mitteilungen aus der Ägyptischen Sammlung*, vi (Berlin, 1965). On Egyptian deities in general see G. Hart, *Egyptian Gods and Goddesses* (London, 1986).

[67] I. Gamer-Wallert, *Fische und Fischkulte im alten Ägypten* (Wiesbaden, 1970).

[68] Liverpool Mus., *op. cit.* (note 50), pl. 12; Roeder (1965), *op. cit.* (note 66), 46; J. G. Wilkinson, *Manners and Customs of the Ancient Egyptians*, III, rev. S. Birch (London, 1878), 12, fig. 496.

[69] Cairo 38836; Daressy, *op. cit.* (note 66), 208 and pl. XLII.

[70] F. G. H. Price, 'Notes upon a rare figure of Amen-Re', *Proc. Soc. Biblical Arch.*, xxiii (1901), 35–6.

[71] On this development and the role of the museum see Sir Henry Miers, *A Report on the Public Museums of the British Isles (Other than the National Museums) to the Carnegie United Kingdom Trustees* (Edinburgh, 1928); S. F. Markham, *A Report on the Museums and Art Galleries of the British Isles (Other than the National Museums) to the Carnegie United Kingdom Trustees* (Edinburgh, 1938).

[72] H. S. Smith, 'Walter Bryan Emery', *J. Egyptian Arch.*, lvii (1971), 190–201, at 190.

Assyrian and Babylonian Antiquities

A. R. Millard, F.S.A.

The preface to Joseph Mayer's *Catalogue of the Egyptian Museum ...* (1852) commences:

> The great results which have attended the excavations of our countryman, Mr. Layard, at Nymrood, and the discovery of the alphabet of the arrow-headed inscriptions at Behistun by Major Rawlinson, have given a new impulse to the study of antiquity, and we may prognosticate that the time is not far distant when a knowledge of the habits, manners, and arts of the earliest inhabitants of the earth, will be better understood than it was by the Hebrew, Greek, and Roman historians, who have left us in their works the valuable records of their research and observation.

Mayer was up-to-date in his knowledge of the major discoveries of the day. The forty-four pages that follow, however, contain only five items connected with the discoveries of Layard and Rawlinson. They are four Babylonian seals (p. 16, nos. 61–4) and one 'onyx stone ... described on two sides in the Babylonian or arrow-headed character; the third has on it a name in a sort of double cartouche' (pp. 19f, no. 214), which is a forgery. By the time C. T. Gatty prepared the second edition of his *Catalogue of the Mayer Collection,* i: *The Egyptian, Babylonian and Assyrian Antiquities* (1879), three small fragments of carved stone from Assyria, many more cylinder seals and a collection of cuneiform tablets, a few bricks and other antiquities had reached Liverpool (pp. 75–83, nos. 545–631). The registration numbers for some of the seals show they entered the collection in 1868, as did one relief fragment. Thus the Mayer Collection was able to show representative specimens of Assyrian and Babylonian culture beside its large Egyptian holdings.

Regrettably, nearly all of the cuneiform tablets and many of the cylinder seals were destroyed during the bombing of Liverpool in the Second World War. The tablets had almost all been studied and published in hand-copy[1] in 1885, so their information remains available and they will not be treated here.[2] The cylinders are a different case. Of the fifty-two seals listed in 1879 only nineteen can be identified. They had not been studied or recorded in detail, so their loss is almost complete: Gatty's brief descriptions are the only record. Four examples of these seals are presented here to illustrate this area of Mayer's collection. Cylinder seals are a

71

typical product of Babylonian culture. They came into use during the fourth millennium B.C. and continued into Achaemenid Persian times. Intended as a means of guaranteeing contents of boxes, bundles and jars, and of identifying ownership, they also had amuletic value. The designs often portray the owner and a deity who may be his 'patron' or whose protection he invoked. The style and technique of the engravers varied over the ages.

The Mayer Collection does not have examples of the earliest periods of seal-cutting, but some pieces belong to the Akkadian period (c. 2334–2154 B.C.), a time when some very fine seals were made. M 14238 is a fairly ordinary one, a cylinder of green serpentine with slightly concave sides, 25 mm. high. At the left the seal's owner stands wearing a fringed robe, with his left hand raised in greeting. Before him stand two deities with horned crowns who introduce him to the seated figure of a goddess. She wears a long flounced dress, a horned crown, holds three ears of barley in her right hand, and sits on a stool apparently made of wicker-work (pl. xva).[3] Several centuries later a different fashion was current in the era of the Old Babylonian Dynasties (c. 2000–1600 B.C.). M 14230, cut in haematite, 24 mm. high, belongs to the end of that period. It depicts a worshipper in a long robe facing a god, with his right hand raised. The god holds a crook, and stands with one foot advanced, placed upon a kneeling gazelle. Above the gazelle a small, nude, kneeling figure fills the space between the two principal figures. To the right an inscription states that the seal belonged to Apil-Amurru, son of Shunuma-il, servant of the god Amurru (pl. xvb).[4] Also belonging to the second millennium B.C. is an unusual seal of blue glass (M 14206), which still retains its original gold mounts. It is 35 mm. high. Although part of the surface is damaged, enough is preserved to make the design clear. This seal belongs to the Mitannian style of northern Mesopotamia and Syria in the middle of the millennium. Two tall figures stand facing to the right, with a shorter figure between them, and an eight-rayed star above. The first figure holds what seems to be a sceptre. In front of him is the hind part of a quadruped. The other side of the damaged area shows a squatting man above a kneeling man who reaches out to a gazelle which is turning its head away from the man. The material of the seal is noteworthy, for glass had only recently begun to be used. Blue glass was valued because it could be a substitute for the precious lapis lazuli which had to be imported from Afghanistan (pl. xvc).[5] One characteristic of seals produced during the Assyrian Empire (c. 900–612 B.C.) is the obvious use of the drill. In M 14219 it is seen in conjunction with the strokes of the cutting wheel and the engraving tool. A worshipper stands at the left, facing two divine emblems, the stylus and the spade with ribbons, which represent the gods Nabu and Marduk. Above them is the winged sun-disc. Beyond, a bearded god stands upon a dais, holding a sceptre in one hand, and wearing a sword and two bows crossed on his back. Behind him are the lunar crescent, six-rayed star, and group of seven stars, all divine symbols, and, below them, a mouflon looking backwards (pl. xvd).[6]

Cylinder seals such as Mayer owned had been obtained by a few collectors before the discoveries of Layard and others. The excavations at Nimrud and at Nineveh, following the work of the Frenchman Botta at Khorsabad, revealed for the first time the whole range of Assyrian art. In particular these early excavations uncovered a wealth of sculptures that lined the walls of the Assyrian palaces. When the excavators opened the palace halls, they found that they had been burnt or looted, and many of the stone slabs were cracked or partly destroyed. Layard brought away

PLATE XV

a. Akkadian cylinder seal (height 25 mm.) (M 14238)

b. Old Babylonian cylinder seal (height 24 mm.) (M14230)

c. Mitannian glass cylinder seal (height 35 mm.) (M 14206)

d. Assyrian cylinder seal (height 38 mm.) (M 14219)

Reproduced by courtesy of NMGM

Photographs: a, b, d, Edgar Jones

PLATE XVI

Fragment of Assyrian sculpture (209 × 160 mm.) (10.10.78.33). Reproduced by courtesy of NMGM

what he considered the best or most important carvings. The bulk of his finds (including the 'lion hunt' reliefs) went to the British Museum, but he gave some examples to his relatives and friends. (One fragment, now at the School of Archaeology and Oriental Studies, the University of Liverpool, was a present to the captain of a ship that brought him home from Basra.[7]) Visitors to the sites in Assyria, and the local people, appropriated pieces left in the ruins. Through one or other of these means, one scrap found its way into the hands of a Mr J. H. Armstrong, from whom the Museum bought it in 1878 (pl. XVI).[8] It was described by Gatty in 1879 as follows:

> 546. Fragment; of an Assyrian sculpture in alabaster, portion of a figure of a man, from the interior of the palace of Sennacherib at Nineveh. 10.10.78.33.

By their nature, such crumbs are often hard to place in any known scene or series of reliefs. Here, the background is hill-country, conventionally shown by a scale pattern. An Assyrian soldier, wearing a tall conical helmet and mail shirt, and with carefully curled hair and beard, is carrying a table or stool. In the reliefs the Assyrian soldiers usually engage in more martial acts, except when they are taking booty from a captured city. The best-known case is to be seen on the Lachish reliefs from the palace of Sennacherib (705–681 B.C.).[9] The fragment does not find a place in those, but it could come from a badly damaged series showing the siege and capture of another city also in mountainous country.[10] Sculptures decorating the palace of Sennacherib's grandson, Ashurbanipal (*c.* 668–627 B.C.), included pictures of the capture of a city set in hills, probably in Elam,[11] and this soldier may have fitted in one of those. The design of the helmet may point to the earlier reign.

Mayer wrote that he hoped his collection might 'serve as a ground-work for those who are desirous of seeing the high state of civilization which the Egyptians had attained'.[12] By 1879 he could be satisfied that, in a much smaller way, the state of Assyrian and Babylonian civilization could also be seen in Liverpool, something which was probably not the case in any other northern city.

NOTES

[1] Cuneiform tablets are usually cushion-shaped pieces of clay on which the wedge-shaped signs have been impressed with a stylus. The shape of the tablets makes it difficult to photograph them without distortion, so the usual practice of Assyriologists is to represent the three-dimensional signs in two-dimensional drawings.

[2] J. N. Strassmaier, 'Die babylonischen Inschriften im Museum zu Liverpool', *Actes du sixième Congrès international des Orientalistes,* II (1) (Leiden, 1885), 569–624. Strassmaier published thirty-three tablets, two remain: *ibid.*, nos. 8 and 15; Liverpool Museum, nos. 29.11.77, 2, and 29.11.77, 11 (= Gatty, *Egyptian II*, nos. 611 and 617).

[3] Gatty, *Egyptian II*, no. 580.

[4] *Ibid.*, no. 574.

[5] *Ibid.*, no. 558.

[6] *Ibid.*, no. 567. A mouflon is a wild mountain sheep.

[7] See R. D. Barnett, *Sculptures from the North Palace of Ashurbanipal at Nineveh* (London, 1976), 61, pl. lxxi (h): School of Archaeology and Oriental Studies, the University of Liverpool, no. E 10000.

[8] Height 209 mm., width 160 mm.

[9] The Lachish reliefs are often reproduced: see, recently, R. D. Barnett and A. Lorenzini, *Assyrian Sculptures in the British Museum* (Toronto, 1975), 82; D. Ussishkin, *The Conquest of Lachish by Sennacherib* (Tel Aviv, 1982), 85.

[10] S. Smith, *Assyrian Sculptures in the British Museum from Shalmaneser III to Sennacherib* (London, 1938), pl. lx.

[11] Barnett, *op. cit.* (note 7), pl. xxxiv.

[12] JM, *Egyptian Museum*, preface.

The Etruscan Collection

G. Lloyd-Morgan, F.S.A.,
and Sheila P. Girardon*

Since the early eighteenth century the collecting of Etruscan antiquities has been a rewarding pastime in Italy. Initially this created a large number of private collections, not only in the main cities, but also in many small towns and villages. Generally these were due to the presence in the locality of landed aristocracy and persons of culture and antiquarian taste.[1] But the impoverishment of many Italian aristocratic families, following the political instability of the period, created the ideal conditions for a flourishing market in antiquities, aimed particularly at foreign buyers: it was in the eighteenth century that great collections like those of Sloane and Townley were created. The British aristocracy was then one of the wealthiest in Europe, and a portion of that wealth was enthusiastically spent acquiring antiquities, many of them Etruscan. Already in 1742 Antonio Francesco Gori, a member of the *Accademia Etrusca* of Cortona, writing on the number of collections of Etruscan antiquities outside Italy, says: '*non vi è Nazione che dall'Italia, dalla Toscana e da Roma abbia portato seco maggiori e più singolari tesori in ogni genere di Antichità . . . quanti la Britannica industre, e sempre del buono e del bello estimatrice.*'[2] Thus, by the middle of the eighteenth century Etruscan objects were a constant element in many collections in Britain. The commerce in antiquities was facilitated by the presence in Rome of a number of more or less scrupulous Britons, like James Byres, Thomas Jenkins and Gavin Hamilton, who acted as bankers and dealers for their compatriots. Their customers included several associates of the Society of Dilettanti, Charles Townley being among the most assiduous buyers.[3]

During the nineteenth century the market was opened to a wider circle of collectors, including wealthy merchants like Joseph Mayer and many travellers who wished to bring home a souvenir of the 'Grand Tour'. Two such travellers' accounts, Mrs Hamilton Gray's *Tour to the Sepulchres of Etruria* (1840) and George Dennis's *The Cities and Cemeteries of Etruria* (1848), offer a vivid and entertaining insight into contemporary dealing in Etruscan antiquities.[4] In their pages a Victorian traveller not only learned the rudiments of Etruscan culture, but also found much general information. For example, he or she would know which inns offered hospitality in the remote countryside of Etruria. Again, if he had the misfortune to be struck by a sudden migraine while visiting the imposing surroundings of Tuscania, he would know the address of the local chemist, Signor Lorenzo Valeri, who could provide not only the cachet to cure it, but also a well-stocked selection of Etruscan antiquities which he had for sale.[5] Both Dennis and Mrs Hamilton Gray produced a full and detailed list of the Italian public and private collections, together with the names of many dealers—from the famous Castellani brothers to more obscure provincial dealers—and an up-to-date review of the excavation front, almost entirely carried out in the rich cemeteries. But Etruscan culture presented the apparently intractable problem of a civilization without literary texts: the Etruscans would not speak. So in England, at least, the zeal for Etruscan studies was not sustained much beyond the 1850s. It was not until the 1920s that Randall McIver and others restored the subject to its proper place. Here we are indebted to Mary Johnstone's study of the Mayer material in 1932.[6] The plea she had made a few years before at the international Etruscan conference for 'the location and publication of unknown and neglected material' is still relevant today.[7]

SHEILA P. GIRARDON

Joseph Mayer's Etruscan collection was presented to the Liverpool Museum in 1867, and there catalogued by C. T. Gatty in 1883.[8] Mary Johnstone's enquiry of 1932 will soon be followed by the systematic catalogue which is currently being prepared by Jean Turfa. Here we give a conspectus of the collection, with examples.

As the study of Etruscan culture was still in its youth during the nineteenth century, the greater part of the information and finds being drawn from the cemeteries, it is not surprising that Mayer's collection included cinerary urns. One of the most attractive is the terracotta ash urn with a reclining female worked in the round on the lid (M 10463: pl. XVII). The front of the high, rectangular-shaped chest is decorated with a relief showing the mortal combat between Eteocles and Polynices, the sons of Oedipus, with a vanth (an Etruscan winged female demon) to either side. The scene is framed by lightly fluted pilasters with stylized Corinthian capitals. Gatty notes that this piece was painted 'a dull red and greenish blue and [the colours] are very well preserved'.[9] It has since, unfortunately, been touched up with stronger, more garish colours. The urn can be dated to the second century B.C. by comparison with four other examples from an intact tomb group that was found at Goiella, near Chiusi, in 1973.[10] The female figure on the Mayer urn is similar to one of the Goiella ladies, who also carries a heart-shaped fan in her right hand.

Jewellery and personal ornaments make up about a third of Mayer's Etruscan collection. Here his taste and skills as a jeweller enabled him to select a representative range of pieces. As Johnstone remarked, 'Nearly all of it is in extremely good condition . . . and of high quality.'[11] It had also attracted Gatty's admiration: he illustrates eighteen items of jewellery and only two other pieces, an ivory and the ash urn. Among the delights of this group are the pair of earrings said to have been found in the ash urn itself (M 10464: pl. XVIIIa) and another exquisite pair, cylindrical in shape (*a baule*) and decorated overall (M 10325: pl. XVIIIb). Still another pair is in the form of circular studs (diameter *c.* 25 mm.), again showing a range of technical skills and artistry that would have immediately caught the attention of the manufacturing jeweller (M 10308: pl. XVIIIc). A *bulla* is a small, bag-shaped amulet worn round the neck—one of a number of Etruscan objects and institutions that were taken over by

PLATE XVII

Terracotta ash urn (640 × 470 × 200 mm.) (M 10463). Reproduced by courtesy of NMGM

PLATE XVIII

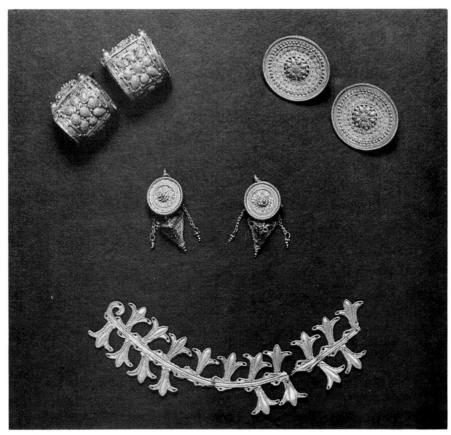

(from top, left to right) a–c. Earrings (diam. 14 mm., 21 mm., 24 mm.) (M 10464, 10325, 10308) *d.* Necklace/appliqué (length 80 mm.) (M 10311)

e. Amulet (diam. 24 mm.) (M 10327)

Reproduced by courtesy of NMGM

PLATE XIX

Ivory mirror-handle (137 mm.) (M 10002). Reproduced by courtesy of NMGM

PLATE XX

Ivory casket-panel (length 109 mm.) (M 10017). Reproduced by courtesy of NMGM

the Romans.[12] There are several examples amongst the various pendants and attachments in the Mayer Collection; M 10327 is illustrated here as an example (pl. XVIII*e*). One necklace has an unusual face pendant (M 10313) and another is a necklace/appliqué (M 10311: pl. XVIII*d*). Although they cannot be strictly described as jewellery, we cannot overlook the perennially fascinating false teeth with gold bridges (M 10334–5), which demonstrate the more practical aspect of the Etruscan craftsman.[13]

Neither Johnstone nor Gatty discusses the bronzes in any detail. This is somewhat surprising, in that they account for a little under half the total number of items in the collection. The mirrors, which are important to Etruscan studies for the engravings of individuals and groups from Etruscan myth and legend, as well as providing a source of names and inscriptions, will be published in the *Corpus Speculorum Etruscorum*.[14] One of the best-preserved examples, typical of the later hand-mirrors, is M 12927. The elegant fourth-century ivory handle (M 10002: pl. XIX) was once attached to the tang of an engraved bronze hand-mirror. It is carved with two standing male figures: the one carrying a *caduceus* is Turms, the Etruscan Hermes or Mercury; the other is a beardless youth with a sword.[15] The other bronzes include a wide range of items. One dramatic-looking hooked implement (M 12925) was originally thought to be a *harpago* or flesh hook, but is now reinterpreted as a torch-holder, on the evidence of an engraved mirror now in the Metropolitan Museum, New York.[16] Somewhat more civilized and elegant are the candelabra on neat tripod stands. Candles of wax or a soft mutton fat were impaled on the spikes arranged around the head. A complete example (M 12935), along with a *thymiaterion* or incense burner (M 12936) and a *situla* (M 12979), is shown in the Mayer portrait of 1840 (pl. I). Even more modest vessels such as *paterae*, buckets and jugs were ornamented by the Etruscan metalworker; the Mayer Collection contains not only complete vessels but also a good selection of their decorative fittings. The foot of a vessel in the form of an animal paw, with the vertical solder plate in the form of a siren or harpy (M 12962), is typical of the workmanship which was admired in Etruria and beyond. Decorative motifs could reflect religious belief—as for instance an ivory plaque with Artumes (the Etruscan Artemis or Diana) catching a stag, which once was part of an inlaid panel on a wooden casket (M 10017; pl. XX). Another important religious activity was the dedication of votives at temples and sanctuaries. Some would be given as thanksgiving to the deity, others would be prayers for help. Of particular interest are those found at healing sanctuaries, where terracotta models of injured limbs or stylized diseased internal organs have been found in some numbers.[17] Although heads and half-heads moulded in high relief are well represented in Mayer's and other collections in Britain, the votive eyes (M 12698–9) are a more unusual and equally attractive dedication.

Apart from these figured votives, Mayer's Etruscan ceramics are surprisingly few: only a Villanovan urn (M 5226), a vessel of *impasto* ware illustrated by Johnstone (M 10478),[18] and an Italo-Corinthian alabastron (M 10706) represent the richness and variety of the potter's craft in Etruria. There is one example of worked amber (M 8802), and a perfect blue-glass perfume bottle or *oinochoe* (M 10159). Four cornelian scarabs complete the tally.[19]

With few exceptions, the sources and the ultimate provenance of Mayer's Etruscan material are wholly obscure. Some items reputedly come from Canino;[20] the ash urn has analogues in the region of Chiusi; and other pieces can be linked with the extensive grave-robbing in and around Vulci in the first half of the nineteenth century.[21] Mayer himself may not have been greatly distanced from that instant archaeology. He was travelling in Italy as early as 1828;[22] and we know for certain that the candelabrum, the incense-burner and the *situla* were in his possession, and prized, by 1840.[23] That was years before his archaeological enlightenment by Roach Smith. This much is clear: that there was a substantial Etruscan presence in Mayer's Egyptian Museum of 1852.[24] If Mrs Hamilton Gray (1840) and George Dennis (1848) marked a new era in the popular apprehension of things Etruscan, then Mayer was in at the start.

G. LLOYD-MORGAN

NOTES

* The authors are particularly indebted to Jean Turfa for her generous help.
[1] P. Barocchi and D. Gallo (eds.), *L'Accademia Etrusca*, Exhibition Catalogue (Cortona, 1985), 109–19, 'Collezionismo e dibattito accademico'.
[2] A. F. Gori, *Difesa dall'alfebeto degli antichi Toscani* (Florence, 1742), ccxlviii sq.
[3] B. F. Cook, *The Townley Marbles* (London, 1985), 9–30.
[4] E. C. H. Gray, *Tour to the Sepulchres of Etruria in 1839* (London, 1840); G. Dennis, *The Cities and Cemeteries of Etruria*, 2 vols. (London, 1848).
[5] *Ibid.*, I, 452; Valeri is one of several local characters mentioned in the chapter on Toscanella (as Tuscania was called at the time).
[6] M. A. Johnstone, 'The Etruscan Collection in the Public Museum of Liverpool', *Studi Etruschi*, vi (1932), 443–52; *ead.*, 'The Etruscan Collection in the Free Public Museums of Liverpool', *Liverpool Annals of Arch. and Anth.*, xix (1932), 121–37.
[7] *Ibid.*, 136–7. As participants in the Second International Etruscan Congress in Florence (1985) we would reiterate that appeal.
[8] C. T. Gatty, *Catalogue of the Mayer Museum*, iv: *Greek, Roman and Etruscan* (London, 1883). This is a rare book; substantially the same text is more accessible in *THSLC*, xxxiv (1881–2), 39–66.
[9] *Ibid.*, 51–5.
[10] H. S. Roberts, 'Later Etruscan mirrors: evidence for dating from recent excavations', *Analecta Romana Instituti Danici*, xii (1983), 31–54: urns nos. 1–3 are illustrated in figs. 1, 12, 13 respectively; urn no. 2 bears the female figure whose head is turned somewhat more to the left than the Mayer example; urn no. 4 with the same combat relief as no. 3 is not illustrated.
[11] Johnstone in *Liverpool Annals*, *op. cit.* (note 6), 121.
[12] J. Ward-Perkins and A. Claridge, *Pompeii A.D. 79*, Exhibition Catalogue (London, 1977), no. 48 with discussion, and description of Naples inv. no. 145490 from the Casa del Menandro, Pompeii.
[13] Johnstone in *Studi Etruschi*, *op. cit.* (note 6), 448–9, discusses these two pieces and gives further bibliography. An example from Praeneste is on display in Room 33 of the Villa Giulia, Rome: M. Moretti, *Il Museo Nazionale di Villa Giulia* (Rome, 1961), 298. There is a good illustration of the teeth in M. Grant, *The Etruscans* (London, 1980), 240–1.
[14] These will be published with the mirrors from Manchester Museum, text by Jean Turfa, in a forthcoming fascicule of the *Corpus Speculorum Etruscorum*, devoted to collections in Great Britain.
[15] N. T. de Grummond, *A Guide to Etruscan Mirrors* (Tallahassee, 1982), 11, figs. 10, 11.
[16] E. Gerhard, *Etruskische Spiegel*, v (1897), 217, with fig.; also illustrated with brief discussion in L. B. van der Meer, *De Etrusken* (The Hague, 1977), 50, fig. 54.
[17] G. Colonna (ed.), *Santuari d'Etruria*, Exhibition Catalogue (Arezzo, 1985), 38–40 (no. 1.26 votives from the temple at Manganello, Cervetri); 151–3 (no. 8.1 sanctuary at Punta della Vipera); 156–7 (no. 8.3 sanctuary at Grasceta dei Cavellari, Monti della Tolfa); 158–9 (no. 8.4 votive deposit found at Ghiaccio Forte); 185 (no. 10.3 from Arezzo). All are well illustrated and discussed.
[18] *Studi Etruschi*, vi (1932), 449–50, pl. xxi.
[19] M 10584, 10598–600.

[20] e.g. the *situla* (M 12979) shown in the 1840 portrait.

[21] Tombs were first discovered at Vulci in 1828.

[22] It was then that the Grand Duke of Tuscany presented JM with a fine maiolica plaque (see below, p. 178). JM returned to Italy in 1835.

[23] M 12935–6 in the Daniels portrait of 1840 or (at latest) repainted in 1843: see pl. I.

[24] JM, *Egyptian Museum*, Rooms 2 and 4 and the Library.

Greek and Roman Antiquities

E. C. Southworth

A broad sweep over the antiquities that Mayer amassed will reveal many treasures and delights. Detailed examination, however, shows the collection to be remarkably variable in terms of quality and quantity. In sheer bulk the Egyptian material is unsurpassed and within this many of the real glories lie. Within the classical material by contrast only a few groups stand out as being of major significance. This is not to deny Mayer's interest in the classical heritage. His early travels in Italy are reminiscent of the Grand Tour, even though there was a strong practical element as befits a designer in training. He sketched in cathedrals and ancient sites.[1] The items he lent to the Pottery Mechanics' Institute in 1838 included 'three water-colour drawings of the interior of the house of Pansa at Pompeii'.[2] As these are not acknowledged as other drawings in the list are, they may well be Mayer's own work. The classical world appears to have made as much impact on Mayer the designer as on Mayer the collector. Most of his designs feature personifications of virtues in fluent classical pose and setting. His early stationery has a simple female bust reminiscent of Athena, another sketch shows Science unlocking the treasure of Antiquity. The 'treasure' reflects his collection: medieval swords and armour, an Egyptian canopic jar and a statuette of Sekhmet, rare Anglo-Saxon glass and pottery, and a prehistoric British cremation urn. Classical antiquity is represented by a single plain globular amphora of little merit.

What then does the classical element of the Mayer Collection comprise? Two significant groups are dealt with in other chapters: the Etruscan items and the classical gems. The Graeco-Roman marbles will be considered elsewhere. The present note is an attempt to bring together some of the remaining material and to discuss it as a whole. We shall be concerned with Greek pottery and terracotta, and Roman metalwork and glass.

In 1856 Charles Roach Smith's publication of the Faussett Collection featured an innovatory essay on the continental parallels for Anglo-Saxon material.[3] Mayer's approach to classical antiquities may have been coloured by the same thinking, in that he acquired large amounts of material from continental excavations, particularly Roman pottery, glass and metalwork from Germany, which would complement material from similar excavations in the British Isles. It is easier to understand Mayer's classical collection in this context of comparative study rather than as the search for artistic achievement in its own right.

The Greek pottery is quite cursorily dealt with in the 1852 catalogue of the Egyptian Museum:

> In the centre case are nearly 600 terra-cotta Vases, found in tombs of ancient Etruria. They are of various elegant and singular forms, and many of them are ornamented with figures, scrolls, and other designs.[4]

Little survives of this section of the collection. Gatty records only some seventy pieces in his museum records, of which barely twenty-two now survive. Of these, only four have even tentative attributions to named painters. A Campanian red figure *oinochoe* (M 10690: pl. XXI*a*) is attributed to the Manchester painter, for example, and a pleasing early Apulian red figure *pelike* (M 10483) is from the workshop of the Tarporley painter. On the other hand, there is a wide variety of forms and periods from proto-Corinthian *aryballoi* to Hellenistic bowls (cf. M 10725: pl. XXI*b*).[5] The group of some twenty terracottas is slightly more coherent. There are Tanagra figurines and Italian votive figures. These are charming, if common, representations of cockerels (e.g. M 8845: pl. XXII*a*), pigs and cattle, some still with their original paint. There is as yet no corpus volume of the classical pottery in the Liverpool Museum, but improved computerized documentation of the holdings has now made this a realistic possibility.

Mayer's interest in jewellery is borne out in a fine series of Hellenistic gold pendants and earrings (e.g. M 10297: pl. XXII*b*; M 8902: pl.XXII*c*), as well as a number of late Roman Italian examples. These serve to enhance the overall spread of techniques and styles represented in addition to the Etruscan masterpieces.

A significant source of Roman material was William Chaffers, 'numismatist and antiquary'. An exhibitor at the first British Archaeological Association congress at Canterbury in 1844, it was he who valued the Faussett Collection for the British Museum and acted as intermediary when Mayer eventually rescued it. A number of glass vessels are described by Gatty in the Museum records as having 'Mr. Chaffers labels' on them, as are Roman pots from London and elsewhere.[6] A letter survives from Chaffers to Charles Roach Smith which includes transcriptions of Roman bronze stamps 'sent herewith just to raise your curiosity as to the rest of the collection from the Rhine and which you must see as soon as you can spare the time to come to London'.[7]

Political uncertainty in Europe in the mid-nineteenth century appears to have made it easier for dealers in London to acquire material from abroad. A detailed list of 120 pieces of glass offered to Mayer still exists in the Mayer Papers.[8] The source is F. R. P. Bööcke of Oxford and London, who was obviously familiar with Mayer's collection. He spoke to the Historic Society of Lancashire and Cheshire about the Dolon vase from Canosa in the collection (M 4516),[9] and was involved, in some as yet undefined way, in the purchase of the Fejérváry Collection.[10] Later he was to arrange and promote the resale of the Hertz Collection at Sotheby's in 1859.[11] The list offered to Mayer includes description, dimensions, findspot and the place where Bööcke purchased them. The places include Paris, Rome and London, and collections specifically mentioned include those of Prince Esterhazy and Count Wiczay. Most of the glass in the Bööcke list was found in Germany or Italy, together with a few Egyptian pieces (pls. XXII*d*–XXIII*b*).[12] Several of these can be easily identified in the collection, most presumably entered it but cannot be recognized from their

PLATE XXI

a. Campanian red figure *oinochoe* (height 290 mm.) (M 10483)   *b.* Hellenistic black-glaze hydria (height 166 mm.) (M 10725)

Reproduced by courtesy of NMGM

PLATE XXII

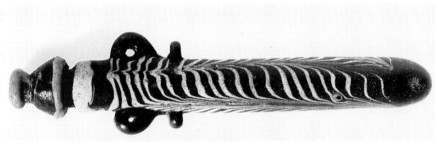

d. Rhodian glass kohl tube and stopper (length 127 mm.) (M 10085)

b. Hellenistic gold earrings (length 15 mm.) (M 10297)

c. Hellenistic gold earring, showing Eros as Pan (length 19 mm.) (M 8902)

a. Terracotta cockerel (height 130 mm.) (M 8845)

Reproduced by courtesy of NMGM

PLATE XXIII

b. Hellenistic glass hydria: (height 75 mm.) (M 10162)

Reproduced by courtesy of NMGM

a. Hellenistic glass alabastron (height 147 mm.) (M 10079)

PLATE XXIV

a, b. Gold glass discs (diam. 52 mm., 53 mm.)
(M 10069, 10070)

c. Roman glass hanging lamp (diam. 105 mm.)
(M 10199)

Reproduced by courtesy of NMGM

verbal descriptions. Possibly the finest from this source, and one of Mayer's finest pieces of glass overall, is a moulded bowl in a marbled fabric with white and amber glass (M 10078). It has been polished and is complete. Equally fine and very rare are two gold glass medallions of the type found in the catacombs in Rome (M 10069–70). These are of pale green glass, one engraved with figures of two boxers, the other with a portrait of a boy (pls. xxiv*a, b*). More mundane, but in an excellent state of preservation is a hanging lamp of thin clear glass with the original bronze chains for suspension (M 10199: pl. xxiv*c*).

The extent of the ancient glass in the Mayer Collection implies not mere casual accumulation but a deliberate collecting policy, albeit from a limited range of sources. Of the 400 or so items which were originally acquired, some 250 still exist. Second- and third-century Rhenish glass forms the largest and most comprehensive group. These pieces are in a variety of colours from dark green to blue and yellow with all shades in between. Decoration is usually in the form of a thin trail of glass in a contrasting colour, either round the neck and body or pulled down into elaborate loops and handles. Other decorative techniques include polishing, engraving and fluting. Another method of producing glass vessels is to enclose the blown, molten glass in a mould. This enables the craftsman to produce intricate shapes which have very angular lines or elaborate, repeated decoration. This can be in the form of a fluted edge or a pictorial representation (M 10062). Less common is the inclusion of an inscription as part of the moulding process (M 10129).

The unsolved puzzle of Mayer's collection as a whole is the purchase (1856) and disposal (1857 and 1859) of the Hertz Collection. We have scarcely any information about the 1857 sale; but it is clear that in 1859 some items were bought back again on Mayer's behalf.[13] As regards the Greek and Roman material, sixty-five items returned to Mayer in this way.[14] They were in restricted categories. They include twenty-three items of classical metalwork, five pieces of glass, eight ivories, at least six classical gems, three seals and one Greek pot. Many of these items cost only a few shillings, apart from the ivories and better bronzes, and the total cost was well under £200. The sale as a whole realized £10,011. 2*s*. 6*d*. with over 3,000 lots. It is hard to discern a collecting policy apart from deliberate caution. The single Greek pot bought is of interest. Described as a 'Phiale Omphalos from Nola', it is a small Hellenistic black glaze dish with a projecting centre, around which is a moulded scene of chariots and winged deities (M 10302). Smith paid £20. 10*s*. for it and it is a fine piece. Why did he buy this and not a splendid amphora from the Prince of Canino's collection which went for £87? There were seventy Greek pots in the sale, many of high quality, which would have enhanced Mayer's collection greatly. It is worth mentioning too that a group of three Mexican objects of great rarity was also in the sale. A mask, knife and skull, inlaid in mosaic with turquoise, obsidian and coral, fetched £133 altogether. Described as unique, these would have complemented the Mexican codex Mayer had recently obtained from the Fejérváry Collection. Given his penchant for exceptional pieces, it is hard to avoid the conclusion that in the late 1850s Mayer had overstretched himself financially.

The value of Mayer's Greek and Roman material lies in its potential as a foundation for the future development of the Museum's collections. Thanks to Mayer, there is representation of almost all aspects of classical civilization in a fairly balanced spread. No one group of items has dictated through its prestige or bulk a path for collecting and research which blocks other avenues. So far, the sources of this material are less clearly understood than in other areas of the collection, but the quality of individual pieces and small groups is manifest and there will still be surprises in store.

NOTES

[1] e.g. a sketch of a statue of St Charles Borromeo in Milan Cathedral: Liverpool City Record Office, Hg 942.7204.

[2] MPL, Thomas Ryder to JM, 7 July 1838.

[3] C. Roach Smith, *Inventorium Sepulchrale* (London, 1856), ix-lvi.

[4] JM, *Egyptian Museum*, 8.

[5] e.g. also M 10932.

[6] See e.g. M 10247, 10250.

[7] MPL, W. Chaffers to C. Roach Smith, undated.

[8] MPL, F. Bööcke to JM, 5 Jan. 1855.

[9] *THSLC*, vii (1855), 81–2.

[10] MPL, F. Bööcke to JM, various dates 1854–5.

[11] See Henig below, pp. 94–6.

[12] The examples shown (M 10085, 10079, 10162: pls. xxIId, xxIIIa, b) are fine Hellenistic vessels of a type usually found in Egypt.

[13] See Henig below, pp. 94–6.

[14] Sotheby's, 20 Apr. 1859. The copy in Liverpool Museum records appears to have been annotated by Joseph Clarke: MPL, letter from JC to JM, 1855. It was later cross-referenced to the Museum collection, possibly by C. T. Gatty. The copy annotated by Sotheby's is now in the British Library: S. C. Sotheby. (1).

[15] Now British Museum St. 399–401 (Museum of Mankind); bought at the Hertz sale by Henry Christy. See further E. Carmichael, *Turquoise Mosaics from Mexico* (London, 1970), 33–5, 37.

Ancient Engraved Gems

Martin Henig, F.S.A.[*]

Joseph Mayer was not one of the great connoisseurs of engraved gems. There is no indication that he acquired intaglios and cameos on the basis of an intimate knowledge of their style and iconography like his contemporaries, the Revd C. W. King and Revd S. S. Lewis, both Cambridge dons; still less can he be ranked with Sir Arthur Evans, a pioneer in approaching gems as archaeological artefacts.[1] However, unlike these gentlemen, he was a jeweller and 'dealer in precious stones, cameos, intaglios' and he had a good opportunity to acquire gems which came into his shop by way of trade.[2] It is clear from the 1852 Catalogue of the Egyptian Museum, that he owned over 160 'antique gems, in cameo and intaglio, of Greek, Roman and modern work'. A few items were singled out for especial mention: 'an engraved Bloodstone, with Gnostic figures and inscriptions', indicative of his interest in gnostic or magical amulets of which we get a hint from remaining portions of his collections, and 'a ring set with a garnet on which is engraved an eagle, found in ancient Etruria', providing something of a provenance.[3] British interests evidently brought in a few gems such as an early Byzantine garnet intaglio of a lion from Sibertswold (Faussett Collection) and a cornelian intaglio of Minerva from St Martin's, Canterbury (pl. xxva), of Roman date (Rolfe Collection), both set in seventh-century gold pendants.[4] A thirteenth-century silver seal at one time in Mayer's possession and later in that of Philip Nelson was set with a cornelian intaglio depicting Cybele; it seems to have been found in north Cheshire in 1850, and the medieval legend SIGILL.PHILIPPI.PVLE refers to an owner from Poole in Wirral.[5]

These are casual acquisitions of glyptic material on a relatively modest scale. Mayer's interest as a gem collector lies in his attempt first to acquire Bram Hertz's collection in its entirety in 1856 and then, after the sale of the gems at Sotheby's between 7 and 24 February 1859, his subsequent purchase of many fine gems from that collection.

The Hertz Collection was of considerable size, comprising almost 1,800 gems thought to be ancient as well as others of more recent date. It had been assembled between 1830 and 1850 by a German collector living in London and was catalogued (anonymously) by Dr Koner of Berlin in 1851. In his introduction Koner presents the admirable aims of the collector, so characteristic of the age and, indeed, of the year of the Great Exhibition:

The collection of Antiquities, described in the present Catalogue, was formed with the intention of gathering, so far as possible, the scattered monuments of ancient art, in order to illustrate the rise, progress and decline of the Fine Arts, and to obtain satisfactory corroboration of the veracity of ancient traditions respecting the religious habits, arts, and employments of bygone nations and the achievements of illustrious men and heroes.[6]

A review in *Archäologische Zeitung* in the same year, by an even more eminent German scholar, Professor Eduard Gerhard, provides a useful appreciation:

By purchasing beautiful and costly articles belonging to all periods of art, Mr Hertz has acquired a practised eye, and a power of discrimination which he has further exercised by making a selection from the acqusitions he has secured, in order to sift out the collection . . . This collection is not indeed to be considered as having been formed on the methodical plan of a professional collector, but rather as a brilliant and instructive display of antiques of every kind belonging to an important department, being both most valuable and numerous, and suitable to the choicest of all collections, A Cabinet of Gems.[7]

Such testimonials, it might have been thought, would have secured fame for the Hertz Collection and hence for its offspring, the Mayer Collection, like that enjoyed by other cabinets, for instance those of Praun and Montigny. This was not the case and the reason for it may lie in the sentiments expressed by King in an ungenerous and peptic paragraph.

The sole object of its founder (Bram Hertz) was, in unreasoning emulation of Stosch's celebrated cabinet, to accumulate every type ever engraved, when it was swollen to its enormous extent by the frequent admission of spurious works (through his want of all critical knowledge) . . . In truth such a motley assemblage of works of every degree of merit (though perhaps desirable in a national museum, as illustrating in a continuous series the history of the art, provided only they be duly classified), is quite out of character with a *private* cabinet, where the aim of the possessor should be to admit only a limited number of works and those the best of their kind.[8]

Elsewhere King states that 'the Hertz Collection derived almost everything of value that appeared amidst its multifarious rubbish' from Dr Nott's collection.[9]

In 1856 Mayer was a leading member of 'an association of Liverpool merchants', as Michaelis later describes them, who wished to give this large collection of gems and other antiquities to their native city.[10] The sum of £12,000 was involved, a very great deal of money, and Joseph Clarke in a letter to Roach Smith expressed his reservations: 'Mr Mayer no doubt has an astounding collection in Hertz's but I am astounded at the price given for it, why the British Museum people would have niggled about as many hundreds as he has given thousands for it!'[11] In a letter to Mayer, however, Clarke was more positive: 'I cannot but congratulate you on the purchase of the Hertz Collection. I have heard inadvertently that it is worth from fifteen to twenty thousand pounds . . .'[12]. The problem was that nothing like £12,000 had been paid and while formal ownership now resided with Mayer, the consortium seems to have fallen apart. Mr F. Böocke, who had been a broker in the original transaction, which left him like Mayer financially embarrassed, is now seen in another role as co-ordinator of the great Sotheby sale which took place between 7 and 24 February 1859.[13] The sale realized £10,011. 2*s.* 6*d.* but this was less than the original figure by almost £2,000 and after commission had been paid Mayer's loss was even greater. Joseph Clarke wrote to F. W. Fairholt: 'Mr Mayer and Barry's executors lose at the least £3,000 by the Hertz [sale] which I am afraid prey on his spirits.'[14] Financial loss was not, however, the end of the matter. Although the original Hertz Collection was broken up, to the benefit of various dealers and collectors and, incidentally, the British Museum as the result of the purchases of A. W. Franks,[15] Mayer's friends were active. Joseph Clarke seems to have purchased a few gems together with other items on Mayer's own instructions, spending £23. 13*s.* 0*d.* in this way, as well as further material on his own account.[16] Charles Roach Smith bought a great many more gems, as is proved by the following extract from a letter sent by Clarke to Mayer dated 27 April 1859, coupled with the frequent appearance of the name 'Smith' as purchaser in the annotated sale catalogue:

> Your letter fills me with vexation. It seems as if the Hertz collection was to be a source of nothing but trouble to you. I have received no missive as yet; whenever I do I shall be careful in my answer. I never supposed I was purchasing for you any more than Mr Roche (i.e. Roach) was, but I hope the bother will soon be over, and then the best way will be to think no more of it.[17]

It says much for the loyalty and consideration of Mayer's friends that a substantial part of the Hertz Collection was back in Mayer's hands in 1879 when Charles Tindal Gatty published his *Catalogue of the Engraved Gems and Rings in the Collection of Joseph Mayer, F.S.A.* Amongst the gems from the Hertz Collection *ex* Mayer which I have identified in Cambridge (see below) only two were not Roach Smith purchases: namely Hertz no. 116 (= Gatty no. 132) bought by Clarke, and Hertz no. 1469 (= Gatty no. 782) purchased by another friend, William Chaffers Jun.

Gatty's catalogue is the primary document for the study of Mayer's gems, at least of those kept at Bebington for it excludes the gems which he presented to Liverpool Museum in 1867.[18] Unfortunately, this work is completely lacking in scholarly distinction. It is not illustrated and does not give any clue as to provenances of individual stones. Reading like a sale catalogue, it did indeed form the basis of Sotheby's catalogue for the auction of Mayer's collection in May 1887. This Pennant House (Bebington) collection contained some 817 gems, both ancient and post-classical, with others set in rings. Quite a number clearly are *ex* Hertz Collection (as Gatty tells us), but by no means all. This assemblage, which must have vied in quantity and, it can be shown, in quality with other contemporary cabinets such as King's, which became the centrepiece of the gem collection of the Metropolitan Museum, New York, appears to have excited no contemporary comment. The Mayer sale was for the most part dominated by dealers rather than antiquaries (a contrast with the earlier disposal of the Hertz gems), although King seems to have purchased a few lots of modern gems of little importance.[19] It realized the very modest total of £1,394. 1*s.* 6*d.*, which may be a measure of the decline of interest in the minor arts over thirty years. Fortunately, a connoisseur of fine art, not otherwise known as a gem collector, Frank McClean, purchased a number of the more interesting lots (viz. lots 275, 279, 284, 289, 296, 309, 313, 317, 331, 337, 339, 342, 347 and 349). He also purchased coins at the sale. At his death (1904) he bequeathed his collection to the Fitzwilliam Museum, Cambridge. Although a catalogue of this munificent gift was prepared by an excellent scholar, O. M. Dalton, his work on this occasion shows signs of great haste and the account of the gems is incomplete and sketchy. There is no mention of where McClean had bought the bulk of his collection.[20] In addition the Revd Samuel Savage Lewis bought seven Mayer gems from dealers (including the three Graeco-Egyptian amulets comprising lot 346). These are indeed ascribed to the Mayer Collection in Middleton's catalogue of the Lewis gems—and could hardly fail to be, as this is indicated on their settings at least in four instances. These gems were bequeathed by Lewis to Corpus Christi College, Cambridge. Further research would doubtless reveal other Mayer gems in collections at home and abroad. One important example of the very highest quality must here suffice, the only gem in fact to be illustrated in Gatty's catalogue where it provides a frontispiece. It is a small chalcedony bust in the round, once in the Hertz Collection and identified by both Koner and Gatty as a bust of Livia (pl. xxv*b*). More recently it has been designated by Erika Simon as portraying Antonia Minor as a priestess of *Divus Augustus*. It was in a Swiss private collection before being acquired by the Getty Museum in Malibu in 1981.[21]

A total of sixty-three gems (including thirty-four which can be identified from the Hertz catalogue) provides a fair sample from which to judge the quality of Mayer's gems. In addition, there are the gems in Liverpool deriving from the 1867 gift and perhaps for the most part reflecting an earlier stage in his collecting career before he tried to buy the Hertz Collection.

Any assessment of Mayer as a gem collector is beset by imponderable factors. With regard to written sources, how far does Gatty's commonplace text, in many respects inferior to that of Dr Koner, reflect Mayer's own knowledge or lack of it? Mayer's business interests suggest that as a younger man he could have done a better job himself and Gatty, normally a capable antiquary, is somewhat apologetic in his introduction. The catalogue was produced in a hurry to guide the visitor and the informed scholar (who perhaps never came) through the collection in Pennant House. Secondly, what discrimination did Mayer employ in enlarging his holding? There are quite a few Graeco-Egyptian amulets in Liverpool as well as in Cambridge collected by Mayer and I cannot resist the impression that these reflect his special interest in Egyptian civilization. Thirdly, to what extent does the high quality of the gems now in Cambridge reflect the good taste of Mayer and his friends rather than that of McClean and Lewis? At the Mayer sale the gems were sold in lots of three to five stones. Thus, when McClean bought, he may have had particular pieces in mind but his capacity for close discrimination was limited. Lewis, buying from dealers, could be more choosy. Yet even the McClean bequest, the gift of a man who would seem to have known little about gems, is of impressive quality and interest. We can, I think, suggest that Roach Smith was very clever at the Hertz sale, and that he and Mayer both had a good eye for gems. The observations which follow are an attempt to say something about some of the highlights of Mayer's collecting as they are now preserved in Liverpool and Cambridge. Full descriptions of intaglios in Cambridge will be found in the relevant catalogues (see below, Appendix: Concordance Tables).[22] Here they are cited by Gatty's numbering.

The earliest classical gems[23] belonging to Mayer are two Graeco-Persian chalcedony scaraboids of the later fifth century B.C. One, in Liverpool, portrays a seated camel (pl. xxvc); the other, now in the Fitzwilliam Museum, depicts a winged bull. The latter was said to be Sassanian in the Hertz catalogue and 'probably Persian' by Gatty. Both thought the subject was Pegasus.[24]

An agate scarab, an Etruscan gem probably cut in the fourth century B.C., is a lively representation of Oedipus confronting the sphinx. This gem, now in Liverpool, illustrates the Etruscan love of Greek mythology (pl. xxvia).[25] Sphinxes remained common in the art of Italy; the emperor Augustus inherited two gems cut with the device of a sphinx which he used to seal letters. We may compare the opaque black ring-stone, jasper or agate, depicting a sphinx and dating from late Republican times (pl. xxvib).[26] Later on Augustus employed the gem-cutter Dioskourides to engrave a gem bearing his image and, although this has not survived to our day, we possess other stones from his hand including a fine intaglio in Cambridge showing Hermes enveloped in a *chlamys*. Mayer owned a most interesting parallel to this gem, also now in the Fitzwilliam Museum (pl. xxvic). Here the figure of Hermes is surrounded by a hatched border in Etruscan style emphasizing the mixed Greek and Italic pedigree of gem-engravers working in Italy in the first century B.C.[27]

This double heritage is demonstrated by other intaglios belonging to Mayer. Representations of a Greek philosopher (Chrysippos according to Gisela Richter), a dwarf riding upon an amphora, Eros with the attributes of Herakles (all Fitzwilliam Museum), a fight between a pygmy and a crane, and Aphrodite Euploia crossing the sea upon a ram (both Lewis Collection) clearly belong to the Hellenistic tradition.[28] Italic motifs such as a peacock, Odysseus and Diomedes stealing the Palladion, and Diana Nemorensis are strongly archaizing in character.[29] Rather more mixed in pedigree are two very interesting intaglios in the Lewis Collection. An amethyst portrays the Vestal Virgin, Claudia Quinta, pulling the ship carrying the goddess Cybele off a sandbank in the Tiber (pl. xxvid). This event happened at the time of the triumphal installation of the Magna Mater in Rome at the end of the third century B.C. while Hannibal was still threatening Rome. The figure of Claudia Quinta is surely based on an Archaic statue, not true to its period, but nonetheless imparting to the scene a timeless, heroic atmosphere.[30] Enthusiasm for the archaic is also shown by a burnt sardonyx intaglio showing Apollo or an image of that god holding a deer by its front legs (pl. xxviia).[31] It is possible to see this gem as a 'pendant' to the Italic 'Diana Nemorensis', but the style here is no longer sub-Etruscan but belongs to the sophisticated art of the Augustan age.

Amongst Roman Imperial gems is a fine study in onyx of Cupid standing in front of a circular shrine of Venus, just such an *aedicula* as housed Praxiteles' *Aphrodite of Knidos* (pl. xxviib).[32] A blue onyx (nicolo) intaglio depicts Dea Roma holding a bust, perhaps of *Divus Augustus*. Here it is instructive to observe that, although the Hertz catalogue had correctly described the subject as Roma, Gatty has her as a 'warrior, wearing a helmet, seated on a heap of armour, and holding in his right hand a laureated head'.[33] Learning is not necessary in order to enjoy the wonderfully realistic lizard cut upon a cornelian (pl. xxviic) which seems about to scuttle away.[34]

The category which may have interested Mayer most was that of gems with an Egyptian theme. As an example I illustrate an impression of a magnetite amulet in the Fitzwilliam Museum bought by Clarke for Mayer at the Hertz sale (pl. xxviid). It shows an Isiac priestess or perhaps Isis herself.[35] It is the measure of the

PLATE XXV

a. Cornelian intaglio depicting Minerva, reset in seventh-century gold pendant from St Martin's, Canterbury ($\frac{2}{1}$) (M 7014). Reproduced by courtesy of NMGM

b. Miniature chalcedony bust of Antonia Minor as a priestess of *Divus Augustus* (height 50 mm.). Reproduced by courtesy of the J. Paul Getty Museum, Malibu

c. Graeco-Persian chalcedony scaraboid depicting a camel ($\frac{4}{1}$) (M 10542). Reproduced by courtesy of NMGM

Photographs: a, c, Robert Wilkins

PLATE XXVI

a. Etruscan agate scarab showing Oedipus and the sphinx ($\frac{4}{1}$) (M 10601). Reproduced by courtesy of NMGM

b. Late Republican dark agate ring-stone cut with a sphinx ($\frac{4}{1}$) (M 10528). Reproduced by courtesy of NMGM

c. Roman cornelian intaglio of Hermes (impression) (*ex* Mayer Collection) ($\frac{4}{1}$). Reproduced by courtesy of the Fitzwilliam Museum, Cambridge

d. Amethyst intaglio: Claudia Quinta pulling the ship containing the image of Cybele off the Tiber sandbank (impression) (*ex* Mayer Collection) ($\frac{4}{1}$). Reproduced by courtesy of Corpus Christi College, Cambridge (Lewis Collection)

Photographs: Robert Wilkins

PLATE XXVII

a. Roman sardonyx intaglio of Apollo (impression) (*ex* Mayer Collection) ($\frac{4}{1}$). Reproduced by courtesy of Corpus Christi College, Cambridge (Lewis Collection)

b. Roman onyx intaglio of Cupid before the shrine of Venus (Aphrodite Anadyomene) (impression) (*ex* Mayer Collection) ($\frac{4}{1}$). Reproduced by courtesy of the Fitzwilliam Museum, Cambridge

c. Roman cornelian intaglio of a lizard (impression) (*ex* Mayer Collection) ($\frac{4}{1}$). Reproduced by courtesy of the Fitzwilliam Museum, Cambridge

d. Graeco-Egyptian magnetite amulet of Isis (impression) (*ex* Mayer Collection) ($\frac{4}{1}$). Reproduced by courtesy of the Fitzwilliam Museum, Cambridge

Photographs: Robert Wilkins

inaccessibility of the Pennant House collection that King made no use of Mayer's holdings in his pioneering study, *The Gnostics and their Remains* (London, 1864), the second expanded version of which was published in London in 1887. In the same year King did publish two of Mayer's amulets which had come to the Lewis Collection, but he ascribes their provenance to the Montigny Cabinet sold in Paris during the same year.[36]

Mayer had medieval seals and Renaissance and modern gems, some of them evidently quite good pieces. If here, as elsewhere, the collection lacked works of the highest quality and rarity, there is no doubt that it contained much of great interest. Unlike so many later archaeologists and antiquaries, Mayer realized that art did not become less important when it was executed on a miniature scale and that the progress of civilization is to be seen reflected in the minor arts, nowhere more so than in glyptics.

APPENDIX: CONCORDANCE TABLES

The catalogues compared below illustrate six chapters in the history of the Mayer Collection:

1851 Koner/Hertz	Koner's catalogue of the Hertz Collection (see below, note 6)
1859 Sotheby's	Sale of the Hertz Collection (see below, note 7)
1879 Gatty	C. T. Gatty's catalogue of gems in JM's collection in Bebington (see below, note 5)
1887 Sotheby's	Sale of JM's effects in Bebington (Lugt 46620; see below, p. 227)
1975 Henig/Lewis	M. Henig's catalogue of the Lewis Collection of gems now in Corpus Christi College, Cambridge
1988 Henig/Fitzwilliam	M. Henig's catalogue of the collection of gems now in the Fitzwilliam Museum, Cambridge

I: Gems from the Mayer Collection (Bebington) now in the Fitzwilliam Museum, Cambridge

Gatty 1879	Sotheby's 1887	Koner/Hertz 1851	Sotheby's 1859	Henig/Fitzwilliam 1988
75	275	334	901	671
76	275	284	735	193
77	275	—	—	295
78	275	342	909	301
91	279	452	1142	174
92	279	471	1300	176
93	279	477	1306	686
94	279	—	—	262
111	284	613	1605	183
112	284	567	1559	289

continued

I: Gems now in the Fitzwilliam Museum, Cambridge, continued

Gatty 1879	Sotheby's 1887	Koner/Hertz 1851	Sotheby's 1859	Henig/Fitzwilliam 1988
113	284	—	—	149
129	289	374	941	267
130	289	377	944	265
131	289	378	945	266
132	289	116	875	514
133	289	—	—	316
153	296	—	—	88
154	296	823	2125	138
155	296	777	2010	336
184	309	—	—	222
185	309	—	—	221
186	309	845	2147	217
187	309	—	—	631
199	313	—	—	689
200	313	—	—	132
201	313	—	—	306
202	313	1236	2704	867
215	317	—	—	659
216	317	—	—	185
217	317	1055	2473	141
218	317	849	2151	280
271	331	—	—	318
272	331	—	—	340
273	331	—	—	658
274	331	979	2338	209
275	331	—	—	202
294	337	1361	2897	651
295	337	1360	2896	83
296	337	1367	2965	652
297	337	—	—	650
298	337	1313	2849	361
304	339	1442	3040	375
305	339	1395	2993	445
306	339	1405	3003	370
307	339	1454	3052	353
308	339	—	—	153
317	342	—	—	512
318	342	—	—	493
319	342	—	—	513
330	347	1510	3108	501
331	347	—	—	500
332	347	—	—	515
336	349	30	617	66
337	349	—	—	409
338	349	—	—	440

II: Gems from the Mayer Collection (Bebington), now in the Lewis Collection, Corpus Christi College, Cambridge

Gatty 1879	Sotheby's 1887	Koner/Hertz 1851	Sotheby's 1859	Henig/Lewis 1975
55	270	388	955	15
120	287	123	80	193
327	346	—	—	247
328	346	—	—	244
329	346	—	—	239
767	449	786	3019	45
782	455	1469	3067	184

NOTES

* I am indebted to Roger White and Michael Rhodes for details of the Hertz affair, to Robert Wilkins, F.S.A., for pls. xxva, xxvc–xxviid, and to the Department of Antiquities, J. Paul Getty Museum, Malibu, for pl. xxvb.

[1] Revd C. W. King, author of *Antique Gems and Rings* (London, 1872) and other works. His own collection was sold to John Taylor Johnston, who presented it to the Metropolitan Museum of Art, New York, in 1881; see G. M. A. Richter, *Metropolitan Museum of Art, New York: Catalogue of Engraved Gems* (1920; 2nd edn. 1956). King's friend, the Revd S. S. Lewis, bequeathed his substantial collection to his college, Corpus Christi, Cambridge, in 1891; see J. H. Middleton, *The Lewis Collection of Gems and Rings in the Possession of Corpus Christi College, Cambridge* (Cambridge, 1892) and M. Henig, *The Lewis Collection of Gemstones in Corpus Christi College, Cambridge*, Brit. Arch. Rep. Suppl. ser. 1 (Oxford, 1975). Evans's interest was heralded by a note on ancient gems which he had collected in Dalmatia: A. Evans, *PSA*, 2nd ser. ix (1882), 175–9; cf. *id.*, *An Illustrative Selection of Greek and Graeco-Roman Gems* (Oxford, 1938).

[2] 'J. M. has on Sale an Extensive Collection of ANTIQUE GEMS, in CAMEOS, INTAGLIOS . . .': Science Museum Library, South Kensington, 'Prospectuses of Exhibitors', xv, xxiii–xxvi, *Manufacturer's Catalogue (c.* 1856), 1.

[3] JM, *Egyptian Museum*, 25, drawers 21 and 22; 20, no. 221; 21, no. 227. Also see p. 17, drawer 1, no. 77.

[4] C. Roach Smith, *Inventorium Sepulchrale* (London, 1856), 131 and pl. iv, fig. 17; cf. S. C. Hawkes, J. M. Merrick and D. M. Metcalf, 'X-ray fluorescence analysis of some Dark Age coins and jewellery', *Archaeometry*, ix (1966), 111 no. L 23 (M 6528 Sibertswold), 105 no. L 9 (M 7014 Canterbury).

[5] C. T. Gatty, *A Catalogue of the Engraved Gems and Rings in the Collection of Joseph Mayer, F.S.A.* (Liverpool, 1879), no. 883, though the provenance is not noted; cf. P. Nelson, 'Some British medieval seal-matrices', *Arch. J.*, xciii (1936), 18 no. 25, pl. ii(4).

[6] *Catalogue of the Collection of Assyrian, Babylonian, Egyptian, Greek, Etruscan, Roman, Indian, Peruvian and Mexican Antiquities* (London, 1851), iii. The authorship is given in *Archäologischer Anzeiger*, no. 34 (Oct. 1851), cols. 91–104, no. 35 (Nov. 1851), cols. 107–15, the review which was reprinted in translation in the sale catalogue (see below, note 7). The total of ancient gems given is: oriental 54; cut gems (i.e. intaglios) 1,517; cameos 223.

[7] Lugt 24633 (7–24 Feb. 1859, Sotheby's), ii.

[8] King, *op. cit.* (note 1), 282–3.

[9] *Ibid.*, 461.

[10] A. Michaelis, *Ancient Marbles in Great Britain* (Cambridge, 1882), 177–8.

[11] MPL, Joseph Clarke to C. Roach Smith, 22 Nov. 1856.

[12] MPL, Joseph Clarke to JM, 11 Dec. 1856.

[13] MPL, F. Bööcke to JM, 18 Jan. 1858 and 30 Jan. 1859. Bööcke asked JM for a £300 float to enable him to run the bidding up (30 Jan.); JM's reply is lost.

[14] MPL, Joseph Clarke to F. W. Fairholt, 14 Apr. 1859. £3,000 is an inflated figure: on an outlay of £12,000 JM had recovered all but £1,989, plus expenses. He had already sold Hertz material at Phillips in 1857 for an unknown sum: see above, p. 11.

[15] H. B. Walters, *Catalogue of the Engraved Gems and Cameos, Greek, Etruscan and Roman in the British Museum* (London, 1926), *passim*; see, e.g., nos. 614 (Hertz sale no. 692), 662 (Hertz sale no. 1662) and 3231 (Hertz sale no. 2188).

[16] The relevant letters from Clarke to Mayer are dated 1 and 9 Mar. 1859 (MPL) (information from Roger White).

[17] Clarke frequently made play with people's names; the Norman spelling of Roche (rather than Roach) was often used by Smith himself, when he wished to allude to his Norman roots and associate himself with the influential European family so named, a member of which he visited during one of his many study tours to France (information from Michael Rhodes).

[18] What JM presented to Liverpool was the Egyptian Museum collection, with only casual additions (if any) from Hertz.

[19] King purchased lots 353 (Gatty nos. 348–50), 388 (Gatty nos. 611–13), 422 (Gatty nos. 697–8), 460 (Gatty nos. 795–6) and 470 (Gatty nos. 823–5). Mayer's friend Thomas Wright, whose interest in gems is shown by a short paper, 'Roman engraved stones found on the site of Uriconium, at Wroxeter, Salop', *JBAA*, xix (1863), 106–11, purchased lot 341 (Gatty nos. 314–16). It should be possible to recognize other Mayer gems. Two reached the Southesk Collection (now itself dispersed) and were evidently of high quality: H. Carnegie, *Catalogue of the Collection of Antique Gems formed by James, Ninth Earl of Southesk* (London, 1908), 9 no. A13 (Mayer sale lot 253), 63–4 no. E10 (Mayer sale lot 270). See also the Lewis Collection below.

[20] O. M. Dalton, *Fitzwilliam Museum, McClean Bequest: Catalogue of the Mediaeval Ivories, Enamels, Jewellery, Gems and Miscellaneous Objects bequeathed to the Museum by Frank McClean* (Cambridge, 1912).

[21] Hertz, 79 no. 117 (= Gatty, no. 164, 1859 sale, lot 300); E. Simon, 'Vier Iulisch Claudische Büsten: Augustus und Antonia Minor in Kurashiki, Japan', *Archäologischer Anzeiger* (1982), 342 n. 16 and figs. 25–7. For another Mayer gem, in a British private collection in 1936, see above, note 5. I am indebted here to Jeffrey Spier, who informed me of the Malibu head, and to Marion True, Curator of Antiquities, J. Paul Getty Museum, who provided me with the photographs for pl. xxv*b*.

[22] M. Henig, *Classical Gems, Ancient and Modern Cameos in the Fitzwilliam Museum, Cambridge* (Cambridge, 1988) and *id.*, *op. cit.* (note 1), for the gems in Cambridge.

[23] For the Egyptian scarabs and Near-Eastern cylinder-seals see above, pp. 58–9, 71–6.

[24] M 10542: J. Boardman, *Engraved Gems and Finger Rings* (London, 1970), 354, pl. 917. It is set in a gold swivel-ring of ancient form but perhaps not antique and almost certainly an addition. For the winged bull (Gatty no. 336; Boardman, *op. cit.* (this note), pl. 919) see Henig (1988), *op. cit.* (note 22), no. 66.

[25] M 10601.

[26] M 10528; cf. Pliny, *Natural History*, xxxvii.10.

[27] Pliny, *Natural History*, xxxvii.8; Gatty no. 91.

[28] *Ibid.*, nos. 275, 113, 76, 782 and 767. This interpretation of Aphrodite Euploia (where I have followed Gatty and Middleton) seems preferable to that of Koner, *op. cit.* (note 6), and more recently of Richard Nicholls, *Classical Heritage: Greek and Roman Art from Cambridge College Collections* (London, 1978), 28 no. 191, that she is Helle, for the figure is almost nude and is accompanied by Erotes. She shows no sign of being about to fall from her mount into the sea. I assume the ram refers to Ares of the Zodiac and of course, in anthropomorphic guise, to Aphrodite's paramour.

[29] Gatty nos. 308, 154, 200.

[30] *Ibid.*, no. 120.

[31] *Ibid.*, no. 55.

[32] *Ibid.*, no. 78.

[33] *Ibid.*, no. 218.

[34] *Ibid.*, no. 304.

[35] *Ibid.*, no. 132.

[36] C. W. King, 'Observations upon four Gnostic gems lately added to the Lewis Collection', *Communications of the Cambridge Antiquarian Society*, vi (1887), 349–54 nos. 2 and 3; Gatty nos. 328–9.

Late Antique and Medieval Ivories

Margaret Gibson, F.S.A.

The Fejérváry and Mayer Collections

In November 1851 Count Gabriel Fejérváry, exiled from Hungary after the 1848 revolution, died in Paris. He bequeathed his collection of antiquities to his nephew Franz Pulszky, another exile (and politically of some weight, being a friend of Kossuth), who had settled in London.[1] Pulszky exhibited the Fejérváry Collection as a whole at the Royal Archaeological Institute in 1853, and in the years that followed he sold first the maiolica and then in 1855 the ivories. As in the case of the Faussett Collection, the Trustees of the British Museum were unable to make the purchase and Joseph Mayer—in the view of his antiquarian friends—stepped in and saved the day.[2] The Fejérváry ivories were acquired for *c.* £1,500 and displayed in the Egyptian Museum. Pulszky himself wrote the catalogue, published in 1856.[3]

The Fejérváry Collection accounts for just over half of Mayer's ivories, and for all of the most famous pieces: the Asclepius-Hygieia diptych, the *Venatio* panel, the consular diptych of Clementinus.[4] Nonetheless, Mayer had already assembled an interesting and representative collection of medieval ivories, including Byzantine, as well as Chinese and Indian pieces that cannot concern us here. These ivories were originally kept with other material, for example gems, in historical categories: 'Egyptian', 'Assyrian', 'Etruscan', 'Greek and Roman', 'Byzantine', 'Western', 'English', and so forth. Such at least is the implication of a list now preserved in one of the Museum's Guard Books.[5] The ivories have there been extracted from a more comprehensive list reflecting an indiscriminate (or 'integrated') display. The Fejérváry ivories are not included; the list represents what Mayer had acquired on his own account, probably before 1855. In today's terms the most remarkable items are the two panels from the Magdeburg antependium (pl. xxix*b, c*), a Byzantine triptych, which though not of first quality is complete, and a fine Gothic casket-lid.[6] For Mayer himself it was perhaps equally important to have examples from all periods—not easy with ivory, as we understand better then he did. In this respect the Anglo-Saxon nativity panel in walrus ivory, which he acquired from W. H. Rolfe,[7] and the handful of Romanesque pieces in whalebone and bone[8] were as interesting as the casket-lid. His Byzantine material has yet to come into its own: it is provincial in style and virtually undatable, for we still know nothing of Byzantine ivory-carving outside Constantinople and Venice.[9]

Mayer acquired the Fejérváry ivories just in time to send some of the finest pieces to the *Art Treasures Exhibition* in Manchester in 1857, where they found a place in J. B. Waring's commemorative volume.[10] In C. T. Gatty's catalogues for the Liverpool Museum they are awkwardly divided between *Greek, Roman and Etruscan* (1883) and *Mediaeval and Later* (1883). Much of the collection was included in the Burlington Fine Arts Club exhibition of *Carvings in Ivory* in 1923; the descriptions in the accompanying catalogue, which owed much to Margaret Longhurst, are the basis of the British Museum handlist of 1954 for the exhibition *Liverpool Ivories*.[11] A new catalogue is in preparation; meanwhile two examples must stand for all.

The *Asclepius-Hygieia diptych* (pl. xxviiia)

The late antique ivories that have survived best are the diptychs commemorating a consul's year of office, as in Mayer's collection the diptych of Clementinus, eastern consul in 513. They span the early fifth to the mid-sixth century A.D. and, with the related pieces that are strictly imperial rather than consular, some fifty panels in all are known. They may always have been plentiful, but a factor in their preservation has been their elaborate inscriptions, which were attracting serious scholarly attention by the eighteenth century. By contrast diptychs commemorating lesser public office, or showing the figures of Roman religion (equally a public matter), or of private reference are so rare that the entire list scarcely comes to a dozen panels.[12] Of these three were in the Fejérváry Collection: the two panels Asclepius-Hygieia, and the single panel *Venatio*. We may look briefly at the former.

The Asclepius-Hygieia diptych shows two statues.[13] On the left is the god Asclepius, whose cult came to Rome from Epidaurus in the third century B.C., clad as a philosopher, his serpent twisting up his rough wooden staff, and at his feet to the right an oxhead (*boucranion*) and to the left the underworld child-deity Telesphoros, displaying an open scroll. Point for point the image compares well with a long tradition of full-scale stone statues of Asclepius in Italy and elsewhere.[14] In Rome the temple of Asclepius on the Tiber island had in Ovid's day the god standing—'in his left hand a staff with the bark still on it, his right hand pulling at the hair of his long beard'.[15] Even the *boucranion* is matched by the stone *boucrania* on the flood-wall at the southern tip of the island, still visible today.[16] On the right panel the statue of Asclepius' daughter Hygieia, confronted by a somewhat unexpected Cupid (bottom left), is a much less common image, but the identification is not in doubt. It is the context of the diptych—its purpose and social circumstances—that is hard to understand.

Stylistically Asclepius-Hygieia is generally attributed to a Roman workshop *c*. A.D. 400. That is entirely reasonable—for instance by analogy with contemporary silver.[17] It would relate to the cult of Asclepius, particularly on the Tiber island, but that such public observance was discontinued by law in 381 and in subsequent enactments;[18] either the date of the diptych is moved back a quarter of a century, or we seek another explanation. Domestic observance persisted, though the public cults had ceased; and the most specific evidence here is the commemorative diptych of which the badly-damaged left panel is in the Musée Cluny in Paris and the right panel in the Victoria and Albert Museum in London (pl. xxviiib). In both priestesses perform traditional rites, the two families being named above: NICOMA-CHORUM and SYMMACHORUM.[19] Stylistically this diptych has little in common with Asclepius-Hygieia: but both diptychs are, so to say, at ease with traditional Roman religion. How the service of the gods was understood is another question. For some intellectuals Apollo, Asclepius and the rest were cosmic or philosophical principles (the sun, justice, health); they still had meaning, they could still be represented well into the fifth century.[20] Whether or not the Asclepius-Hygieia diptych should be read in this philosophical sense, it certainly belongs to a society in which the old religion was legally dispossessed. It cannot be understood as a routine manifestation of established belief.

The Magdeburg panels

By the later tenth century—to try to see the picture in Mayer's own terms—the classical world had vanished. Even its Carolingian reflection scarcely persists in the three panels (pl. XXIX) that were made for Archbishop Adalbert of Magdeburg *c.* A.D. 970. They belong to a series of which sixteen panels are still extant, scattered across the world.[21] They show the life of Christ, with one exception: the donor-panel now in the Metropolitan Museum, New York. There Christ sits in glory, receiving the gift of Magdeburg Cathedral from the emperor Otto I.[22] The two panels with the wide margins (pl. XXIX*b, c*) Mayer himself acquired, quite possibly from the Possenti Collection in Fabriano (March of Ancona).[23] In one, Christ lays on his disciples their apostolic mission: Go out and preach. In the other, St Peter breaks open the fish's mouth to take the tribute-money, looking back in astonishment at Christ as he does so.[24] We know from a pilgrim's guide of *c.* 1520 that both panels were set in a reliquary box in the archbishop's church at Halle, near Magdeburg (pl. XXX): 'Christ commissioning the Apostles' is visible, 'Peter and the Tribute-money' was on the other long side.[25] Eight panels were on the reliquary, uncut but screwed on to their base at the four corners. Four further panels survive on a book-cover now in East Berlin, and the rest here and there—several with the margins reduced, one with only the figures remaining in silhouette. 'The Woman taken in Adultery' (pl. XXIX*a*) was in the Fejérváry Collection, and so to Mayer; the margins are cut down and the surface worn and highly polished. It is the only case of a Magdeburg panel being reunited with its fellows.

Where the panels were made is an open question that cannot be tackled here. But that they were made for Adalbert of Magdeburg, in his new eminence as archbishop, is reasonably secure. How did he display them? As an altar-frontal, a door, a screen, an archiepiscopal throne? There is no contemporary information, beyond the certainty that the object (whatever it was) had already been dismantled by the mid-eleventh century.[26] The panels are pierced to let the light through, as in the windows of the Temple and the two types of criss-cross in the panels shown, and similarly in all the rest. This feature would suggest a door or a screen. Analogies are hard to find, but it is worth remembering the three ivory and silver doors in the late eighth-century furnishings of St Denis, one of which may still have been there *c.* 1140.[27] In liturgical terms, a door is hard to justify if the ivories were within the church. The other main option is an archiepiscopal throne or *cathedra*, such as the sixth-century chair of Maximian at Ravenna: a potent influence on Carolingian art and presumably still in

PLATE XXVIII

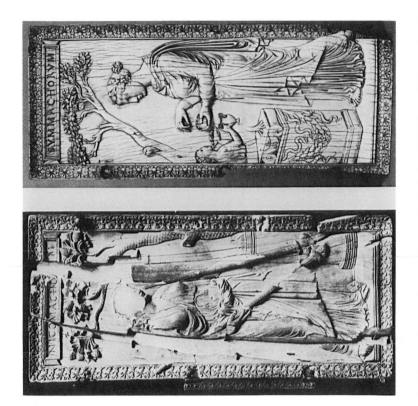

a. Asclepius-Hygieia diptych (height 314 mm.) (M 10044). Reproduced by courtesy of NMGM

b. Nicomachorum-Symmachorum diptych (height 298 mm.). Reproduced by courtesy of the Musée Cluny, Paris, and the Victoria and Albert Museum, London

PLATE XXIX

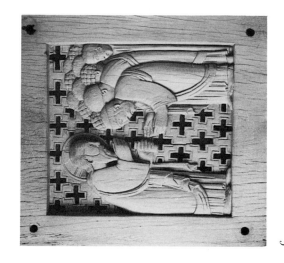

Three Magdeburg panels (*left to right, a.* 130 × 117 mm.; *b.* 129 × 118 mm.; *c.* 110 × 102 mm.) (M 8061, 8062, 8017). Reproduced by courtesy of NMGM

a

b

c

PLATE XXX

Reliquary box in the Hallesches Heiltum, showing Christ and the Apostles (M 8061) second from left. MS Aschaffenburg 14, fo. 255^v, reproduced by courtesy of the Hofbibliothek, Aschaffenburg

ceremonial use in Ravenna in the later tenth century.[28] Whether as screen or door or throne, the panels reinforced Archbishop Adalbert's authority as the representative of Christ and the emperor on the northern frontier.

The collection today

No ivories were added to the collection between 1867 and 1941. In the fire of that year eleven Gothic devotional panels were lost, plus (curiously) all the antique and early medieval panels that were thought to be spurious.[29] Several interesting pieces have been acquired since: notably the fourth-century figure of a shepherd carrying a lamb (*criophore*),[30] Gothic panels from Philip Nelson, late antique furniture inlay from the Wellcome Trustees,[31] and most recently another very provincial Byzantine 'diptych' to supplement Mayer's own and a fine Embriachi mirror-frame, which serves as a point of reference for the several fragments of the genre that were already in the collection.[32]

NOTES

[1] See further above, pp. 10–11. Pulszky's life as a politically active exile in the 1850s and 1860s is chronicled by T. Kabdebo, *Diplomat in Exile*, East European monographs 56 (New York, 1979).

[2] See below, pp. 118–21. The Hungarian prehistoric metalwork and the Mexican deerskin codex (Codex Fejérváry-Mayer) may have been part of the deal: no details survive beyond Pulszky's own account (above, p. 11, and note 81).

[3] F. Pulszky, *Catalogue of the Fejérváry Ivories, in the Museum of Joseph Mayer, Esq., F.S.A.* (Liverpool, 1856).

[4] M 10044 (Asclepius-Hygieia), M 10042 (*Venatio*), M 10036 (Clementinus). See M. Gibson, *Liverpool Ivories* (Liverpool, 1983), slidepack nos. 1–4.

[5] Liverpool Museum, Department of Antiquities, Guard Book I, 90. I am indebted to Margaret Warhurst for this reference.

[6] M 8061, 8062 (Magdeburg: Gibson, *op. cit.* (note 4), slidepack nos. 8–9), M 8063 (triptych; *ibid.*, slidepack no. 10), M 8052 (casket-lid).

[7] M 8060 (*ibid.*, slidepack no. 11), acquired 1857. For Rolfe see further above, p. 12.

[8] M 8018 (vintage: bone), M 8016 ('Presentation in the Temple': whalebone; Gibson, *op. cit.* (note 4), slidepack no. 12), M 8065 (evangelist box: bone).

[9] M 8013 (crucifixion panel from triptych), M 8014 (St John the Baptist), M 8019 (nativity/crucifixion panel), M 8020 (deesis panel from triptych), M 8032–9 (casket-panels: bone), M 8063 (triptych; *ibid.*, slidepack no. 10).

[10] J. B. Waring, *Art Treasures of the United Kingdom: Consisting of Examples Selected from the Manchester Art Treasures Exhibition* (London, 1858), 6–7, 9–11, 23–4.

[11] *Catalogue of an Exhibition of Carvings in Ivory*, Burlington Fine Arts Club Exhibition Catalogue (London, 1923); *Liverpool Ivories: Special Exhibition,* British Museum Exhibition Catalogue (London, 1954). M 8003, 8010–11, 8014, 8016–19, 8021–2, 8037–9, 8049, 8052, 8056, 8060–2, 8064–5, 10036, 10044 were exhibited at Manchester in 1976: *MRT*, nos. 99–110, 113–14, 116–19, 122.

[12] R. Delbrueck, *Die Consulardiptychen und verwandte Denkmäler*, 2 vols. (Berlin, 1929), I, xxvi–xxxiii; W. F. Volbach, *Elfenbeinarbeiten der Spätantike und des frühen Mittelalters*, 3rd edn. (Mainz, 1976), with full bibliography.

[13] The best description is still Delbrueck, *op. cit.* (note 12), I, no. 55.

[14] C. Kerényi, *Asklepios: Archetypal Image of the Physician's Existence* (London, 1960), pls. 40–3.

[15] Ovid, *Metamorphoses*, xv.654–6.

[16] For a vivid, if dramatized, rendering see G. B. Piranesi, 'Veduta dell' Isola Tiberina', *c.* 1760: *Vedute di Roma* (Focillon, no. 836), conveniently reproduced by H. Levit, *Views of Rome Then and Now* (New York, 1976), no. 3.

[17] K. J. Shelton, *The Esquiline Treasure* (London, 1981), 64–5, and *passim*.

[18] *Theodosian Code*, XVI.x.7–18.

[19] The diptych may well have belonged to the circle of Quintus Aurelius Symmachus (*ob. c.* A.D. 402), who argued for the restoration of the Altar of Victory in the Senate, and Virius Nicomachus Flavianus, who committed suicide as consul in A.D. 394 on Theodosius' defeat of the pagan Eugenius. Symmachus' daughter married Nicomachus' son. The most illuminating account is still H. Bloch, 'The pagan revival in the west at the end of the fourth century', in A. Momigliano, *The Conflict between Paganism and Christianity in the Fourth Century* (Oxford, 1963), 193–218; see now A. H. M. Jones, J. R. Martindale and J. Morris, *The Prosopography of the Later Roman Empire*, 2 vols. (Cambridge, 1971–80), I, ad loc.

[20] Macrobius, *Saturnalia*, i.20.5–6. For the dating see Alan Cameron, 'The date and identity of Macrobius', *J. Roman Stud.*, lvi (1966), 25–38.

[21] A. Goldschmidt, *Die Elfenbeinskulpturen aus der Zeit der karolingischen und sächsischen Kaiser*, 2 vols. (Berlin, 1918), II, nos. 8, 11 and 13; C. T. Little, *The Magdeburg Ivory Group: a Tenth-century New Testament Narrative Cycle* (New York University unpublished Ph.D. thesis, 1977).

[22] Goldschmidt, *op. cit.* (note 21), no. 16 (then in Seitensetten); photograph in D. Gaborit-Chopin, *Ivoires du Moyen Âge* (Fribourg, 1978), 192.

[23] Goldschmidt, *op. cit.* (note 21), nos. 8 and 11; cf. 9: an unsupported statement but (being Goldschmidt's) to be taken seriously.

[24] Matt. 28:16–20; and (tribute-money) cf. Matt. 17:24–7.

[25] P. M. Halm and R. Berliner, *Das Hallesche Heiltum* (Berlin, 1931), 58–9 and pl. 153. The text below the picture reads: 'a silver gilt box with viii ivory panels carved with eight scenes from the gospels'.

[26] The four panels on the *Codex Wittekindeus*, now in East Berlin, were already part of the binding in the time of Archbishop Engelhard (1052–63): V. Rose, *Verzeichniss der lateinischen Handschriften der königlichen Bibliothek zu Berlin*, II (1) (Berlin, 1901), 42 (MS theol. fol. 1).

[27] Suger, *De consecratione*, ed. E. Panofsky, *Abbot Suger on the Abbey Church of St Denis and its Art Treasures*, 2nd edn. (Princeton, 1979), 116 and 248.

[28] For Maximian's throne see Volbach, *op. cit.* (note 12), no. 140, and Gaborit-Chopin, *op. cit.* (note 22), 32–5, 183. The archiepiscopal status of Magdeburg was confirmed at Ravenna in 967: P. Jaffé and S. Löwenfeld, *Regesta Pontificum Romanorum* (Leipzig, 1885), i.3715.

[29] The lost Gothic ivories are: M 8001, 8005, 8050, 8058–9, 8066, 8071,8073–4, 8076–7. The lost *spuria* are M 10040 and 10041 (the consular diptychs of Areobindus (a. 505) and Philoxenus (a. 525), and two 'Romanesque' pieces, Christ enthroned (M 8015) and a Virgin and Child with Four Evangelists (number unknown).

[30] From Norwich Museum: see *Carvings in Ivory*, *op. cit.* (note 11), no. 31.

[31] The six Philip Nelson ivories are: 53.114.227–8, 280–3; cf. *Liverpool Ivories*, *op. cit.* (note 11), nos. 53–6 (= 53.114.277–8, 280–1). The Wellcome material is unpublished.

[32] Christie's Sale Catalogue, London, 15 July 1986, nos. 1 and 7, both illustrated.

'Limoges' Enamel

Margaret Gibson, F.S.A., and Pauline Rushton

In 1862 Joseph Mayer exhibited at the Royal Archaeological Institute '25 specimens of the art of enamel', medieval and later, there summarily listed.[1] This little collection passed to the town of Liverpool in 1867; Llewellyn Jewitt noticed it in 1870,[2] and finally C. T. Gatty gave a workmanlike account of nearly every item in his catalogue of 1883.[3] Meanwhile the Mayer Museum had contributed two pieces to the Liverpool Art Club exhibition of *Bookbindings* (1882).[4] No further printed literature appeared thereafter. Several pieces of JM's Limoges enamel were included in the exhibition catalogue *Seven Centuries of Metalwork* (Liverpool Museum, 1975), and all will find a place in Mme Gauthier's great *Corpus des Émaux Méridionaux*. For the interim we provide a simple check-list. The metal appears to be in all cases copper alloy.

M 3: *head of processional cross*, thirteenth century.
Damaged enamel corpus (133 × 163 mm.), mounted on wood. Gatty, *Mediaeval and Later*, no. 93.

M 5: *crucifix, c.* 1200.
Figure of Christ only (192 × 229 mm.), Virgin and St John missing. Gatty, *Mediaeval and Later*, no. 84; *MRT*, no. 149.

M 6: *panel from book-cover*, thirteenth century.
Crucifixion with Virgin and St John (155 × 225 mm.). Inscription in Latin, Greek (and blank left for Hebrew); kneeling donor at foot of cross. Nowhere described.

M 7: *panel from book-cover*, thirteenth century.
Crucifixion with Virgin and St John (105 × 215 mm.). Gatty, *Mediaeval and Later*, no. 92.

M 8: *panel from book-cover, c.* 1200.
Crucifixion with Virgin and St John (114 × 229 mm.). *THSLC*, iv (1852), 134–5, fig. opp. 135 [JM exhibits panel to Society]; Ll. Jewitt, 'The Mayer Museum', *Art J.* (1870), 118, showing same engraving; Gatty, *Mediaeval and Later*, no. 91; *MRT*, no. 147.

M 9: *panel from book-cover*, thirteenth century.
Crucifixion with Virgin and St John (113 × 210 mm.). Gatty, *Mediaeval and Later*, no. 89.

PLATE XXXI

a. Becket reliquary (height 170 mm.) (M 17)

b. Pyx (length 81 mm.) (M 21)

Reproduced by courtesy of NMGM

PLATE XXXII

Thurible cover (height 95 mm.) (M 23)
Reproduced by courtesy of NMGM

M 17: *Becket reliquary*, first half of the thirteenth century (pl. XXXIa).
Becket's martyrdom: two murderers with swords and a third with an axe. The nimbed saint is shown with two angels on the roof above; the other long side (not shown) has an abstract quatrefoil pattern; a saint on each end (length 123 mm., width 70 mm., height 170 mm.). *PSA*, 2nd ser. i (1860), 152 (brief reference by A. W. Franks à propos of a Becket shrine from Hereford); *Arch. J.*, xix (1862), 283 (JM exhibits 'a shrine or *cofra* of the work of Limoges'); Gatty, *Mediaeval and Later*, no. 86.

M 18: *reliquary box*, thirteenth and ? nineteenth centuries.
Saint (thirteenth century) on lid and Virgin and Child (? nineteenth century) on base (123 × 170 × 70 mm.). The box is probably composite, whatever the dates of its several elements. Gatty, *Mediaeval and Later*, no. 90.

M 21: *small rectangular pyx*, first half of the thirteenth century (pl. XXXIb).
Two angels on each of the long sides and on each side of the lid; another angel on each end (71 × 81 mm., height without lid 46 mm.). Nowhere described. On permanent display in the Decorative Art Gallery, Liverpool Museum.

M 22: *conical pyx*, beginning of the thirteenth century.
Continuous decoration of angels in roundels (height 155 mm., base 91 mm.). Gatty, *Mediaeval and Later*, no. 85 (wrongly called M 21); *MRT*, no. 148.

M 23: *fragments of thurible(s)*, first half of the thirteenth century (pl. XXXII).
The cover is shown (width 122 mm., height 95 mm.). The circular plate (diam. 58 mm., height 35 mm.) now attached to the cover with a piece of wire is enamelled in a different pattern and may well belong to some other object. Gatty, *Mediaeval and Later*, no. 88; *MRT*, no. 151.

M 26: *pair of candlesticks*, thirteenth century.
Quatrefoil design on dark blue enamel ground (height 205 mm., base 124 mm.). Gatty, *Mediaeval and Later*, no. 87. On permanent display in the Decorative Art Gallery, Liverpool Museum.

M 5875–8: *appliqué figures*, thirteenth century.
All found in quasi-archaeological contexts in Kent in the eighteenth and nineteenth centuries.

M 5975
Thickness (29 × 61 mm.).

M 5876
Hammel (21 × 68 mm.). Exhibited by W. H. Rolfe, 8 May 1845: *Arch. J.*, i (1845), 163.

M 5877–8
Wodensburg (24 × 75 mm. and 21 × 53 mm.). Gatty, *Mediaeval and Later*, no. 94.

NOTES

[1] *Arch. J.*, xix (1862), 283.
[2] *Art J.* (1870), 118: cf. M 8.
[3] Gatty, *Mediaeval and Later*, 26–9; the medieval 'Limoges' items are nos. 84–94. M 21 is omitted, by a confusion with M 22.
[4] *Catalogue of a Loan Collection of Ancient and Modern Bookbindings*, Liverpool Art Club Exhibition Catalogue (Liverpool, 1882), nos. 4 and 5; cf. M 6–9.

Mayer and British Archaeology

Roger H. White*

Joseph Mayer's best remembered and indeed his most important contribution to British archaeology was his purchase of the Faussett Collection of Kentish antiquities in 1854. The story of its acquisition is one that is little told, and its significance in the creation of and publicity for a national collection is underplayed. Nevertheless, it was not his only contribution, as those who study prehistoric metalwork know.[1] Major purchases of prehistoric pottery, medieval artefacts, post-medieval pottery and a collection of local antiquities make Mayer's collection one of the finest and most varied of its type. Allied with his extraordinary range of interests was a commitment to and indefatigable support of contemporary British archaeologists: a support which resulted in a unique programme of direct funding for archaeological and historical works based largely on his own collection. Considered together, these elements make one of the most unusual and interesting chapters in the history of British archaeology.

The Faussett Collection, the first large body of British antiquities that Mayer purchased, was formed by the Revd Bryan Faussett (1720–76) of Heppington in Kent.[2] During the later years of his life (1757–73) he devoted as much time as his health would permit to the excavation of barrows in and around the area where he lived. In all, he excavated eight cemeteries one of which, Crundale, was later recognized to be Roman. From the evidence of Crundale, and by the discovery of Roman coins in a few of the graves, Faussett interpreted his finds as graves of 'Britons Romanized' and it was not until Revd James Douglas printed some of the finds after Faussett's death in his *Nenia Britannica* (1793) that their significance as Anglo-Saxon graves of the pagan period was realized. In common with all excavations of the period, the finds were kept by the excavator at his house along with the most valuable part of the collection, the five volumes of the excavator's journal which recorded the various graves and their associations, the account being supplemented by sketches. It is the combination of the journal and the grave contents that gives the collection its signifcance. Without the record, the objects would have lost nearly all of their archaeological value and have become instead *objets d'art*, the majority being more *objet* than *art*.

The collection remained undisturbed and forgotten after Douglas's publication until 1842 when Charles Roach Smith, the prominent London archaeologist and collector, walking in the vicinity of Heppington, paid a visit to Faussett's grandson, Henry Godfrey-Faussett. The impact of that visit on Roach Smith can be felt in the excited letter that he sent to his great friend and fellow antiquarian W. H. Rolfe: 'My visit to Heppington has more than answered my expectations . . . Douglas will give you some idea of the rarity and interest of these antiquities, but no correct opinion can be formed but by an inspection . . .'[3] An official inspection was carried out the next year under the aegis of the British Archaeological Association, of which Roach Smith was one of the founder members. Godfrey-Faussett was keen to have the collection published by the Association but, as Roach Smith laments, there was little impetus to such an effort from that organization as they had neither the time nor the money to do such work.[4] In 1853 Godfrey-Faussett died and his executors contacted Roach Smith in accordance with his wishes to see if the collection could be sold intact. Roach Smith suggested that it should be purchased for the nation by the British Museum and William Chaffers, a fellow antiquarian and friend of Roach Smith who ran an antiques business, valued it for the Museum. The staff of the Department of Coins and Antiquities, as it then was, under the Keepership of Hawkins, were very keen to acquire the collection recognizing its value both as the most substantial collection of Anglo-Saxon antiquities then in existence and in the uniqueness of the recorded details of the excavations. Hawkins accordingly added £500 to his projected purchasing budget for the following year, giving a total of £4,000. He also added that the total of £3,500 should be seen as an alternative if the Trustees did not wish to purchase the collection. It was this lower amount that the Trustees agreed to.[5] As Kendrick has shown, this attitude was one that was consistent with the current thinking on the quality of British material: it was not 'high art' and therefore not worth purchasing.[6]

Practising archaeologists and historians of the period saw the matter in a different light, however, and they found a vociferous champion in Roach Smith who used his occasional publication, *Collectanea Antiqua*, to pursue the campaign. Roach Smith's opposition to the Trustees' decision was not isolated, as his references to the proceedings of the Archaeological Institute and the British Archaeological Association show, and it is reflected also in questions tabled in the House of Commons on the subject.[7] The antiquarian community saw the decision as a missed opportunity to begin a collection of 'National Antiquities'. At a time of high patriotism, when History and Archaeology were being used in near-Darwinian fashion to demonstrate the perfection of the Victorian era in comparison to earlier times, they felt that judgements on the artistic quality of British archaeological objects were inappropriate.[8] This general mood is reflected in the meetings of the Historic Society of Lancashire and Cheshire. In 1850 Mayer stated that he had

> . . . noticed the great want of Public funds for furthering the object of Archaeology & a petition was spread to be presented to the Lords of the Treasury praying that a grant of money be made, to be expended under their own control for preserving and collecting objects of National interest.[9]

The status of British archaeology was compared, unfavourably in all cases, with that of the national archaeology of European countries. In particular the Danes, Germans and French were far in advance of the British Museum which had no gallery for British material before 1850. Hawkins and his staff fought hard against such defects but with little success, although the appointment of A. W. Franks in 1851 has rightly been seen as a turning point.[10] Franks's commitment to the Faussett

Collection is reflected in letters written to him by Mayer. On 24 November 1853 Mayer wrote to him: 'Hurrah! for the Faussett collection. I hope you will get them ... I wrote to the Rev. Faussett to ask about them if you refused them—but of course nothing more as they should be yours but if you refuse them they shall not be separated if I can help it.'[11] However, it became increasingly clear to Roach Smith and Mayer that the Trustees were 'not to be dictated to' on this matter and thus Mayer made arrangments to move swiftly, contacting the Faussetts himself to avoid the possibility of an auction. On 18 February 1854 the offer to the Trustees lapsed and Mayer travelled to Kent on the 21st to purchase the collection. By the 28th Faussett had received the first instalment of the £700 that was now being asked for the collection.[12] On 26 February he wrote to Franks confirming the purchase, noting in passing that 'the trustees were much to blame in not having them'.[13] Roach Smith, in characteristically aggressive fashion, called on the

> ... Corporation of the City of Liverpool ... [to] ... come forward and occupy the place repudiated by the managers of the Anti-British Museum, and establish an Institution devoted to NATIONAL ANTIQUITIES ... The ground is unoccupied ... Let her rulers step forward ... and take up a position which would ... place her second to none ... in patriotic devotion.[14]

The call was answered by the British Museum two years later (see below). In the meantime, the collection had been sent by rail to Liverpool, and Mayer with characteristic alacrity requested that Thomas Wright, an eminent archaeologist and historian, give a lecture to the Historic Society of Lancashire and Cheshire at the Philharmonic Hall in Liverpool later that same year on the subject of Anglo-Saxon antiquities. The lecture soon became a joint venture with the British Association whose annual conference was that year held in Liverpool. On 28 March 1854 Wright wrote to Mayer, 'As I told Dr Hume, I will try and make a nice *popular* paper on Anglo-Saxon Antiquities.'[15] Wright's lecture was a great success and is commemorated in a splendid water-colour of the massed audience in the Philharmonic Hall (pl. XXXIII). Naturally the collection was on show for the guests, courtesy of its new owner.[16] The lecture was published in the *Transactions* of the Historic Society (1855) and 1,500 copies were printed to be distributed to the audience.

At the same time, Roach Smith was already starting on the publication of *Inventorium Sepulchrale*, the Faussett archive, with the direct sponsorship of Mayer. The book was illustrated with twenty plates newly engraved by Fairholt, the best archaeological illustrator of the day, and woodcuts which were based on the original excavator's sketches. Again Mayer moved with all speed. The proofs were ready in 1855 and the volume, issued to subscribers and underwritten by Mayer, was available in April 1856.[17] As Roach Smith wrote in the introduction, even if the British Museum had purchased the collection, it was extremely doubtful whether they would have been able, or willing, to publish it.[18] The publication was minimal, in that the notebooks were largely copied word for word with the editor's footnotes brief and to the point. The introduction placed the whole in its historical context as far as that was then understood. The fact that *Inventorium Sepulchrale* is still essential to the study of the pagan period of Anglo-Saxon history is a tribute not only to Mayer and Roach Smith but also to the superbly accurate account rendered by Faussett.[19]

There is no doubt of the impact on the archaeological world of both the purchase of the Faussett Collection and its publication. Roach Smith wrote to Mayer on 20 February 1856, responding to a letter of his on the expense incurred in the purchase of the collection, that

> ... if I did not feel that the work will inevitably bring you *great* returns in honourable fame, I should regret them. I am *sure* of this:- many will envy you: and many will regret they are not in your position. There are chances, my dear Sir, which occur only once in an age, & the Faussett collection was a *chance of chances.*[20]

Joseph Clarke, Keeper of the Saffron Walden Museum, wrote a rather more formal note of congratulation:

> ... I have heard ... that the Faussett collection ... are [*sic*] come into your possession, and I sincerely hope that it is correct . . . I believe them to be invaluable . . . and from the enlightened policy which you have invariably persued, I trust they will be of more use, and become more known to the archaeological world, than they would have been had they gone to the National collection . . . I quite envy you your purchase . . . [21]

Revd J. Collingwood-Bruce, the eminent Newcastle antiquarian, later wrote that 'those attached to Archaeological persuits are deeply indebted to you for the preservation of the Faussett collection.'[22] Thomas Wright passed on a request from the eminent French archaeologist l'Abbé Cochet that he would like a copy of *Inventorium Sepulchrale* and that he would be prepared to exchange any of his own publications for it. Wright himself wrote that 'you ought to be immortalised if it were only for your most munificient gift to the town of Liverpool.'[23] Franks, writing from the British Museum, congratulated Mayer also, adding that 'you have surely conferred on English Archaeologists a great and valuable boon. The publication of the work is the only thing which in any measure reconciles me to the loss of the collection to the National Museum.'[24] How contemporaries saw the purchase is vividly recorded by Joseph Clarke. Writing from Cambridge on 6 July 1854 after attending a meeting, he says that

> ... Prince Albert being here ... there were about 570 persons in the senate house yesterday ... Lord Talbot de Malahide[25] alluded in strong terms to the refusal of the B. M. trustees to purchase the Faussett collection: he said any nation in Europe; France, Belgium, Austria, Russia would have grasped at the offer of them, but as a set off to his disappointment he had the great satisfaction of informing them that a highly spirited gentleman of Liverpool had secured them and a general round of applause followed the mention of your name.[26]

The saga of the Faussett Collection has an interesting sequel in the negotiations for the purchase of the private collection of Charles Roach Smith. The story has been recently told by Dafydd Kidd and is soon to be explored more fully by Michael Rhodes.[27] Nevertheless, it is interesting to note that the asking price of £3,000 was much greater than that for Faussett and that, although this was later reduced to £2,000, it still represented a substantial amount of the Museum's budget. The campaign to organize the purchase was long and hard-fought. The Trustees, who, as Roach Smith said scathingly, were 'incompetent to judge' the quality of the collection, were the target of questions in Parliament and a major petition from antiquarians throughout the country (including fifty-three signatories from the Historic Society of Lancashire and Cheshire alone). A further petition was addressed to the Treasury, who would have to approve the finances.[28] The outcome on this occasion was more fortunate as the purchase was approved by April 1856 and the collection now forms the basis of the Department of Prehistoric and Romano-British Antiquities at the British Museum.[29] Although the Faussett and Roach Smith Collections were different in character, the latter being of much greater quantity and of a local interest in that the bulk was from London, it is probable that it was the uproar over the refusal to purchase the Faussett Collection that in a great measure led to the purchase of the Roach Smith Collection. From now on, attention would have to be paid to the formation of a national collection of antiquities from the British Isles, irrespective of a spurious assessment of their worth as 'art'.

Purchase of the Faussett Collection also led directly to two further acquisitions, one minor and one major. The minor collection consisted of grave goods excavated by J. Y. Akerman at Broughton Poggs and Filkins (Oxon.) and at Fairford and Kemble (Glos.). The context of the objects is published in his account in *Archaeologia*, at the end of which he states that he will be depositing his collection with the British Museum.[30] All the material, however, now seems to be in Liverpool and it appears likely, although no documentation survives, that the collection was donated or sold by the excavator to Mayer, in retaliation for the Trustees' refusal to buy Faussett. This action was paralleled by W. M. Wylie who had offered to donate his substantial collection of Anglo-Saxon objects from Fairford (published in *Fairford Graves* in 1852) to the British Museum, if they purchased the Faussett Collection. Their refusal led to Wylie's donation to the Ashmolean, Oxford.[31] The second collection was that of W. H. Rolfe, purchased in 1857. Rolfe was an antiquarian from Sandwich and the grandson of the antiquarian William Boys. He was a great friend of Roach Smith, who appears to have been instrumental in negotiating the sale between Rolfe and Mayer, although Clarke certainly knew of the deal at an early date.[32] The collection consisted largely of objects from Anglo-Saxon cemeteries, including Gilton which had also been excavated by Faussett (pl. xxxiv). There was also a large collection of medieval antiquities, most of which were later catalogued by Gatty (pl. xxxv).[33] The involvement of Roach Smith and Clarke in the purchase is evident in the surviving correspondence, with the latter fighting strongly until as late as 1868 to try to get Mayer to purchase what remained of Rolfe's important collection of coins but Mayer was (he wrote) 'not much of a coin collector; only where they demonstrate some subject in hand'.[34]

Clarke's concern extended even to helping Mayer pack the collection up in an attempt to avoid the problems that had arisen over the sale of the Hertz Collection, where some of the material was unaccounted for when the collection arrived in Liverpool.[35] Rolfe's gratitude to Mayer is expressed in a letter written shortly before his death which reads in part, 'My regret at parting with my Collection is daily giving way to a feeling of pride at the distinguished fate to which you have kindly assigned them.'[36]

Given Mayer's background, it is not surprising that his first and most important interest in his adopted native town was the study of the Liverpool pottery industry.

His paper 'On Liverpool Pottery' (1855) remains a seminal work, despite some errors, mainly because he was still able to make personal contact with the various families who had established the industry in Liverpool.[37] A. Smith, the author of the most recent work on the Liverpool potteries, notes that 'no student of Liverpool ceramics can begin his work without reference to the first writer on the subject, that extraordinary collector and benefactor Joseph Mayer . . . [who] . . . was the first man to take the subject seriously.'[38] Mayer's account of Sadler, who had invented and marketed the process of transfer printing on earthenware and creamwares, is particularly valuable. In contrast to some of his other writings, this article flows well and there is a nice use of anecdote to bring life to the story. Mayer visited the sites of the potteries himself, and in particular used a beautiful water-colour he had drawn at the age of twenty-two while the Herculaneum Works were still in operation to illustrate his work (pl. XXXVI*a*). Mayer's interest was not confined to the sites and archives of the potters: he was also an avid collector of Liverpool ceramics.[39] Visits to the various surviving relatives of the potters noted in his article nearly always seem to result in the gift or purchase of some piece of pottery (pl. XXXVI*b*). His collection was not, however, limited to Liverpool wares: his Wedgwood collection is justly famous, and the rescue and purchase of the Wedgwood archive resulted in two books by Eliza Meteyard, both directly sponsored by Mayer.[40] Clarke, Roach Smith and Franks appear to have supplied quantities of pottery of all dates, only some of which has survived the Blitz, and Wright even suggested that the two men should collaborate on a 'History of English Pottery' for which Mayer would have been eminently suitable.[41]

Mayer's acquaintance with Hume, a co-founder of the Historic Society of Lancashire and Cheshire, seems to have been founded on their mutual interest in the rural site of Dove Point, Meols, Cheshire. Hume had been collecting there since 1840, Mayer joining him in 1846. The site is located at the mid-point of the short, west end of the Wirral peninsula and, as Hume's work shows, it had been eroding steadily throughout the historic period, much in the manner of its more famous East Anglian counterpart, Dunwich. Hume and Mayer formed the largest collection of objects from the site (over 1,800 pieces) and Ecroyd Smith's collection brings the total to over 3,000 items.[42] For a minor rural site this is a prodigious amount, and recent speculation based on the unusual coins (including Iron Age Armorican types) and the quantity of Dark Age material indicates that the site was an entrepôt: a northern equivalent of Hengistbury Head, Dorset, or *Hamwih*, Hants (ancient Southampton).[43] The fact that such speculation can be entertained is purely the result of the collecting activities of these three men. Their mutual interests led to the foundation of the Historic Society and Mayer provided much material for its meetings, exhibiting objects and presenting papers on local vernacular architecture and other subjects which may also be the result of local field trips.[44] He put his continental travels to good use in a paper entitled 'On Ancient Shoes', which attempts to compare ethnographical material with excavated shoes. He refers in that discourse to a visit to Charles Roach Smith's London Museum, which he considered to be 'perhaps the most interesting private collection in Europe'.[45] In 1849 we have a glimpse of Mayer on a rare field trip to an archaeological excavation, when he and Hume visited the important Roman industrial site at Wilderspool, Cheshire.[46] It was in the same year that he became genuinely involved in the British archaeological scene. That summer the congress of the British Archaeological Association was held at Chester, with the active involvement of the Historic Society. Mayer and others hosted an excursion to study the antiquities of Liverpool. On 2 August they took the members on a Wirral steamer to the ancient ferry at Eastham, a tour by sea of the Cheshire coastline, and then to visit Speke Hall, Sefton Church and Ince Blundell in Lancashire where the notable Blundell Collection of Ancient Sculpture was situated. Mayer organized a dinner at the Adelphi hotel and also arranged an exhibition there of his own antiquities.[47] In the longer term, however, there is no doubt that the real importance of the congress to Mayer was his introduction to Roach Smith, Clarke and Wright (pl. XXXVII).[48] These three men demonstrate the varied interests and commitments which then operated on the British archaeological scene. Roach Smith was a chemist by trade, a business that enabled him to purchase antiquities for his vast collection.[49] Clarke was a natural historian who had become interested in archaeology and had attended the first congress of the British Archaeological Association in 1843.[50] Wright by contrast was the first 'professional' archaeologist, in that he derived his livelihood purely from writing about the subject; he was also the only one of the three to have a degree.[51] The British Archaeological Association had enabled all three men to break away from the metropolitan bias of the established societies and use the railways to travel the country and broaden their outlook. This is reflected particularly in the Association's congresses, which were held in various cities all over the country. Indeed, the growth of the railways also produced some of the material that they discussed, in the same way that motorways fuelled the growth of archaeology in the 1960s and 1970s.

Roach Smith, Clarke and to a lesser extent Wright became good friends with Mayer, advising him on his collection but also sharing in his interest in horticulture and the local militia. Roach Smith and Clarke in particular seem to have become attached to the 'Lord (Street) Mayer', as the latter, with characteristic humour, referred to him. All three recognized in Mayer a man committed to the cause and, more importantly, one who had the means to make his commitment concrete. Roach Smith had already demonstrated his interest in 1849 when he donated examples of Roman shoes which had been dredged from the Thames to the Historic Society, no doubt in response to Mayer's paper.[52] It was through their contacts in the archaeological world that they were able to help Mayer actively, however. Much of the correspondence in the 1850s and 1860s from Clarke and Roach Smith, and some from Wright and Franks, is taken up with offering antiquities for sale. The objects acquired indicate the range of Mayer's collecting interests:

> I have received for you a fine British [Bronze Age] urn ... found ... at Felixstowe ... I got it ... for a little above £2. It is a fine specimen of the kind. [Roach Smith, 12 Dec. 1852][53]

> I yesterday secured a Roman vessel, from Blackfriars Bridge & two old English vessels from the Fleet Ditch for you ... I have bought a bit of *Roman* enamel work also (£2) a rare example. [Roach Smith, 11 Apr. 1856][54]

> I hope you have received Mr. Wickham's Saxon casket [the Strood Anglo-Saxon Horn Mount]. It is a gem & I should be most vexed if any accident befel it. [Roach Smith, 2 July 1856][55]

PLATE XXXIII

Thomas Wright's lecture on the Faussett Collection (27 Sept. 1854); Joseph Mayer receives an illuminated address, by W. Herman. MPL, reproduced by courtesy of Liverpool City Record Office

Photograph: Roger White

PLATE XXXIV

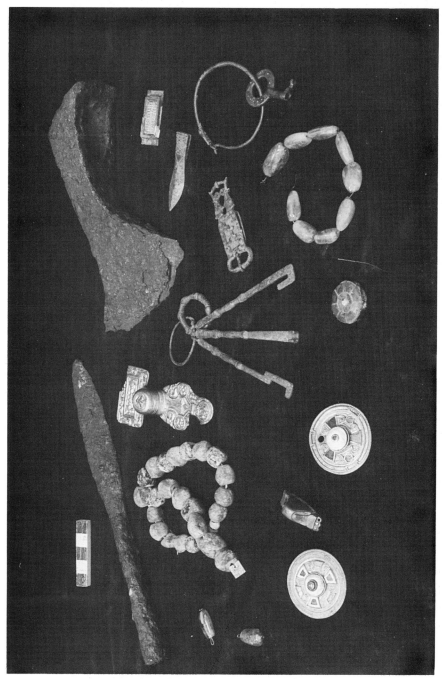

Anglo-Saxon cemetery finds, mainly of the sixth and seventh centuries A.D. These include a pair of keystone garnet disc brooches, a small gilt bronze square-headed brooch, amber and amethyst beads, a girdle hanger, a spearhead and a francisca (throwing axe) from Great Chesterford (*ex* Faussett and Rolfe Collections). Reproduced by courtesy of NMGM

Photograph: Roger White

PLATE XXXV

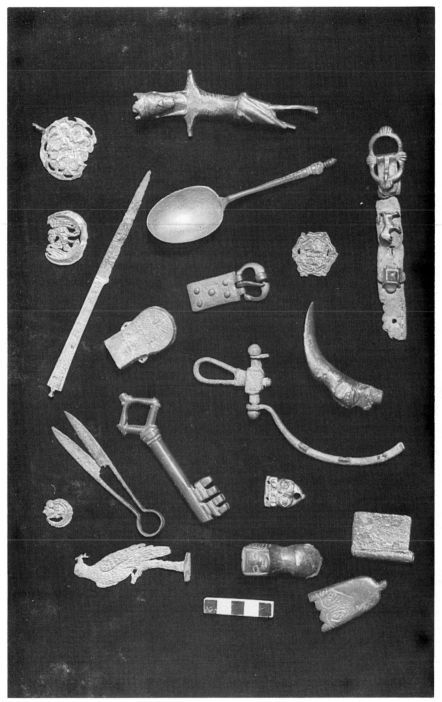

Medieval metal objects, mainly from Kent and London. Included in this collection are a purse frame, examples of lead pilgrim badges showing a dove and ampullae for holding holy water, a spout in the shape of a female head, the corpus from a crucifix, a key and a dagger chape (*ex* Faussett and Rolfe Collections). Reproduced by courtesy of NMGM

Photograph: Roger White

PLATE XXXVI

a. View of the Herculaneum Pottery, 1825, by Joseph Mayer. MPL, reproduced by courtesy of Liverpool City Record Office

b. Transfer-printed Liverpool porcelain; prominent in the foreground is one of the popular 'George Washington' plaques; late eighteenth to early nineteenth century. Reproduced by courtesy of NMGM

Photographs: Roger White

PLATE XXXVII

b. Charles Roach Smith. MPL, reproduced by courtesy of Liverpool City Record Office

a. Joseph Clarke, by John Harris. WAG 7632, reproduced by courtesy of NMGM

PLATE XXXVIII

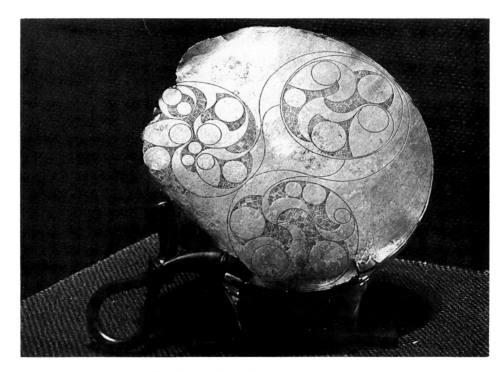

a. The Mayer Mirror (length 224 mm.) (M 6395)

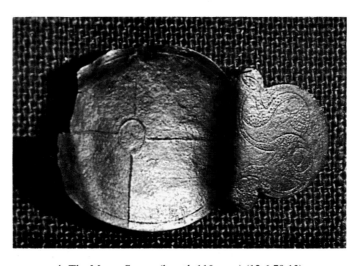

b. The Mayer Spoon (length 110 mm.) (12.6.79.13)
Reproduced by courtesy of NMGM
Photographs: Roger White

I feel rather elated at the idea of its [post-medieval slipware tyg] having been the first thing exhibited in your new [Museum] room. [Clarke, 22 Dec. 1854][56]

saxon broach [*sic*] 2″10″0
Colchester antiquities
piece of copper and celt from Braintree, Essex 16.0
The Felsted, Essex find consisting of Celt & broken *do*, part of a bronze sword, part of the spoke on a bronze wheel, piece of rough metal and *Roman* cannonball at 19 . 6
Francisca [Throwing Axe] from [Great] Chesterford 6.0; . . . making altogether, I think, about thirty pounds!!! [Clarke, Dec. 1854][57]

It was principally through such contacts that Mayer obtained his British and some of his foreign antiquities.

There were pitfalls, however, in the acquisition of such a prodigious collection. Principal among these, of course, was the danger of purchasing forgeries. The Simonides forgeries we still unhappily associate with Mayer's name (see above, pp. 53–4). But this was not the only incident. Another famous example of fraud that Mayer was involved in was the case of the Shadwell pilgrim signs.[58] These were manufactured by two Thames rakers or mudlarks known as Billy and Charley. The inspiration for the objects came from articles on medieval pilgrim badges, such as those written by Roach Smith for his *Collectanea Antiqua*, which had created a market far exceeding the limited supply from the Thames foreshore. The two rakers thus decided to fill the gap in the market by creating 11,000 pieces of varying size and believability, selling them as the cargo from a wrecked ship. Their entire stock was purchased by Eastwood, a London dealer who sold them as legitimate antiquities, which is what he thought they were. The forgeries were almost instantly recognized as such by some archaeologists although others stoutly maintained their authenticity: Eastwood was forced to sue the detractors or lose his livelihood. He lost his case. Mayer purchased a large number of these objects, and these were later catalogued with the medieval material by Gatty;[59] but Mayer was clearly doubtful of their character. A letter from Wright responds to his query: 'I have been examining those leaden things, and do you know I am quite satisfied they are genuine . . . nobody could have insinuated them.'[60] Yet as early as 1863 Mayer himself was exhibiting them as forgeries to the Historic Society.[61] Such problems are hinted at in other instances by the surviving correspondence. In a letter dated 10 January 1857, Joseph Clarke writes to Roach Smith that:

Mr. Mayer purchased a collection not far from York for a hundred and forty pounds, I did not see . . . it . . . but . . . [having seen] . . . plates of them . . . a painful impression came across me of his having been taken in. Mr. Bateman [the Derbyshire archaeologist] refused to purchase this same collection on the grounds of its spuriosity.[62]

The collapse of the consortium to purchase the Hertz Collection (see above, pp. 94–6) probably marks the end of Mayer as a major purchaser of collections. Certainly there were no major acquisitions after that incident and it is possible that Mayer's losses from the Hertz sale wiped out his capital. Other reasons may be cited, however, in that after 1857 Roach Smith wrote to Mayer that he no longer wanted to collect for himself although he offers to buy for Mayer if necessary, and in 1868 Clarke wrote to Mayer saying, 'In fact I am utterly tired of collecting anything . . . if you would but come and see me . . . and take the pick of all my collections nothing would delight me more.'[63] Sad though the loss of these contacts was, the impression that Mayer relied totally on his friends for his acquisitions is erroneous. The purchase of the Anderson Collection is a case in point. This consisted of a number of Bronze Age urns and other material from barrows on Danby and Goathland Moors in Yorkshire and seems to have been purchased by Mayer directly from the excavator in 1854. Indeed, they paid a visit to the site together, on which occasion Anderson presented Mayer with a flint arrowhead. Mayer responded in characteristic fashion with a silver-mounted and engraved pipe.[64] Letters survive also listing objects for sale from the Anglo-Saxon cemetery at Faversham, Kent; the Iron Age Trawsfynydd Tankard was purchased in the same way.[65] The two objects actually named after Mayer, the Mayer Mirror and the Mayer Spoon (pl. xxxviiia, b), both also of Iron Age date, were acquired respectively by Mayer in Paris and on Mayer's behalf by Roach Smith.[66] In a letter to Mayer, however, Franks claims that the provenance of the mirror could have been Barnes, Surrey, and anxiously tries to purchase it for the British Museum as a companion to the recently discovered Desborough, Northants, mirror.[67] Indeed, the mirror is of the utmost importance in the study of Iron Age art as it has a typologically early design. The spoon is also of the highest quality and derives from Ireland but cannot be provenanced further.

In the long run, perhaps Mayer's greatest contribution to the development of British archaeology lies not in the range of his collection, inevitably soon to be surpassed by the national collection, but in his support of his archaeological friends. When Collingwood-Bruce wrote to Mayer to congratulate him on his purchase of the Faussett Collection, he added that 'I seem to be doubly attached to you for your adherence in sunshine and storm to that worthy man C. Roach Smith.'[68] The adherence was both personal—the two were great friends—and professional. Roach Smith was paid 200 guineas for writing *Inventorium Sepulchrale*, a payment which he had neither sought nor expected.[69] Mayer's relationship with Wright, to judge from the latter's correspondence in the British Library, was on a more formal basis. Wright could provide Mayer with the contacts he needed in the archaeological world and Mayer reciprocated with work that he paid for out of his own pocket and even with direct loans. For example, a fee of fifty guineas was agreed for the second volume of Wright's *Anglo-Saxon and Old English Vocabularies*.[70] On his part, Wright was unstinting in his praise of Mayer and energetic in getting Mayer's name spread in antiquarian circles, particularly those abroad. He often sent letters to Mayer from antiquarians who had corresponded with him on his latest works as these often also complimented Mayer. Altogether, Wright was commissioned to write three publications, for which a total of nearly 200 guineas was paid.[71] Mayer was also instrumental in helping Wright to excavate the important site at Wroxeter (Roman *Viroconium Cornoviorum*), giving £50 for the 1867 season so that Wright could show the site to the visiting members of the congress of the British Archaeological Association which was then being held at Shrewsbury. His effort was in vain, however, as the excavations folded after that season.[72]

Mayer's generosity was not restricted to antiquarian publications alone; both Bell and Thorpe were funded in their publications on historical documents, and Roach

Smith had two non-archaeological papers funded directly by Mayer.[73] The former, *On the Scarcity of Home Grown Fruits,* was reprinted in two editions after appearing in the *Transactions* of the Historic Society. Finance of publications by Mayer took two different forms: either the work was commissioned and a fee agreed between Mayer and the author,[74] or the work was funded only partly by Mayer who would, for instance, take out fifty subscriptions of a publication to make it viable. Mayer's rewards were hardly material as he received no remuneration from this activity. The only reward he appears to have received was in dedications made to him in volumes in addition to those he funded directly, for example by Wright in 1861, Roach Smith in 1868 and Jewitt in 1870.[75]

However ready Mayer's friends were to acknowledge their debt to him, it is clear that the rest of society did not respond to his generosity in the same way. After the laying of the foundation stone for William Brown's Free Public Library and Museum, Clarke complained angrily to Roach Smith that:

Mr Browne [*sic*] was greatly laudated, and everybody else concerned except our friend who was one of the most active and liberal of the committee, he thought to have it marked up to him the next week in Dr. Hume's report to the Illustrated [London] News, and although he bribed the Doctor with ten sovereigns towards any charity he might choose, still the only credit he got was that he made the trowel...[76]

The problem seemed already to have occured at the Manchester Exhibition. Clarke continues:

Here are a parcel of snobs and charlatans at the head of affairs at Manchester whose vocation it occurs to be to cringe and tody to the great who would have served him [Mayer] just the same, but for the utmost perserverance on his part, promising him six cases, and when his things were there, almost refusing him one. I think he began to see things in rather a different light...[77]

The problem with the Manchester Exhibition, as Wright pointed out to Mayer, was that 'people in England ... are not yet sufficiently educated to art and antiquities to appreciate such an exhibition in sufficient numbers.'[78] The judgement is echoed in a letter from Roach Smith to Mayer immediately before the publication of *Inventorium Sepulchrale*:

Having given Liverpool a rich present, I see you are tutoring her how to understand it! There are certain classes to whom the gift of food is nothing, unless at the same time you chew it for them; and I expect you will find the Liverpool Cit[izen]s ... of this class. Gratitude nor appreciation can never possibly spring from them. You will be esteemed and honored—but never *really*, at *Liverpool*. There are higher and better regions for you.[79]

It is Liverpool's good fortune that the opinion of Roach Smith has not been wholly fulfilled but rather that the prophecy of Joseph Clarke has proved true:

Your gatherings will go somewhere where they will be taken care of; mine will go to destruction. Your museum has been nobly given and has most deservedly earned you a niche in the temple of Fame, and your name will float down the stream of time as a benefactor to art and an encourager of science.[80]

NOTES

* I should like to acknowledge here the many kindnesses shown me in the compilation of this article. Margaret Gibson provided many of the Franks letters in addition to much advice. Michael Rhodes discussed aspects of Roach Smith and British archaeology in the mid-nineteenth century. The staff of Liverpool Museum and Liverpool City Record Office were most helpful with my demanding requests. Finally, Margaret Warhurst encouraged me to write the article and provided me with the full benefit of her background knowledge on Mayer.

[1] Nicholson, *Prehistoric Metalwork*, passim.

[2] The best account is still Roach Smith's preface to his *Inventorium Sepulchrale* (London, 1856), i–vii.

[3] Liverpool City Record Office, C. Roach Smith, *Material Relating to Retrospections Social and Archaeological*, II, fo. 33.

[4] id., *Collectanea Antiqua*, 7 vols. (London, 1848–80), III, 181.

[5] *Ibid.*, 266–7.

[6] *Ibid.*, 187; cf. T. Kendrick, 'The British Museum and British antiquities', *Mus. J.*, lxxxi (1951), 139–42.

[7] Roach Smith, *op. cit.* (note 4), III, 189–92, 268–9.

[8] P. Levine, *The Amateur and the Professional: Antiquarians, Historians and Archaeologists in Victorian England 1838–1886* (Cambridge, 1986), 78–80.

[9] *THSLC*, ii (1849–50), 212.

[10] D. M. Wilson, *The Forgotten Collector: Augustus Wollaston Franks of the British Museum*, Walter Neurath Memorial Lecture 16 (London, 1984), 11–12.

[11] BM, Department of Medieval and Later Antiquities, JM to A. W. Franks, 24 Nov. 1853.

[12] MPL, Godfrey Faussett to JM, 18 and 28 Feb. 1854.

[13] BM, Department of Medieval and Later Antiquities, JM to A. W. Franks, 26 Feb. 1854.

[14] Roach Smith, *op. cit.* (note 4), III, 299.

[15] BL, MS Add. 33346, fo. 8, Thomas Wright to JM, 28 Mar. 1854.

[16] *THSLC*, vii (1855), 4*–6*.

[17] 'On Saturday I sent you by railway a copy of the *Inventorium Sepulchrale* directing it to be delivered without delay': MPL, C. Roach Smith to JM, 15 Apr. 1856.

[18] Roach Smith, *op. cit.* (note 2), vi.

[19] Recent excavations by Hawkes and Grainger in some of the same Kentish cemeteries have demonstrated the accuracy of Faussett's account beyond doubt (pers. comm. G. Grainger).

[20] MPL, C. Roach Smith to JM, 20 Feb. 1856.

[21] MPL, Joseph Clarke to JM, 24 Feb. 1854.

[22] MPL, J. Collingwood-Bruce to JM, 7 July 1856.

[23] BL, MS Add. 33346, fos. 71ᵛ and 62, Thomas Wright to JM, 19 July 1856 and 14 Apr. 1856.

[24] MPL, A. W. Franks to JM, 22 Apr. 1856.

[25] Proposer of the Treasure Trove law (1858) and President of the Royal Archaeological Institute (1863–83).

[26] MPL, Joseph Clarke to JM, 6 July 1854.

[27] D. Kidd, 'Charles Roach Smith and his Museum of London Antiquities', *Brit. Mus. Yearb.*, ii (1977), 105–35, at 126–8. M. Rhodes is at present working on a thesis concerning Roach Smith and his contribution to British archaeology.

[28] Roach Smith, *op. cit.* (note 4), IV, App., 1–32.

[29] Kidd, *op. cit.* (note 27), 128–31; Wilson, *op. cit.* (note 10), 24.

[30] J. Y. Ackerman, 'An account of researches in Anglo-Saxon cemeteries at Filkins, and at Broughton Poggs in Oxon.', *Archaeologia*, xxxvii (1857), 140–6, at 146.

[31] Roach Smith, *op. cit.* (note 2), v; W. M. Wylie, *Fairford Graves* (Oxford, 1852).

[32] MPL, Joseph Clarke to JM, 6 and 17 Aug., 12 Sept. 1857.

[33] Gatty, *Mediaeval and Later*, passim.

34 MPL, Joseph Clarke to JM, 25 Feb. 1868. Quote from a letter by JM to Roach Smith, 8 Mar. 1858, now bound into BL 12983 H 14 (*Anglo-Saxon and Old English Vocabularies* by T. Wright). Some of Rolfe's coins were acquired by Sir John Evans in or *c.* 1858, whence they passed to the Ashmolean.

35 Liverpool Museum, Department of Antiquities, Guard Book I, 200, Joseph Clarke to C. T. Gatty, 3 Feb. 1875.

36 MPL, W. H. Rolfe to JM, 17 Nov. 1857.

37 JM, 'On Liverpool pottery', *THSLC*, vii (1855), 178–210.

38 A. Smith, *The Illustrated Guide to Liverpool Herculaneum Pottery 1796–1840* (London, 1970), 132.

39 C. T. Gatty, 'The Liverpool potteries', *THSLC*, xxxiii (1881), 123–68.

40 E. Meteyard, *Life of Josiah Wedgwood*, 2 vols. (Liverpool, 1865); *ead.*, *A Group of Englishmen (1795–1815), being Records of the Younger Wedgwoods* (Liverpool, 1871). See below, p. 200.

41 MPL, JM to A. W. Franks, 24 Nov. and 19 Dec. 1853; BL, MS Add. 33346, fo. 40, T. Wright to JM, 29 Mar. 1854. On Roach Smith's contribution, see the letters quoted below, notes 53–5.

42 A. Hume, *Ancient Meols, or Some Account of the Antiquities Found near Dove Point on the Sea Coast of Cheshire* (Liverpool, 1863), 50–1.

43 J. A. A. Rutter, 'The pottery', in D. Mason, *Excavations at Chester, 26–42 Lower Bridge Street 1974–6: The Dark Age and Saxon Periods*, Grosvenor Museum Archaeological Reports 3 (Chester, 1985), 40–55, at 40. See also G. Chitty and M. Warhurst, 'Ancient Meols', *J. Merseyside Arch. Soc.*, i (1977), 19–42.

44 JM, 'The old halls of Cheshire: no. 1, Tranmere Hall', *THSLC*, iii (1851), 107–11.

45 JM, 'On ancient shoes, as used in this and other parts of the country', *THSLC*, i (1849), 117–21, at 121.

46 A. Hume, 'Notes on a Roman road, near Warrington', *THSLC*, ii (1850), 27–38, at 29.

47 *THSLC*, ii (1850), 238–40.

48 C. Roach Smith, *Retrospections Social and Archaeological*, 3 vols. (London, 1883–91), I, 64–7.

49 Kidd, *op. cit.* (note 27), 108–10.

50 Roach Smith, *op. cit.* (note 48), II, 38–43.

51 B.A. Trinity College, Cambridge, 1834.

52 *THSLC*, ii (1850), 2.

53 MPL, Roach Smith to JM, 12 Dec. 1852.

54 MPL, Roach Smith to JM, 11 Apr. 1856.

55 MPL, Roach Smith to JM, 2 July 1856.

56 MPL, Clarke to JM, 22 Dec. 1854.

57 MPL, Clarke to JM, Dec. 1854.

58 Roach Smith, *op. cit.* (note 4), v, 252–60.

59 Gatty, *Mediaeval and Later*, 37: 'forged by two shore rackers at Shadwell some years ago'. For a modern account of the forgeries, see R. Halliday, 'The Billy and Charley forgeries', *London Archaeologist*, v (9), 243–7.

60 BL, MS Add. 33347, fo. 1, Wright to JM, 28 Jan. 1859.

61 *THSLC*, xv (1863), 248.

62 MPL, Clarke to Roach Smith, 10 Jan. 1857.

63 MPL, Roach Smith to JM, 11 Apr. 1857, and Clarke to JM, 28 Mar. 1868.

64 Nicholson and Warhurst, 4.

65 Liverpool Museum, Department of Antiquities, Guard Book I, 19, James West to Gatty, 2 Apr. 1885 (Faversham); Nicholson, *Prehistoric Metalwork*, 34 (Trawsfynydd Tankard).

66 *Ibid.*, 30 and 50.

67 MPL, A. W. Franks to JM, 22 Dec. 1857.

68 MPL, J. Collingwood-Bruce to JM, 7 July 1856.

69 Roach Smith, *op. cit.* (note 48), I, 69. This amount was enough for Roach Smith to purchase a retirement home at Strood in Kent (pers. comm. M. Rhodes).

70 BL, MS Add. 33347, fo. 97, Wright to JM, 6 Nov. 1865.

71 T. Wright, *Anglo-Saxon and Old English Vocabularies*, 2 vols. (London, 1857 and 1873; 2nd edn. 1884); *id.*, *Feudal Manuals of English History* (London, 1872); *id.*, *Uriconium: an Account of the Ancient Roman City at Wroxeter* (Shrewsbury, 1873). The estimate is based on Wright to JM, 28 Mar. 1854, and other letters: BL, MSS Add. 33346 and 33347, fo. 8 sqq.

72 Wright (1873), *op. cit.* (note 71), vi.

73 W. Bell, *T. Sprott's Chronicle of Profane and Sacred History Translated from the Original Manuscript* (Liverpool, 1851); B. Thorpe, *Diplomatarium Anglicum Aevi Saxonici* (London, 1865); C. Roach

Smith, *On the Scarcity of Home Grown Fruits, with Remedial Suggestions* (Liverpool, 1863; 2nd edn. 1874; *id., The Rural Life of Shakespeare, as Illustrated by his Works* (London, 1870; 2nd edn. 1874).

[74] Examples are Roach Smith, *op. cit.* (note 2); Wright (1857 and 1873), *op. cit.* (note 71); Meteyard (1865), *op. cit.* (note 40).

[75] T. Wright, *Essays on Archaeological Subjects, and on Various Questions Connected with the History of Art, Science and Literature in the Middle Ages* (London, 1861); C. Roach Smith, *Remarks on Shakespeare, his Birthplace etc.* (London, 1868; 2nd edn. 1877); Ll. Jewitt *Grave Mounds and their Contents: a Manual of Archaeology* (London, 1870).

[76] MPL, Clarke to Roach Smith, 21 May 1857.

[77] *Ibid.*

[78] BL, MS Add. 33346, fo. 146, Wright to JM, 20 May 1857.

[79] MPL, Roach Smith to JM, 11 Apr. 1856.

[80] MPL, Clarke to JM, 28 Mar. 1868.

III. MANUSCRIPTS

Introduction

JM acquired manuscripts from time to time, as they caught his attention in book-shops or the sale-room. Such few purchases as can be dated belong to the 1840s: M 12012 (by 1849), M 12032 (1847+: H. F. Lyte), M 12107 (1844: Sussex sale), M 12108 (1843+: D. J. Bles). Certainly by the time Mayer opened his Egyptian Museum in 1852 he had a number of both western and oriental manuscripts, illustrative of the art of book-production. They were displayed, or kept, in the library of the Egyptian Museum, which contained 'many manuscripts in Hebrew, Sanscrit, Persian, Irish, etc.'. He continued to buy here and there: M 12046 was acquired in 1854; M 12096 (Arabic) has a scribal colophon of 1843; and 11.9.73.1 (Burmese), shown by its number, (18)73, to be a late donation, was written as recently as 1848.

About a dozen manuscripts of the Mayer Collection were exhibited by the Free Public Library and Museum at the Liverpool Art Club in 1876.[1] Mayer exhibited under his own name an illuminated Shepherd's Calendar and two Persian manuscripts (all now lost to view) and a roll of documents from Battle Abbey.[2] The western manuscripts were first described in Gatty, *Mediaeval and Later*; for the oriental the first account is in the present volume. We have omitted M 12091 (Koran: nineteenth century) and six Hebrew and two Samaritan manuscripts for mundane considerations of time and space.

MARGARET GIBSON

NOTES

[1] *Catalogue of a Loan Collection of Illuminated Manuscripts*, Liverpool Art Club Exhibition Catalogue (Liverpool, 1876), nos. 23–42 (LFPLM) and nos. 131–4 (JM).

[2] The Persian manuscripts and the Battle Abbey roll were sold at Sotheby's, 19 July 1887, lots 122/41 and 148. Lugt omits this sale: see below, p. 227.

Western Manuscripts, Latin and Vernacular

Michael Perkin

In January 1872, when his portrait was presented to him by the Chairman of the Mayer Library in Bebington, Joseph Mayer in his reply, reported by the *Liverpool Mercury*, remarked that 'he was ever a lover of early records, and he believed that the first start of his private library was due to an old illuminated missal that fell into his hands'. The word 'illuminated' is significant since the appeal to the eye was obviously of great importance to Mayer. He collected manuscripts not primarily for their texts but for their physical and decorative properties: their materials and construction; bindings; calligraphy, illumination and decoration. Much to his credit he made no attempt to restore or rebind them: they were regarded as the raw material for his long-projected history of the arts. As Gatty states in the introduction to his Catalogue of 1883, 'it was . . . [Mayer's] special intention, in making this collection and presenting it to the town, that it should be a means of education to the local art students'.[1] Unfortunately, since any documentation concerning the manuscripts was dispersed at the sale of the bulk of his papers in 1887, we have very little knowledge of how, when or where Mayer acquired individual manuscripts. They were obtained at auction sales, by private treaty and by gifts and exchange with friends, and probably during his extensive travels on the Continent from 1828 to 1857, perhaps especially his visit to Austria and various German states in 1854.[2] The total collection now consists of 126 manuscripts, about half of them Near- and Far-Eastern, the remainder being medieval and later western. They were deposited on indefinite loan in Liverpool University Library in the session 1947–8. Of the medieval and later items, some twenty-seven (including one printed book) were listed in Gatty's catalogue and thirty-eight were described comprehensively and with great authority by Neil Ker in 1983.[3] From another point of view thirteen of the illuminated manuscripts were described by Jonathan Alexander in his catalogue of the Whitworth Exhibition of 1976.[4] The account which follows is deeply indebted to these descriptions.

The thirty-eight medieval manuscripts fall into five groups.[5] Liturgical (the largest) contains: twelve books of hours, two psalters, a version of the Penitential Psalms, three breviaries, one processional and two bibles. There are seven books of devotions and sermons, five of history and chronicles, three literary and philological, and two classical texts. Because of the growth of interest in illuminated manuscripts at both the scholarly and popular level, these are singled out for particular attention in the present account. If illuminated manuscripts have a three-fold importance, in the history of the book, the history of art and the history of ideas,[6] it is probably true to say that they are most used by the art historian since they preserve the major portion of medieval painting.[7] The Mayer Collection contains examples of many styles of illumination in the western tradition, including a number of identifiable artists and schools. One of the earliest manuscripts is the so-called 'Ochsenhausen Psalter' (M 12004), written in south Germany in the first third of the thirteenth century, which has very distinctive illuminated roundels, zodiac signs, occupations of the months, miniatures (pl. xxxixa) and initials. The provenance of this manuscript is further discussed by Nigel Palmer in this volume. Also from Germany, a mid-fifteenth-century Cologne breviary (M 12010) has a decorative style comparable with that in books of hours attributed to Stefan Lochner; it also includes the painted arms of the Archbishop of Cologne, Hermann IV, Landgraf von Hessen (1480–1508).[8] Of the two thirteenth-century French one-volume bibles in the collection, M 12038 has historiated initials attributable to the artist known as 'Master Alexander' (from Bibliothèque Nationale, Paris, MSS Paris, lat. 11930–1, signed '*Magister Alexander me fecit*'). He was probably a master-craftsman, and his workshop may be identified in about a dozen manuscripts, nearly all bibles, in the first quarter of the thirteenth century.[9] Also from France, one early fifteenth-century book of hours (M 12022) has eleven miniatures, with some odd quirks of iconography; another of about the same date (M 12033: use of Rouen) has eight miniatures, the borders and initials identified as 'provincial work partly using compositions of the Boucicaut Master'.[10] But perhaps the most sumptuously illuminated manuscript of all is another French book of hours, made about a generation later, M 12001. It has no less than twenty-eight miniatures with decorative borders full of grotesques, animals and birds; it is 'related in style and iconography to later products of the workshop of the Bedford Master' (pl. xxxixb).[11] The Deposition (pl. xla) is a version in miniature of the centre panel of a triptych by the Master of Flémalle. The artist has reversed the original, which he probably knew only indirectly, and adjusted it to include the traditional motif of the Virgin kissing her son's hand.[12] The Boucicaut Master (named from a book of hours made for Jean II le Meingre, the Maréchal de Boucicaut) and the Bedford Master (named from manuscripts made for John of Lancaster, Duke of Bedford)[13] were contemporaries and on one occasion, apparently, collaborators. It has been recently suggested that they can be identified with two artists documented in Paris in the first quarter of the fifteenth century, Jacques Coene and perhaps Jean Haincelin.[14]

The most notable English illuminated manuscript is a roll of Peter of Poitiers' *Compendium genealogiae Christi* (M 12017), written in England in the mid-thirteenth century, which has a number of scenes in roundels, pen drawings with colour grounds 'in a style reminiscent of Matthew Paris',[15] the scribe, illuminator, painter, goldsmith and historian of St Albans who flourished *c.* 1236–59. Two manuscripts illuminated in Italy form a distinct contrast. A breviary (M 12027) from the first half of the fifteenth century, probably Florentine but with litanies suggesting a special devotion to the Sienese saint, Ansanus, is an imperfect but still thick and very lavishly decorated volume, with fantastic birds, gold blobs, pink, green and blue scrolls and blue cornflowers 'common in Florentine illumination'. In contrast, a

PLATE XXXIX

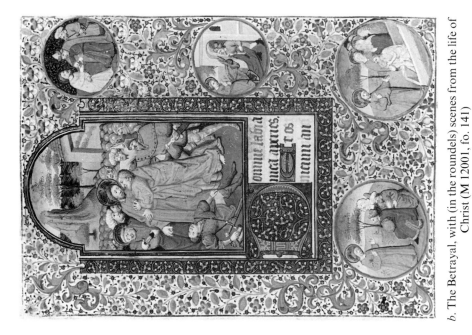

b. The Betrayal, with (in the roundels) scenes from the life of Christ (M 12001, fo. 141)

Reproduced by courtesy of NMGM

Photographs: Ian Qualtrough

a. The Maries at the Sepulchre; the Harrowing of Hell (M 12004, p. 20)

PLATE XL

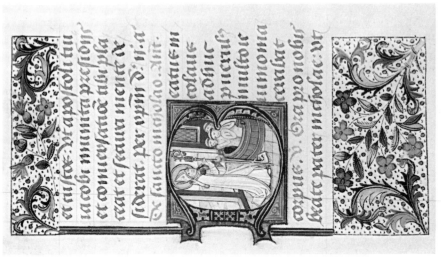

b. St Nicholas restores three boys to life
(M 12006, p. 443)

a. The Deposition (M 12001, fo. 151)

Reproduced by courtesy of NMGM
Photographs: Ian Qualtrough

volume containing texts of Eutropius and Festus written in Italy, probably Rome, in the second quarter of the fifteenth century (M 12068) has Renaissance white-vine border illumination and initials, and is in a contemporary blind-stamped Italian binding.[16]

Finally, in this survey of the illuminated manuscripts, four books of hours from the Low Countries. Written in the first quarter of the fifteenth century for use in England, M 12009 contains fourteen miniatures and decorative borders 'by the Master of Nicholas Brouwer working in Utrecht'.[17] Brouwer was one of a group of illuminators at work from 1415–*c.* 1435/40, at first in Guelders and then in Utrecht.[18] Recent research by J. D. Farquhar has shown that a miniature in this manuscript bears a stamp to identify the manuscript painter on page 62. 'It is a small red circle, apparently made by a woodcut stick print, with the white of the parchment showing through as a gothic minim or i.'[19] The volume is also of interest for its inscriptions: an obituary (in the Calendar) of William Boleyn, grandfather of Anne, 10 October 1505, and notes of the Ewer family of Pinner, Middlesex (second quarter of the sixteenth century). From Bruges in the south, M 12006 is a book of hours written in the second quarter of the fifteenth century, decorated with miniatures and initials in tones of grey, with some silver and blue 'from the atelier of Willem Vrelant' (pl. xl*b*).[20] Originally from Utrecht, the very prolific illuminator Vrelant moved to Bruges *c.* 1450 and worked there until *c.* 1480.[21] Another book of hours (M 12020) is also illuminated by the school of Vrelant: this was written for a Carmelite nun. It is contained in an early sixteenth-century panel-stamped leather binding with the 'Flemish animals' panel, and other animal stamps. Also in a contemporary stamped binding, with four distinct stamps, is M 12023 (use of Utrecht). The full-page miniatures are both strange and idiosyncratic, as are the borders, although two of the compositions were copied from published engravings.[22]

Many of the remaining medieval manuscripts in the collection, while perhaps not outstanding for their decorative qualities, are nonetheless of interest because of their texts, provenance, bindings and other related features. In the space available it would be impossible to describe them all, but the following notes are given of some of the outstanding items in approximate chronological order. Gulielmus Peraldus, *Summa de vitiis* (M 12048), written probably in England in the second quarter of the thirteenth century, has the armorial bookplate of Sir William Betham, Ulster King of Arms. Also from the later thirteenth century are the *Distinctiones Magistri Mauricii* (M 12107),[23] perhaps written in France, and acquired from the Duke of Sussex's library in 1844. From the end of the thirteenth century we have a text of Thomas Aquinas, *Summa theologiae, Secunda secundae* (M 12037), written by 'frater Theodericus de Bopardia' for the nearby Franciscan convent at Koblenz. In the seventeenth century, from the evidence of another inscription, this same volume was in the Cistercian abbey of Bredelar, diocese of Paderborn, Westphalia. The fifteenth-century blind-stamped binding has a number of interesting stamps. A manuscript of Eugippius and others (M 12036) was written in England *c.* 1300 and has an interesting inscription of John Manbe, a Durham monk at Durham College, Oxford, in the 1470s and later sub-prior of Durham Cathedral Priory, who used the book as his own and pledged it in an Oxford loan-chest.[24] A *Psalterium* and *Hymni cum notis*, etc. (M 12016), written in England in the mid-fifteenth century, is in a contemporary leather-over-boards binding with strap-and-pin fastenings, and has a fifteenth- or sixteenth-century ownership inscription of the church of Cardington,

Bedfordshire. Another example of a signed and dated manuscript is a Juvenal (M 12070), partly written in Italy in 1471 by an otherwise unrecorded scribe, Antonius Lulmanus. Part of M 12069, Pseudo-Augustinus, *Sermones ad fratres*, was written in (south ?) Germany by N. Schelhammer in 1490; an earlier part of the manuscript can be dated 1473. Finally, a Renaissance manuscript of Sulpicius Severus, Coluccio Salutati, and others (M 12046), was in part written in the Camaldolese abbey of St Michael at Murano, the island near Venice; it too was in the library of Sir William Betham.[25]

The later western manuscripts in the Mayer gift are a heterogeneous collection, which can be described here in only a summary fashion. One clearly defined group consists of eight Irish manuscripts (M 12029, 12051–2, 12065, 12075–6, 12079, 12095) containing eighteenth-century transcripts of early Irish tracts, tales, chronicles, etc., in both verse and prose. This group was described in detail by Ailfrid MacLochlainn in 1958.[26] Of the remainder, the earliest item is Venetian (20.9.83.37), a matriculation book for a confraternity of ferrymen, the *Traghétto di S. Thomà*, with entries in the Venetian dialect in various hands dating from 1487 to 1571.[27] A rental of Great Malvern Priory, dated 8 June 1520 (19.5.81.1), written on twelve parchment strips of various sizes sewn together, is one of eleven English deeds dating from the fifteenth to the eighteenth centuries. There are other deeds in Latin and German. The only French manuscript is also a collection of documents: edicts and ordinances of Elizabeth I, 1562–4, translated into French in the latter year, and illuminated with large initials in gold and colours (M 12043). A Greek manuscript with Byzantine neumatic notation (M 12053) contains the liturgies of St Chrysostom, St Basil and others, and was written, the colophon tells us, in 1662; a Cretan origin is suggested by references to 'Demetrius and the singers of Crete'.[28] From the eighteenth century comes an English commonplace book of verse and prose (M 12094), in the form of separate sections loose in a leather binding case. All save one item were transcribed in the last quarter of the century. Mainly anonymous, they include pieces by Beilby Porteous, Bishop of Chester (1777–87), Christopher Anstey (1724–1805), Thomas Gray (his *Elegy* with a Latin version on facing pages), and George Steevens. Finally, there is a missal, for use at a pontifical mass, with the bishop's preparations, private prayers and various musical settings, probably eighteenth-century Italian work (M 12045): it is lavishly illuminated with borders, miniatures and initials in colours, gold and gold-foil. The very elaborately gold-tooled morocco binding is probably contemporary.

There are thirteen printed items with Mayer numbers which are not described here. They are mostly late in date and, as with the manuscripts, appealed to Mayer as art objects rather than texts. Some items complement the manuscripts; for example, there is a fine Paris *Heures a l'usage de Rome* (M 12040), printed on vellum for Thielman Kerver in 1497, lavishly illustrated with woodcut miniatures and borders.[29]

NOTES

[1] Gatty, *Mediaeval and Later*, iv.
[2] Nicholson and Warhurst, 4.
[3] N. R. Ker, *Medieval Manuscripts in British Libraries*, iii: *Lampeter–Oxford* (Oxford, 1983), 214–54.
[4] *MRT*, 16–37.
[5] Not 39 as stated by Ker, *op. cit.* (note 3), 214.

[6] D. M. Robb, *The Art of the Illuminated Manuscript* (New York, 1973), 15.

[7] C. de Hamel, *A History of Illuminated Manuscripts* (London, 1986), 7.

[8] *MRT*, no. 43.

[9] de Hamel, *op. cit.* (note 7), 110.

[10] *MRT*, nos. 24–5.

[11] *MRT*, no. 32.

[12] Only a fragment of the original triptych survives, but the composition (which is also reflected in the Turin Hours: A. Chatelet, *Heures de Turin* (Turin, 1967), pl. xxi; cf. E. Panofsky, *Early Netherlandish Painting* (Cambridge, Mass., 1953), 167 and n.) is known from a copy that was made within a generation for St Julian, Bruges: see M. J. Friedländer, *Rogier van der Weyden and the Master of Flémalle* (Leiden, 1967), no. 59. This copy, now WAG 1178 *ex* Roscoe, was on display in the Royal Institution gallery when JM was in Colquitt Street; thus he himself may well have noticed the coincidence.

[13] Robb, *op. cit.* (note 6), 290–8.

[14] de Hamel, *op. cit.* (note 7), 173–6.

[15] *MRT*, no. 14.

[16] *MRT*, nos. 68 and 70.

[17] *MRT*, no. 34.

[18] L. M. J. Delaissé, *A Century of Dutch Manuscript Illumination* (Berkeley and Los Angeles, 1968), 21.

[19] J. D. Farquhar, 'Identity in an anonymous age: Bruges manuscript illuminators and their signs', *Viator*, xi (1980), 379 and fig. 8.

[20] *MRT*, no. 38.

[21] Delaissé, *op. cit.* (note 18), 74–7.

[22] *MRT*, nos. 39–40.

[23] A widely-used preaching tool: F. Stegmüller, *Repertorium Biblicum Medii Aevi*, 10 vols. (Madrid, 1940–79), III, no. 5566.

[24] This manuscript has just been identified (by its *secundo folio*) as one of the few surviving books from the library of the Augustinian Hermits at York (pers. comm. K. W. Humphreys).

[25] Purchased at the Betham sale (Sotheby's, 1 June 1854, lot 130). The binding is contemporary with the manuscript: wooden boards, slightly bevelled; remains of quarter leather covering on spine; two star-shaped studs on upper board holding remains of clasp (upper to lower).

[26] A. MacLochlainn, 'Irish manuscripts at Liverpool', *Celtica*, iv (1958), 217–38.

[27] C. H. Clough, 'Twenty soldi to cross the Grand Canal: the manuscript guildbook of the ferryman of San Tomà in the Sydney Jones Library', *The University of Liverpool Recorder*, cii (Feb. 1987), 36–41.

[28] I am indebted to Dr J. Pinsent for help in identifying this manuscript.

[29] Hain, no. 8854: cf. *Catalogue of Books Printed in the Fifteenth Century now in the British Museum*, 12 vols. (London, 1908–85), VIII, 213–14.

Parzival Fragments from the Binding of a Latin Psalter in Liverpool[1]

Nigel F. Palmer

The Mayer Collection contains as MS 8951 a fragment of two leaves from a manuscript of the Middle High German poem *Parzival* by Wolfram von Eschenbach, the composition of which may be dated to the first decade of the thirteenth century.[2] The lost manuscript from which they derive, known as 'e' in the literature on *Parzival*, may be dated on palaeographical evidence to the later thirteenth century, and if it had survived complete it would have been one of the most reliable manuscripts of the text and a mainstay of the critical edition. Manuscript e belongs to a small group of texts closely associated with D, the St Gall *Parzival* (Stiftsbibliothek cod. 857), rather than to the great mass of manuscripts in the G group.[3] Within the D group it is particularly closely associated with three fifteenth-century Alsatian manuscripts m, n and o, whose special importance for the text of *Parzival* was set out by Ernst Martin in 1900.[4] But e is a hundred and eighty years earlier. It so happens that the two surviving leaves of e contain the text of two remarkable catalogues of the names of knights which were omitted in the G recension, lines 770, 5–30 and 772, 3–22, and here the text of e is of prime importance for our knowledge of what Wolfram originally wrote. It may be said that in general they confirm the quality of D.

The *Parzival* fragments were removed in the late nineteenth century from the binding of a Latin psalter, now M 12004, which was written in the second quarter of the thirteenth century and is especially notable for its fine cycle of miniatures depicting the life of Christ.[5] The purpose of the following remarks is to reconsider how the *Parzival* fragments came to lie as paste-downs in a Latin psalter earlier than the manuscript from which they themselves were taken, and to set out what can be learned about the psalter and *Parzival* MS e by looking at them together.

The psalter was originally made up of four main parts: (1) a calendar extending over six leaves with illustrations of the signs of the zodiac and the labours of the months in roundels (pp. 1–12); (2) a series of what were originally sixteen full-page miniatures, which tell the story of the life of Christ, culminating in the Last Judgement and a picture of the damned being led away by a demon, the first six pictures now missing (pp. 13–22); (3) a complete Gallican Psalter (pp. 23–257); (4) an appendix, following on without a break after Psalm 150, which consists of antiphonally arranged prayers to the Holy Spirit, the Virgin Mary, John the Evangelist and St

Catherine, the customary fourteen canticles,[6] and a litany (pp. 257–89). Large initials for Psalms 1, 26, 38, 52, 68, 80, 97, and 109 mark the beginning of matins from Sunday to Saturday and vespers on Sunday according to the Roman office.[7] In addition, the tripartite division of the Psalter is marked by illuminated initials extending over a whole page for Psalms 1, 51, 101, and a similar initial marks the first of the ferial canticles. This gives what Hughes calls the 'ten-fold' division of the Psalter. The individual psalms and their verses are decorated by smaller gold initials and line-endings. In the first part of the psalter (up to p. 109), crudely drawn demons and grotesques fill the ends of the lines.[8] The brightly coloured decoration combines with the large and rather spiky jet-black script to produce a sumptuous, Byzantine effect which is characteristic of the illuminated Swabian books of the period. The quality of the book lies rather in its design than in the painters' artistic talents, which are only modest. It is a large and rather heavy volume (257 × 185 mm., 145 leaves), such as might have been made as a gift for an abbess or noblewoman, and it lacks the sense of being a private devotional book, which marks out some of the psalters of this period, when they were used regularly as private prayer books, particularly by women, and occupied a place in devotional life comparable to that of the French and Netherlandish books of hours in the later Middle Ages.[9]

Two short German vernacular texts have been added in a late fourteenth-century hand to the last leaf of the psalter (pl. XLIb).[10] The first is a short list of prognostics for children born on the seven days of the week, the second is a German prose recension of the beginning of the *Somniale Danielis*, a widely circulated handbook of dreams in which the dream images with their interpretations are arranged in alphabetical order.[11] This manuscript, which has been entirely overlooked in the literature on dream books, is the earliest known copy of the *Somniale Daneilis* in German.

The calendar and the litany in M 12004 are closely related to those in a Paris psalter (Bibliothèque Nationale, nouv. acq. lat. 187),[12] to which Wolfgang Irtenkauf was able to ascribe a provenance on the basis of the final prayer of the litany, which refers to the Virgin Mary, Saints Peter and Paul, James, Blasius, George and Benedict.[13] This combination of saints points specifically to the Benedictine house of Ochsenhausen in east Swabia, a double monastery for monks and nuns founded from St. Blasien in 1093 and still associated in the thirteenth century with St. Blasien and the Hirsau reform movement.[14] Notwithstanding some very minor differences in the calendar, Irtenkauf extended the Ochsenhausen provenance to the Liverpool manuscript as well, and this hypothesis was presented as a fact in *MRT*. There are, however, reasons for doubting that the psalter was made for Ochsenhausen and that it was used there. Ker considered that it was more likely to have been written for lay use and pointed to the absence of the Benedictine divisions in the Psalter and to the fact that the canticle *'Audite celi'* is not divided in the Benedictine manner. It should also be added that the final prayer of the litany, the only feature which specifically links the Paris manuscript with the Benedictines of Ochsenhausen, is not included here. The calendar, although otherwise more richly illuminated than that of the Paris manuscript, is all in black and does not mark red-letter days. There are no later additions of any kind in the calendar, suggesting that it has never been used in a community. On the other hand, the evidence against Benedictine use is certainly not conclusive, and the *preces* preceding the litany (on p. 257), which are evidently marked up to be recited antiphonally with 'A' and 'B' for the two groups, suggest that conventual use was envisaged by the scribe. The Paris manuscript, which has the prayer showing that it was designed to be used in a particular Benedictine monastery (Ochsenhausen), does not have the Benedictine divisions of the Psalter either. Whatever the early history of the Liverpool psalter, which will probably remain unknown, it was undoubtedly most closely associated with the Ochsenhausen psalter in Paris. The calendars of the two manuscripts are so similar in their content, script and layout that they may well have originated in the same scriptorium at about the same time.[15] This scriptorium must surely have been one of the Swabian Benedictine abbeys associated with St. Blasien and the Hirsau reform movement.

The *Parzival* fragments cannot have been included in the original binding, indeed the manuscript from which they were taken was most probably written some thirty or forty years after the psalter. They provide clear evidence that the psalter has been rebound.[16] They were used as paste-downs and consist of two single sheets (*c.* 245 × 165 mm.) hooked around and sewn in with the outer quires of the manuscript.[17] It is most improbable that such paste-downs were added later, and they indicate that the quires of the psalter were resewn sometime after 1265 (the approximate date of the *Parzival* fragments). There is no other evidence of secondary sewing. The binding is of simple construction and consists of flat unbevelled beech boards of Romanesque appearance, covered with green-stained alum-tawed skin (pl. XLI*a*). Under the leather there is a layer of fabric. The manuscript is sewn on three slit alum-tawed straps which enter the boards through tunnels and then pass along bifurcating channels on the exterior surface of the board, where they are anchored with round pegs. Whereas the flat unbevelled boards are a conservative feature and might easily be mistaken for twelfth-century, the Y-shaped tunnels and channels for the straps exemplify, in Mr Clarkson's opinion, a later medieval technique.[18] The secondary endbands at the head of the spine were of brightly coloured red and yellow silk thread. All three edges of the book are decorated with a pattern in red, blue and gold. When the manuscript was new its exterior must have betrayed something of the brightly coloured decoration within. The clasps, which are intact, consist of bronze doves fixed to canvas straps and are held in position by edge-pins set in the fore-edge of the lower board.[19]

The date of the rebinding must be sought in the fourteenth century. Strictly speaking, the *terminus post quem* is provided by the date of the paste-downs (*c.* 1265), but as these leaves derive from a fine copy of *Parzival* which had been rubricated and most probably also bound, some time is likely to have elapsed before the manuscript was discarded and used as scrap. Folio II recto of the fragments (the upper leaf of the back paste-down: pl. XLI*b*) contains a magic formula inscribed in its upper margin ' + melch.o + er + schrai + su + schrai', which is in the same style (and most probably in the same ink and by the same hand) as the German prognostics and dream book on the verso of the last leaf of the psalter. These additions are in a late fourteenth-century hand, and it follows that the psalter was probably rebound using the two leaves from *Parzival* as paste-downs by the end of the fourteenth century. There is no evidence of early use, but there are clear indications that the psalter continued to be used after it was rebound. A number of wrong initials have been corrected (e.g. pp. 44, 184, 186, 213), and there are textual corrections in a sixteenth-century hand (e.g. pp. 244 and 253). The fore-edge of the upper board has been worn, suggesting that at some period after the rebinding the psalter was in continual use.

On the basis of the information assembled so far the history of the psalter and its paste-downs may be set out as follows.

PLATE XLI

a. Psalter, showing binding and 'dove' clasps (M 12004)

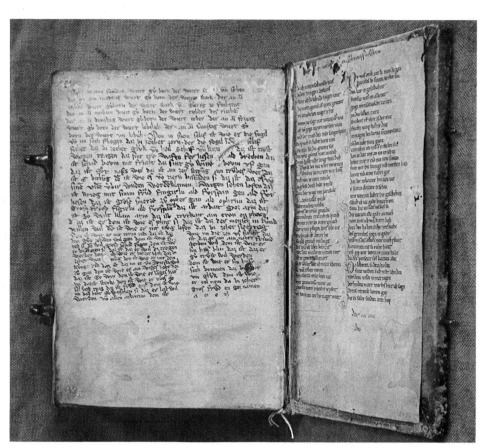

b. The second *Parzival* fragment (M 8951, fo. II) replaced in its original position as a paste-down in M 12004

Reproduced by courtesy of NMGM

Photographs: Chris Clarkson

Second quarter of thirteenth century: Psalter copied.

Third quarter of thirteenth century: *Parzival* manuscript copied.

Later (?) fourteenth century: destruction of the *Parzival* manuscript.

Later (?) fourteenth century: psalter rebound with leaves from *Parzival* as paste-downs; the dove-shaped clasps may have been added at this stage.

End of fourteenth century: addition of German prognostics and dream book on p. 290.

First half of sixteenth century: corrections made to the psalter, which was probably still in regular use.

It is remarkable that the *Parzival* manuscript, itself a fine book, had already been dismembered and used as scrap within a century of being written. This exceptionally early example of a manuscript of a German romance being used as 'Makulatur' needs to be taken account of in the general discussion of book survival in the Middle Ages. Peter Jörg Becker put forward the view a number of years ago that this did not take place until the sixteenth century.[20] Bernd Schirok has recently tabulated the evidence for the *Parzival* fragments, for thirty-four of which there is some evidence of the date when they were used as scrap, and established that thirteen had been so used in the fifteenth century; his earliest example is the fragment f, in Berlin, which may have been used for binding as early as *c*. 1404.[21] The Liverpool fragment antedates this by perhaps a quarter of a century, and in our present state of knowledge it is the earliest example of a German verse text being cut up for binding.

NOTES

[1] The manuscripts should be cited as Liverpool Museum, M 8951 and M 12004. They are on long-term deposit in Liverpool University Library (Sydney Jones Library).

[2] R. Priebsch, 'On a fragment of the Parcival of Wolfram von Eschenbach in the Mayer Museum', *Bulletin of the Liverpool Museums under the City Council*, i (1898), 119–22, with a complete facsimile of the *Parzival* fragments; K. Lachmann (ed.), *Wolfram von Eschenbach*, 7th rev. edn. by E. Hartl, *Lieder, Parzival und Titurel* (Berlin, 1952), xlvi no. 10; B. Schirok, *Parzivalrezeption im Mittelalter*, Erträge der Forschung 174 (Darmstadt, 1982), 33 no. 10.

[3] See G. Bonath, *Untersuchungen zur Überlieferung des Parzival Wolframs von Eschenbach*, Germanische Studien 238–9 (Lübeck/Hamburg, 1971), esp. ii, 11 n. 1; B. Schirok, *Der Aufbau von Wolframs 'Parzival': Untersuchungen zur Handschriftengliederung, zur Handlungsführung und Erzähltechnik sowie zur Zahlenkomposition* (Dissertation, Freiburg in Breisgau, 1972), 66–78 and 122 f. (brief description of M 8951).

[4] E. Martin (ed.), *Wolfram von Eschenbachs Parzival und Titurel*, Germanistische Handbibliothek IX, 1–2 (Halle a./S., 1900–3), i, xxx–xlvi (with some variants of e).

[5] H. Swarzenski, *Die lateinischen illuminierten Handschriften des XIII. Jahrhunderts in den Ländern an Rhein, Maas und Donau* (Berlin, 1936), i, 133 f. no. 53 and ii, 77, 115–17 (ill. 456, 647–60); N. R. Ker, *Medieval Manuscripts in British Libraries*, iii: *Lampeter–Oxford* (Oxford, 1983), 216–18; C. T. Gatty, *Catalogue of Mediaeval and Later Antiquities contained in the Mayer Museum* (Liverpool, 1883), 6 no. 1; *Medieval and Early Renaissance Treasures in the North West* (= *MRT*), with descriptions by J. J. G. Alexander (Manchester, 1976: exhibition catalogue), 18 f. no. 10 and pl. 3; M. R. Perkin, 'Western Manuscripts, Latin and Vernacular' (this volume), pl. xxxixa.

[6] For the canticles see A. Hughes, *Medieval Manuscripts for Mass and Office: A Guide to their Organization and Terminology* (Toronto/Buffalo/London, 1982), 67 and 365 f. n. 50.

[7] For the subdivisions of the Psalter and their significance see R. Kahsnitz, *Der Werdener Psalter in Berlin Ms. theol. lat. fol. 358: Eine Untersuchung zu Problemen mittelalterlicher Psalterillustration*, Beiträge zu den Bau- und Kunstdenkmälern im Rheinland 24 (Düsseldorf, 1979), 134 ff.; Hughes, *op. cit.* (note 6), 225 ff.

[8] According to *MRT*, 18, the line endings are fourteenth-century additions. They are certainly incongruous, but I am not convinced that they are necessarily later additions.

[9] For the use of psalters by women see R. Kroos, 'Zu den Psalterien', in Philipps-Universität, Marburg (ed.), *Sankt Elisabeth: Fürstin, Dienerin, Heilige* (Sigmaringen, 1981), 345–52.

[10] Both published by Priebsch, *op. cit.* (note 2), 121 f. A fresh collation of Priebsch's text with the manuscript yielded the following significant corrections: *Progn.* 1 Der . . .; 5 erber; *Somn. Dan.* 3 daz; 9 bittung; 11 frůnd; fv́rspan gen (= geben!); 16 trvrkait; 27 daz ist frv̊ad capᵗ (= caput, lemma from the Latin text); 30 gv̊trv̊st; 32 bizehet.

[11] For the Latin text see L. T. Martin, *Somniale Danielis: An Edition of a Medieval Latin Dream Interpretation Handbook*, Europäische Hochschulschriften I/375 (Frankfurt/Bern/Cirencester, 1981); J. Grub, *Das lateinische Traumbuch im Codex Upsaliensis C 664 (9. Jh.). Eine frühmittelalterliche Fassung der lateinischen Somniale Danielis-Tradition*, Lateinische Sprache und Literatur des Mittelalters 19 (Frankfurt/Bern/New York/Nancy, 1984). The German corresponds to version b of the Latin text and extends from '*aves*' to '*domus*' (Martin, *op. cit.* (this note), 97–121). German translations are listed by K. Speckenbach in a review of S. R. Fischer, *The Complete Medieval Dreambook* (Bern/Frankfurt, 1982), in *Arbitrium: Zeitschrift für Rezensionen zur germanistischen Literaturwissenschaft* (1985), 36–40. I have also been able to refer to the complete catalogue of all known medieval German versions in K. Speckenbach, 'Deutsche Traumbücher des Mittelalters', in N. F. Palmer and K. Speckenbach, *Träume and Kräuter* (in press), where the Liverpool manuscript is no. 1.

[12] Described by V. Leroquais, *Les Psautiers manuscrits des bibliothèques publiques de France*, II (Mâcon, 1940–1), 133 f.; H. Bober, *The St Blasien Psalter* (New York, 1963), 12–15. I am most grateful to Dr Patricia Stirnemann (Paris) for examining the manuscript for me. She reports that it has the same divisions of the Psalter as the Liverpool manuscript, but instead of the prayers which in M 12004 precede the litany it has the beginning of John's Gospel (fo. 112ᵛ).

[13] W. Irtenkauf, 'Über die Herkunft des sogenannten St.-Blasien-Psalters', *Bibliothek und Wissenschaft*, i (1964), 23–49; id., 'Noch einmal: Über die Herkunft des sogenannten St.-Blasien-Psalters', *ibid.*, ii (1965), 59–84. See especially the second article, 64 f. The final prayer beginning '*Domine Ihesu Christe ne respicias*' is not contained in the Liverpool psalter, where the litany is concluded with three prayers lacking in the Paris manuscript ('*Actiones nostras*', '*Animabus quesumus*', '*Fidelium*': cf. Ker, *op. cit.* (note 5), III, 216–18).

[14] For Ochsenhausen see M. Miller and G. Taddey (eds.), *Baden-Württemberg*, Handbuch der historischen Stätten Deutschlands 6, 2nd edn. (Stuttgart, 1980), 603–5, and Houben, *St. Blasiener Handschriften des 11. und 12. Jahrhunderts; Unter besonderer Berücksichtigung der Ochsenhauser Klosterbibliothek*, Münchener Beiträge zur Mediävistik und Renaissance-Forschung 30 (München, 1979), with no discussion of the psalters in Paris and Liverpool. Professor James J. John (Cornell University) informs me that the manuscripts of Ochsenhausen were described in 1755 by Hieronymus Wirth, and that the collection did not at that time contain a psalter. Two of the earliest Middle High German poems were copied on originally blank leaves in an eleventh-century Ochsenhausen MS: the *Ezzolied* and *Memento mori* in Bibliothèque Nationale et Universitaire, Strassburg, cod. 1 (Lat. 1; All. 278), fos. 74ᵛ, 154ᵛ and 155; cf. G. Schweikle, 'Ezzo', in *Die deutsche Literatur des Mittelalters: Verfasser-lexikon,* ed. K. Ruh *et al.*, 6 vols. (Berlin/New York, 1978–87, in progress), II, 670–80.

[15] See the plate of fo. 6 of the Paris manuscript in Bober, *op. cit.* (note 12), pl. XX. A significant difference in the script is an unusual F-shaped majuscule E used throughout M 12004 and apparently not used in the Paris manuscript.

[16] In the previous literature the binding has generally been considered original. But see Ker's careful formulation, *op. cit.* (note 5), III, 217: 'Contemporary (?) binding of wooden boards covered with green leather'. I am most grateful to Mr Christopher Clarkson (Bodleian Library, Oxford) for giving his opinion on technical aspects of the binding of M 12004; all the technical judgements expressed here are his.

[17] The stitching holes in the inner margin of the fragments were made when the psalter was bound and are not identical with those of the *Parzival* manuscript. The slits in the inner margins, clearly visible on Priebsch's facsimiles, are not medieval and were made when the fragments were removed from the

psalter in the late nineteenth century. It should further be noted that the last quire of MS M 12004 in its present condition is a modern rehitch, perhaps also dating from the time when the fragments were removed.

[18] Further investigation of German bindings from the thirteenth and fourteenth centuries would be required before this feature could be used alone as a criterion for dating. In M 12004 the late date of the binding is also attested by the palaeographical dating of the paste-downs.

[19] Swarzenski, *op. cit.* (note 5), 133 n., refers to similar clasps, all certainly medieval, on John Rylands University Library, Manchester, MS Lat. 95, and BL, London, MS Add. 22280. Both manuscripts are German psalters of similar type to M 12004, with their medieval bindings intact.

[20] P. J. Becker, *Handschriften und Frühdrucke mittelhochdeutscher Epen* (Wiesbaden, 1977), 240–2.

[21] Schirok, *op. cit.* (note 2), 64. For the fragment f see *ibid.*, 33 no. 11.

ADDENDUM

For a textual and palaeographical study of M 8951, with a diplomatic edition of the text, see Nigel F. Palmer, 'Zum Liverpooler Fragment von Wolframs *Parzival*', in K. Gärtner and J. Heinzle (eds.), *Studien zu Wolfram von Eschenbach: Festschrift für Werner Schröder zum 65. Geburtstag* (forthcoming, Tübingen, 1989); see also G. Bonath and H. Lomnitzer, 'Die Fragmentüberlieferung von Wolframs *Parzival*: Eine Bestandsaufnahme', in Gärtner and Heinzle (eds.), *op.cit.* (above), no. 10. For the Ochsenhausen library (above, note 14) see J. J. John, 'Miscellanea Ochsenhusana', in S. Krämer and M. Bernhard (eds.), *Scire litteras: Forschungen zum mittelalterlichen Geistesleben,* Bayerische Akademie der Wissenschaften, philos.-hist. Kl., Abhandlungen, N.F. 99 (München, 1988), 227–40.

The Burmese Manuscripts

Patricia Herbert

It is not known how or when Joseph Mayer acquired the eight manuscripts from Burma that form part of his eclectic collection. The presence of Burmese manuscripts in Britain can be seen as a by-product of British relations with Burma that passed from diplomatic missions in the eighteenth century to war, territorial annexation and colonial rule in the nineteenth. Manuscripts were often brought back by British envoys, soldiers and administrators for their curiosity value, artistic qualities, scholarly interest and so on. The British Museum acquired some of its earliest Burmese manuscripts (now part of the British Library's collection) in the two decades following the first Anglo-Burmese War of 1824–6 and it seems very likely that Mayer obtained his own Burmese manuscripts in the same period. No doubt he acquired them primarily for their interest as examples of different writing materials, scripts, and religious and literary traditions.

In shape and format Burmese manuscripts are nothing like the conventional western notion of a book or manuscript. The oblong strips of leaves are sometimes mistaken for papyrus and the pile of leaves when strung together has been described as being like a venetian blind. To western bibliophiles, who are used to thinking of writing materials predominantly in terms of parchment, paper and perhaps papyrus, the variety of eastern writing materials and methods can be quite intriguing.[1] In pre-twentieth-century Burma the most commonly used writing material was palm leaves. The process of preparing them was simple: the leaves were separated from the central rib, cut into size, then boiled or soaked, dried and rubbed smooth. The text was then incised on both sides of the leaf using a metal stylus, and the leaf rubbed with lampblack and the surplus wiped off, leaving the incised text clearly legible. The leaves were stacked upon each other, secured by a cord strung through two holes pierced in each leaf and by a pair of wooden binding boards. The edges of the leaves and the covers were usually gilded or lacquered. M 12061 is a typical example of a Burmese palm leaf manuscript (pl. XLII). It took great skill to incise the text without splitting the leaf and the work of copying texts was usually done by Buddhist monk-scribes. The copying of a text was considered a highly meritorious deed. Manuscript colophons often record the pious hopes of the scribe for a better rebirth through the merit acquired by copying the text.

A more ornamental form of Burmese manuscript is represented in Mayer's collection by two fine examples, one ivory (M 12059: pl. XLIII) and the other metal (47.53:

pl. XLIV). These are known as *Kammavācā,* or ordination texts. They are larger in dimension than palm leaf manuscripts, have elaborately decorated binding boards, and a gilded and lacquered writing surface on which the Pali text is painted in dark lacquer in a special form of Burmese script, known as 'tamarind' or square script. *Kammavācā* is the name given to a collection of texts excerpted from the *Vinayapiṭaka,* the section of the Buddhist canon dealing with rules for the monastic order. *Kammavācā* texts are used for the valid performance of such monastic ceremonies as ordination, bestowal of robes, consecration of boundaries, etc.[2] Besides palm leaf, paper was also used for making manuscripts in a concertina 'folding book' format, but none is included in Mayer's collection. However, the much rarer writing material, silver, is represented by a single leaf with inscribed Buddhist text (M 12056). Manuscripts on gold and silver have been found enshrined in Buddhist temples and are often of great antiquity. Descriptions of Mayer's eight Burmese manuscripts follow (cf. pls. XLII–XLIV).

M 12056

A single silver leaf, measuring 455 × 47 mm., with eight lines of a Pali Buddhist text incised in very small neat Burmese characters on one side and with two lines of text roughly incised on the reverse side. The uneven and very tarnished surface of the leaf and the fact that the incised text on each side has left indentations on the other make it very difficult to decipher. Eighteenth or early nineteenth century.

M 12057

Palm leaf manuscript of 148 leaves, numbered *ka-do,*[3] lacking some leaves, 485 × 50 mm., with eight lines of a Pali Buddhist text per side written in Burmese script. The leaves are gilded and red-lacquered on the edges and the manuscript has a single rough wooden binding board, gilded and lacquered red on the sides. The manuscript is incomplete at the end and lacks a title and copying date. Eighteenth or early nineteenth century.

M 12059 (pl. XLIII)

Kammavācā (Buddhist ordination text) on ten ivory sheets, 530 × 85 mm., with four lines of Pali text per side written in Burmese square script in black lacquer. The inner margins of folios 1ᵛ and 2 and of folios 9ᵛ and 10 are decorated in red and gold with a design of prancing lions. The margins of the leaves and the entire outer sides of the opening and closing leaves are decorated with a red and gold floral design. Some of the ivory leaves are splitting and some of the lacquer letters have flaked off. Eighteenth or early nineteenth century.

M 12061 (pl. XLII)

Palm leaf manuscript of seventy-two leaves numbered *ka-cā,*[3] 460 × 45 mm., with six lines of text per side in Burmese script. The palm leaves are lacquered red on the sides and the manuscript has a pair of black-painted wooden binding boards, lacquered red on the sides. A printed chart headed 'The Birman Alphabet' has been pasted on the inside of the upper binding board; and pasted on the inside of the lower binding board is a handwritten English text headed 'Observations', in which it is noted that the Indian scriptures were composed 'before the time of Noah' and that the 'Gentoos' (i.e. Hindus) 'affirm that the Deluge did not reach Hindustan'. The Burmese text is *Shwei-pyei-win-pyó,* a poetical work in classical four syllables per line form, narrating episodes from the life of the Buddha.

The colophon states that the copying of the manuscript was finished on the first day of the waxing moon of the month of Thadin-gyut in the Burmese Era year 1125 (= 22 Sept. A.D. 1763).

PLATE XLII

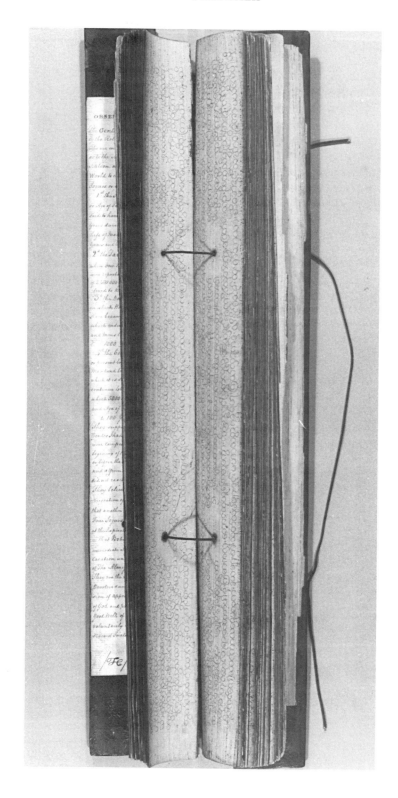

Palm leaf manuscript (M 12061). Reproduced by courtesy of NMGM

Photograph: Ian Qualtrough

PLATE XLIII

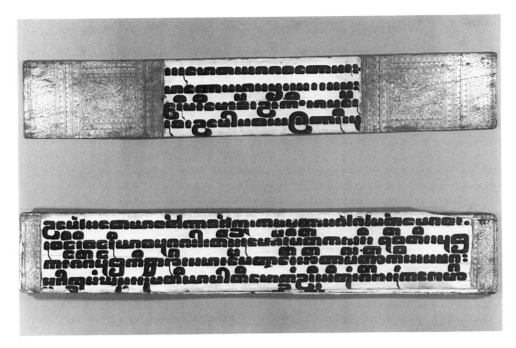

a. Ivory ordination text (M 12059)

b. Detail of *a*

Reproduced by courtesy of NMGM

Photographs: Ian Qualtrough

PLATE XLIV

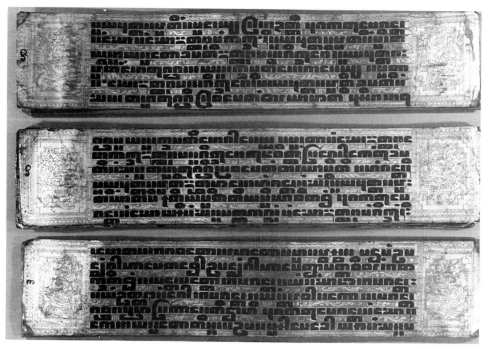

a. Metal ordination text (47.53)

b. Detail of *a*

Reproduced by courtesy of NMGM

Photographs: Ian Qualtrough

M 12062

Palm leaf manuscript of 181 leaves, numbered *dhu-vū*,[3] 490 × 55 mm., with eight lines of text per side in Burmese script. The leaves are lacquered red at the edges, and some are split and damaged; the manuscript lacks binding boards. The text is the *Mahāumagga* (or *Mahosadha*) *Jātaka* in Pali together with a Burmese Nissaya, or gloss. The *Jātakas* are a collection of 550 stories of the Buddha's previous lives. The *Jātaka* related in this manuscript belongs to the last ten stories which are particularly revered. In it, the Buddha-to-be is born as a sage named Mahosadha and subdues a wicked king and brings peace to India. The colophon gives the date of copying as the Burmese Era year 1138 (= A.D. 1776).

M 12105

Six loose and broken palm leaves, with an incised Pali Buddhist text with Burmese gloss in Burmese script; plus six long narrow pointed leaves incised in a script, possibly Javanese, too faint to decipher. Both sets of leaves are badly damaged, very soiled, and of varying dimensions. Eighteenth or early nineteenth century.

47.53 (pl. XLIV)

Kammavācā (Buddhist ordination text) on sixteen metal (cupric alloy) sheets, numbered *ka-khi*,[3] 540 × 105 mm., with six lines of Pali text per side written in Burmese square script in brown lacquer. The leaves are gilded and red-lacquered with a decoration of foliage and cross-hatching patterns between the lines of text, and with figures of *devas* (minor deities) on the cover leaves and margins of the opening and closing leaves. The manuscript has a pair of gilded and red-lacquered wooden binding boards with a worn decoration of panels of *devas* on the outside. The gilding is flaking and damaged on parts of the leaves, revealing the metal underneath. Eighteenth or early nineteenth century.

11.9.73.1

Palm leaf manuscript of seventy-four leaves numbered *ka-chā*,[3] 465 × 55 mm., with nine lines of a Pali and Burmese text per side in Burmese script. The leaves are gilded and lacquered red at the edges and the manuscript lacks binding boards. The text is *Paramattha medani kyàn*, a work on Buddhist metaphysics compiled from various Pali commentaries on the Abhidhamma of the Pali canon.

The colophon states that the copying of the manuscript was finished on the fifth day of the waxing moon of Taw-thalin in the Burmese Era year 1210 (= 5 Sept. A.D. 1848).

NOTES

[1] For a general introduction see A. Gaur, *Writing Materials of the East* (London, 1979).

[2] For a translation of the *Kammavācā* texts see B. Clough, *The Ritual of the Buddhist Priesthood*, Miscellaneous translations from oriental languages 2, Oriental Translations Fund (London, 1834).

[3] The traditional system of foliating Burmese palm leaf manuscripts is not by numerals but by a fixed sequence of combinations of the thirty-three consonants and twelve vowels of the Burmese alphabet. If the manuscript is long enough to exhaust this combination (i.e. over 33 × 12 = 396 leaves), the foliation continues with consonant clusters in place of single consonants.

The Persian Manuscripts

M. I. Waley

In surveying the Persian manuscripts contained in the Mayer Collection, taking one literary genre at a time, we shall concentrate mainly on describing the more unusual items. None of these manuscripts contains texts of great rarity, but several are very attractive from the artistic viewpoint, albeit not outstanding. These exemplify the high standard of craftsmanship which prevailed until relatively recent times in the practice of Islamic calligraphy, illumination, illustration and binding. Indeed it seems likely that Mayer was attracted to several of these manuscripts primarily because of their bindings.

Not surprisingly, several of the best-known Persian classics are represented. These include the *Kulliyyāt* (or collected works) of the great thirteenth-century poet and moralist Sa'dī of Shiraz: an unassuming, but quite well-bound, late eighteenth-century manuscript from northern India (M 12085). Also from India are copies of two classic collections of tales, in versions by Indo-Persian authors which achieved great popularity; many of the tales are themselves of Indian origin. One is the *Ṭūṭi-nāmah* ('Book of the Parrot') by Ẓiyā' al-Dīn Nakhshabī (*ob.* A.D. 1351), copied in 1177 A.H. (= A.D. 1763–4) (M 12099); the second, 'Ināyat Allāh's seventeenth-century *Bahār-i dānish* ('Springtime of Knowledge'), was copied in 1203 A.H. (= A.D. 1789) by a certain Mīr 'Alī Akbar (M 12093).

Several manuscripts contain poetical works. The principal text in a charming small manuscript with excellent calligraphy in the flowing script known as *nasta'līq*, dating from the late eighteenth century (M 12090), is *Laylā va Majnūn*, a romance by Hātifī after the better-known earlier poem of the same title by Niẓāmī; in the margins is the *Subḥat al-abrār*, a Sufi didactic poem by Jāmī (*ob.* A.D. 1492), and at the end of the volume is an Urdu-Persian glossary headed *Ẓābiṭ-i ismhā'-i Fārsī*. Another small volume, still attractive despite extensive water-staining and the loss of its binding, is M 12066, a seventeenth- or late sixteenth-century anthology in which each page is embellished with small triangular and square illuminated panels with floral motifs.

Khamsa ('Quintet') is the collective title of the five narrative and didactic poems by the above-mentioned Niẓāmī, one of the greatest names in Persian literature, who flourished in Azerbaijan during the twelfth century. Like a great many Niẓāmī manuscripts, M 12102 contains all five poems. They are written in excellent *nasta'līq*, extending to 521 folios. The opening of each poem is marked with a

158

PLATE XLV

b. Miniature attributed to Riżā-yi'Abbāsī (M 12078, fo. 12)

a. Court Moghul miniature (M 12078, fo. 3)

Reproduced by courtesy of NMGM

Photographs: Ian Qualtrough

finely-executed illuminated headpiece in gold and several colours, with flowers and floral motifs, birds and butterflies.

An eighteenth-century manuscript (M 12082) of the *Dīvān* (collected poems) of the world-famous mystical lyricist Ḥāfiẓ· (*ob. c.* A.D. 1390), lacking the first and last folios, is one of several of Mayer's manuscripts which have been foliated from back to front as though they were in some European language rather than in the (right-to-left) Arabic alphabet. *Manṭiq al-ṭayr*, the celebrated thirteenth-century allegory of the mystical Path by Farīd al-Dīn 'Aṭṭār, is curiously identified as 'Kifsa-i-Faridudeen' in M 12088 (probably an early nineteenth-century copy). No less renowned is the *Masnavī-'i ma'navī*, a six-volume poem covering virtually every aspect of Islamic spirituality, by Jalāl al-Dīn Rūmī (*ob.* A.D. 1273), found here in a poor nineteenth-century Indian copy (M 12097) which is incomplete at front and back and has suffered from the attentions of worms.

Continuing with religious literature, one may next single out an untitled and unattributed Persian translation of the Four Gospels. The manuscript in question, M 12084, must have been produced in Kashmir or possibly Punjab during the nineteenth century; noteworthy are the good, clear *nasta'līq* calligraphy, the four illuminated headpieces, and especially the fine crackled lacquered painted covers with floral motifs. From the Hindu tradition there is a slim volume (M 12083) with the first chapter of a Persian version from Sanskrit of the great *Mahābhārata* epic.

Rawẓat al-ṣafā' is the title of the work found in another nineteenth-century manuscript, M 12092. This is a general history down to the author's time, by the Timurid historian Mīrkhvānd of Bukhara (*ob.* A.D. 1498). The Mayer manuscript contains the first part, which recounts the history of the Prophets and Patriarchs and that of the kings of ancient Iran down to the end of the Sassanian Dynasty (A.D. 644).

Last, but certainly not least, comes an album (M 12078) which includes some interesting miniatures as well as specimens of calligraphy in the ornate and difficult *shikastah* cursive script. The leaves comprising the album are bound in concertina fashion in a fine lacquered painted binding with floral designs, which must be of Kashmiri origin. In the following descriptions, references are to folios (which do not bear numbers) beginning from what Muslims would regard as the front of the manuscript. Several paintings are mediocre provincial Moghul work. Folio 3 (pl. XLV*a*), however, is a court Moghul miniature datable to *c.* A.D. 1600, though the background has been retouched in a rather muddy green. Two of the figures portrayed are almost certainly Moghul emperors: Akbar, who is seated, and Jahāngīr, dressed in yellow, standing to his right. On folio 6 is a charming provincial Moghul picture of a lady standing beside a stream, with a pearl necklace (or possibly a rosary) in each hand and a peacock on either side of her, as the sun sets behind a hill. Most important of all, however, is folio 12 (pl. XLV*b*): the portrait of a young man wearing a fur hat. Beneath it is an inscription in Persian which reads thus: *raqm-i kamtarīn-i khāksār Riẓā'-i 'Abbāsī*. If this is authentic, the portrait is the work of Riẓā-yi 'Abbāsī, renowned court artist of the Safavid monarch Shah 'Abbās (1588–1629), who greatly influenced the direction of painting in Iran. The elegance and fluency of line evident in the portrait, and the handwriting in the inscription, support the attribution to Riẓā.

A Turkish Manuscript

M. I. Waley

Among Mayer's oriental manuscripts there is but a single volume in Turkish: M 12100[1]. It is an untitled, relatively brief (forty folios, foliated from back to front) collection of miscellaneous official letters (*münşe'āt*) written by (or for) Ottoman Grand Viziers. Some are addressed to rulers of neighbouring states (India, Iran, Transoxiana), others to Ottoman high officials. They are not dated, and this compilation was probably intended primarily to furnish models of administrative epistolary composition.

The manuscript was previously in the possession of the Revd J. H. Hindley, a fairly well-known orientalist bibliophile of the late eighteenth century. Datable to the seventeenth century, it is written in a cursive form of the *rik'a* hand widely used in the Ottoman Empire, and bound in a European-style binding in blind-tooled leather.

The Arabic Manuscripts

C. E. Bosworth

The five Arabic manuscripts here discussed form a most varied group.

M 12021 (parchment; ii + 299 + ii pp.; 189 × 123 mm.)

Like M 12087, this book is technically termed in Arabic a *majmūʿa*, that is one containing more than one component work. In this instance, we have two works by the Shiʿite Persian scholar Mullā Muḥammad Ḥusayn Nūrī, who wrote during the time of the Persian Shah of the Safavid Dynasty, Ḥusayn ibn Ṣafī II Sulaymān (A.D. 1694–1722); since the surviving manuscript is incomplete, it may have contained further works. The first part (pp. 300–96), dealing with theological questions, is in Arabic, in conformity with the extensive use of Arabic in Safavid Persia as the language of theology, law, science and philosophy; whilst the second part (pp. 91–30 and 24–1, misbound), written in the much more flowing and slanting Persian script known as *taʿlīq*, is in Persian, a commentary on a theological work called the *Tajrīd*, dealing with such questions as cosmology, eschatology, the bases of Islamic law, etc. It is composed in the rhymed prose popular for all types of artistic and scholarly subjects, a style which enabled the author to show off his linguistic expertise. The whole work is contained in a recent, unpretentious, European-style medium-brown leather binding, with tooled borders and spine, but no date of copying is given, the latter part of the second work having been apparently not included in this binding.

M 12086 (paper; 114 fos.; 230 × 141 mm.)

An attractively-written manuscript, in black ink with the common red, and in some cases the less common blue, headings of the fifty *Maqāmāt* or 'assemblies' of the Iraqi scholar al-Qāsim ibn ʿAlī al-Ḥarīrī (A.D. 1054–1122). These are sketches, in prose interspersed with verse, depicting incidents involving a picaresque figure, one Abū Zayd al-Sarūjī. They have a certain dramatic quality, and are perhaps the nearest that classical Arabic literature ever came to evolving a dramatic form. But they were chiefly valued by later generations for their bravura literary style, in rhymed prose and with a deliberate use of recondite expressions and rare words to give an effect of dazzling erudition; as such, they were imitated in several of the languages of the Middle East, including Hebrew, Syriac, Persian and Turkish. This manuscript is in the Maghribī script, that is, that used in Muslim North Africa, one in which certain of the consonants are dotted in a different fashion from the standard eastern way. Its colophon (fo. 1ᵛ, rectius 114ʳ) states that it was completed in Dhu 'l-Ḥijja 1222 A.H. (= Jan.–Feb. A.D. 1808) by one Muḥammad ibn Ḥammūda. This is a fairly late date for manuscript copying. Printing by Muslims had begun in Turkey in the eighteenth century, and in Egypt in the early nineteenth, but the invention did not come to Algeria, Tunis and Morocco until the middle or later years of the nineteenth century. The present manuscript thus reflects the social and cultural conservatism of Muslim North Africa. The binding is of the flap variety (see below, under M 12101), but of inferior quality, with crudely-decorated paper-covered boards and leather only for the spine, hinges and edges of the boards and flap.

M 12087 (paper; ii + 194 + 1 fos.; 163 × 130 mm.)

Again a *majmū'a* containing several component works. It bears no date, but the simple yet attractive buff leather binding, stamped with fleurons, is obviously fairly recent, and the deckling of the edges of the folios is a recent western and not an oriental feature. It must emanate from Lebanon or Syria, and a partially-defaced *tamalluk* or 'possession note' in Arabic at the end of the manuscript (fo. 1) says that it once belonged to '. . . son of the priest Ḥannā from the village of Ighzīr [?] . . .'. Its component texts display its Christian origins. They comprise, firstly, the ancient and widespread Near Eastern story of the sage Aḥīqar, said to have been the minister of the Assyrian emperors Sennacherib (705–681 B.C.) and Esarhaddon (681–668 B.C.), and his wise counsels to his nephew and adopted son Nadan. The original Aramaic version became widely used in early Christian circles, in a Syriac linguistic form, for homiletic and educational purposes, and then appeared amongst the Christians of Syria and Iraq in several Arabic versions, once these peoples began to give up their original Syriac speech in favour of Arabic. Other components of the manuscript include homilies by Theodosius Patriarch of Alexandria and St Athanasius, plus pseudepigraphic texts involving David and Solomon. The most interesting feature, however, is that all these texts are in Arabic language but written in Syriac script, specifically its Jacobite form, sc. in the writing system known as Garshuni or Karshuni, an instance of the use of the script of the politically and culturally dominant group by an outside community, paralleling the use of Arabic script in the Near East for writing Hebrew by local Jewish communities there. Since the Arabic alphabet has twenty-eight characters and the Syriac one only twenty-two, various slight modifications to the letters had to be used in Karshuni. In the present manuscript, headings and diacritical points have been picked out from the generally black ink by the use of red ink.

MS 12096 (parchment; iii + 89 + iv fos.; 206 × 135 mm.)

A very nice copy of the *Dīwān* or collected poems of the Egyptian Ṣūfī mystic poet Ibn al-Fāriḍ (A.D. 1181–1235), whose verse, although exiguous in extent, became highly popular in the Islamic world and is regarded as a classic of Ṣūfism. Some of the verses may have been meant to be sung to a musical accompaniment, and most are capable of interpretation on an exterior level, as secular love poems addressed to a human beloved, or on an interior level, as mystical hymns addressed to God. The rectangular upright format is that usually found in all Arabic manuscripts except the earliest ones, for which a rectangular horizontal format is not infrequently found. This manuscript is full bound in the European style (i.e. without flap) in red leather, with gold rules and cartouches on the front and back boards. The contents match this most beautiful binding. Written in 1259 A.H. (= A.D.1843), the two columns of finely-written poetry in each page are contained in red and blue rules, and there is an illuminated gold and blue title-page. This is undoubtedly the most attractive of Mayer's Arabic manuscripts.

M 12101 (parchment; 201 fos.; 208 × 154 mm.)

An Arabic-Turkish vocabulary, arranged alphabetically according to the Arabic roots and with the Turkish equivalents written beneath. Such compilations, virtually copy-book exercises, were common; this one was made by one Maḥmūd ibn Khiḍr ibn Pīr Aḥmad in 964 A.H. (= A.D.1557) and given by him the name *Kitāb Muntakhab al-lugha fī 'ilm al-lugha*, 'Book of selection of words concerning the science of grammar'. The contents are of little interest, but the binding is a worn but handsome red leather flapped one. In this form of binding, a pentagonal flap forms the rear cover board, and this can be folded over the fore edge of the manuscript and tucked like an envelope flap below the front cover board, thus protecting the sewn folios (as here) or even possibly a pile of unsewn leaves, as was not uncommon. The flapped binding is the classic one in the Islamic world, only supplemented by European-type binding in fairly recent times. Examples of it are known from as early as the tenth century A.D. and the technique may have been borrowed from the wrap-round flap systems found in early Christian, and especially Coptic, bookbindings. The boards were often thin after being pared down, and were often (as here) stamped with floral cartouches and ornaments on both front and rear boards; the hinges became worn, hence partial rebinding was often necessary. This has been done here, and a (presumably) British later owner has had a gold-blocked English title added to the spine 'Montakhab Arabic MS'. Islamic books did not have the title written on the spine, and from the time when this manuscript was still in non-western hands, it has (like M 12096) a short title written in black ink on the lower edge of the book; Islamic books were not normally stood upright on shelves in the modern western fashion, but placed flat on them, so that a title on the book's edge would thus be visible.

To sum up, although none of the manuscripts is a rarity, as an ensemble they exhibit a wide spectrum in subject matter and a variety of scripts and countries of origin, this last ranging from North Africa to Turkey and Persia. The bindings are particularly attractive and, in general, the manuscripts illustrate, in a small number of copies, many of the salient features of pre-modern Islamic book production.

IV. RENAISSANCE AND LATER

Introduction

George Heriot and Benevenuto Cellini beckoned the prospective customer into No. 68 Lord Street,[1] where he or she might find Renaissance intaglios and jewellery in the antique manner—such as the 'Dürer' brooch.[2] In the same way Mayer's silver might copy or derive from seventeenth- and eighteenth-century models: in 1851 he ordered from Barnard of London 'a Louis XIV chased boat inkstand', and as an expensive special commission 'a Wafer vase chased Jasper', that is in the manner of early Wedgwood.[3] A few weeks earlier Barnard had supplied 'a Chinese engraved trowel'.[4] Again the Napoleonic memorabilia (below, pp. 212–26) include pieces that are essentially similar to the snuff-boxes and fob-seals that were presented to the Chaplain to the School for the Indigent Blind and other loyal public figures in Liverpool.[5] Here Mayer's collection coincides with his profession as a jeweller and goldsmith.

Notwithstanding Mayer's insistence that he was a 'manufacturing' goldsmith, with his hallmark registered at Chester 1843–73,[6] most of the silver which passed through his shop was to his order, or occasionally to his design, but not of his own manufacture.[7] The exception may be the cases of the clocks and watches that bear his mark. These, together with a very considerable range of English and continental time-pieces from the sixteenth century onwards, are now displayed at the Prescot Museum of Watch- and Clock-making, a few miles north of Liverpool.

Mayer is a provincial player in the great drama of high Victorian design. If his confession of faith is the Mayer shield (1852) commemorating the Great Exhibition,[8] his taste was still founded in Wedgwood; he accepted Stubbs long before he was fashionable.[9] At the same time he himself painted competent architecture in a landscape ('The White Tower of Seville'),[10] and collected oil paintings and water-colours that now seem to epitomize Victorian romanticism: 'Calabrian Peasant Tying the Sandal', 'Scene from *Don Juan*, by R. W. Buss', 'View of the interior of Roslyn Chapel, Scotland, showing the Apprentice's Pillar where he was killed by his master in a fit of rival jealousy'.[11]

MARGARET GIBSON

NOTES

[1] See above, p. 5.

[2] M 238: see above, p. 7 n. 61.

[3] Ledgers of J. Barnard and Sons, now on deposit in the Department of Metalwork, Victoria and Albert Museum, 1851, p.185, account no. 315. The vase 'modelled express' cost £35. 1*s*. 1*d*.

165

[4] *Ibid.*, p. 175.

[5] Liverpool Museum 1966–105: see above, p. 5 n. 40.

[6] C. J. Jackson, *English Goldsmiths and their Marks*, 2nd edn. (London, 1921), 394.

[7] See J. Culme, *Directory of Victorian and Edwardian Goldsmiths, Silversmiths, Jewellers and Allied Trades*, Antique Collectors' Club (Woodbridge, 1987), to whose guidance and advice I am greatly indebted here.

[8] *1851 Exhibition: Official Descriptive and Illustrated Catalogue*, 674, class 23, exhibitor 14, no. 1. The shield was bought by the city of Liverpool in 1887 and is still in the Town Hall.

[9] JM's *Memoirs of Dodds, Upcott and Stubbs* (London, 1879) is still the basis of any biography of Stubbs. The paintings that JM owned were all sold at Sotheby's, 21 July 1887 (Lugt 46763).

[10] WAG 7620: see *Merseyside Painters*, 147 and plates vol. 126.

[11] MPB, unidentified press cutting, JM's bequest to the Bebington Trust, written 1885 and printed in late January 1886.

Arms and Armour

Fiona A. Paton

Joseph Mayer presented over 500 pieces of arms and armour to Liverpool Museum. Despite war damage and the collection's dispersal amongst several departments one can still appreciate the immense range of this material. It consists today of several hundred flintlocks, matchlocks, wheel-locks, swords, daggers, rapiers, axes, halberds, crossbows, suits of armour, powder flasks and spurs, from Europe, Asia and Africa; these date mainly from the fifteenth to the nineteenth centuries.

Mayer's interest in military matters may be traced back to his boyhood and the times he spent with the 34th Regiment of Foot.[1] As his enthusiasm grew Mayer began writing articles on the subject.[2] He seems to have been particularly interested in the history of local defence and its contemporary development. In 1860 he was appointed Commanding Officer of the Liverpool Volunteer Borough Guard and in 1864 Captain of the 4th Bebington Company of the 1st Cheshire Rifle Volunteers.[3] In addition to giving financial support, Mayer presented his section of the 1st Cheshire Rifle Volunteers with two challenge cups for shooting. Joseph Clarke of Saffron Walden, a fellow captain, friend, natural historian and dealer in antiquities, shared Mayer's interest in and concern for local defence organizations. The two exchanged news and views about their respective local companies commenting on such matters as the cost of uniforms, the need for breechloading rifles and the success of inspections.[4]

By the time Mayer opened his Egyptian Museum in 1852, he had amassed over 200 weapons and some armour. This was exhibited in the armoury room on the upper floor. The catalogue actually lists 234 items but this includes a number of curiosities such as an ancient spice mill, a telescope, caps, musical instruments and sandals.[5] If anything there seems to have been a slight bias towards African and oriental material. The following extract from an 1850s press report illustrates quite clearly the extraordinary range of material on view:

> There in one apartment, the visitor is shown almost every shape of instrument that human ingenuity has devised for destroying human life; swords primeval, medieval, and modern with their diminutives in krisses, daggers, and firelocks of various countries and patterns with pistols to match, clubs, spears, shields, helmets, coats of mail etc.[6]

The material on display does not appear to have been organized in any particular fashion. For instance, one finds a Chinese matchlock, a German hunting knife, a war-club from the Sandwich Islands, an Arab gun, and an old English musket listed together in a single section.[7]

It is difficult to ascertain exactly when, where and how Mayer acquired this material. By 1838 he had accumulated enough items to send some firearms, together with pottery and paintings, to the Pottery Mechanics' Institute of Newcastle-under-Lyme.[8] In 1847 he again displayed material, this time in the Grand Polytechnic Exhibition at Liverpool Collegiate Institute,[9] and on several occasions from 1849 onwards showed weapons to the Historic Society of Lancashire and Cheshire. A large wall crossbow and a double-handed sword are illustrated in the *Transactions* for 1851.[10] Mayer probably bought some of this material through dealers. Correspondence between Mayer and Clarke in 1861 refers to a musket from Sebastopol which when last on the market had raised £3, now on offer for 2s. 0d.[11] Other pieces came from collections purchased by Mayer, such as a number of rapiers, spurs and horse bits that he bought from Franz Pulszky in 1855 together with the Fejérváry ivories.[12]

We do know that in 1854 Mayer travelled to Bavaria, Austria, Bohemia, Saxony and Prussia, where amongst other goods he collected swords, guns, pistols, daggers and armour. In an address given to the Historic Society on 8 June 1854, Mayer described some of the difficulties he had had shipping his material back to England. The material was transported by way of the Danube and the Rhine. Unfortunately, one case filled with arms, bronzes, terracottas, manuscripts and glass, weighing a quarter of a ton, was seized by the customs at Hamburg. The weapons were regarded as contraband of war. No sooner had this incident been sorted out than customs at Hull demanded the payment of a 10 per cent duty on all manufactured goods.[13] Some of these recently purchased specimens were used to illustrate Mayer's article 'On the Arming of Levies in the Hundred of Wirral', published in 1859.[14] One of the most impressive pieces is an eighteenth-century Flemish target crossbow made from walnut and inlaid with mother of pearl and ivory, with brass fittings (M 4796: pl. XLVI*b*). Another piece worthy of comment is a seventeenth-century sporting wheel-lock, probably of Spanish origin, with stock, butt and locks elaborately chased in steel with foliage and figures. A most unusual seventeenth-century Silesian flintlock musket-cum-axe also figures in Mayer's article (M 4766; pl. XLVI*g*). It is made from dark wood and inlaid with ivory curvilinear and animal motifs. Charles Beard writing about the collection in 1935 believed that it was almost complete by 1859, suggesting that Mayer could have acquired up to a hundred pieces on the above-mentioned trip.[15]

The collection has a representative selection of European sixteenth-, seventeenth- and eighteenth-century swords, muskets, pistols, crossbows, halberds, spurs, powder flasks and armour. Several sixteenth-century blades bear a running wolf, the mark of the armourers of Passau and Solingen, one of the earliest and most important European blade-making centres.[16] An early court sword is actually signed by its maker, 'JOHANNES WUNDES' who was working in Solingen from *c.* 1560–1610. The hilt of this sword is a plain quillon type with a half-ring to form a knuckle guard level with the quillon. A piece which Mayer displayed on several occasions and seems to have been fond of is a large two-handed double-edged sword, probably from Germany (M 4820). It is engraved with scroll work and mythical characters and beasts. The quillons are swept forward and the knuckle guards are of the plain ring type. This type of sword was the normal arm of the Swiss in the fourteenth and fifteenth centuries. The Italians tried to distinguish their swords, not only by blades but with hilts as well. Some of these elaborately hilted rapiers are represented in the collection (M 4838, M XII, M 4822: pl. xlviiia–c).

The manufacture of a gun involved the work of several craftsmen: blacksmiths, woodworkers, locksmiths and goldsmiths to embellish the mounts and enrich the lock and barrel. The high quality and artistic design of their work is displayed by many of the Mayer pieces. One very fine example is an early seventeenth-century Flemish wheel-lock musket with a walnut stock, heavily inlaid with ivory scrolls and beasts chasing one another, inscribed 'ANNO DOMENI 1616' (M 4762: pl. xlviib, d). It would have been difficult to kill anything but sitting game with such a large and heavy piece. In the seventeenth century the design and decoration of wheel-locks reached its peak. Mayer had a fine German example, the stock beautifully carved in dark wood with hunting subjects and tipped with ivory, signed 'G.M', George Maucher of Swaebisch Gmund (M 4759: pl. xlviic). A sixteenth-century wheel-lock pistol inlaid with various fanciful figures, including foxes, a dolphin, a two-clawed dragon, birds, quatrefoils and stylized horses, bears the mark or spur of Nuremberg where the wheel-lock is believed to have been invented around 1517. No expense was spared in the production of very elaborate pieces, as is shown by a late eighteenth-century Turkish flintlock inlaid with gold at both ends, covered with tortoiseshell and richly decorated with gold, silver, ivory, stone, red coral, pearl and mother of pearl (M 4713: pl xlviia). Fine attention to detail was also shown in the manufacture of powder flasks and cartridge boxes (M 4730: pl. xlvie). A German hemispherical priming flask of the late sixteenth century, again inlaid with ivory circles of animal and foliage motifs, has a central ivory panel bearing the portrait of a German soldier (M 4737: pl. xlvif). In a period when everything from clothes to castles seems to have been lavishly decorated it is not surprising that even the sporting bow, used to hunt game such as deer and wild boar, was superbly fashioned in steel, wood, ivory, and embellished with gold. Several such pieces exist in the Mayer Collection dating from the sixteenth to eighteenth centuries, mainly from Germany (M 4797: pl. xlvia). The Flemish target crossbow (see above, p. 168) illustrates the high standard of craftsmanship required for such weapons (pl. xlvib). The Saxon miner's axe lavishly inlaid with horn (M 4930: pl. xlvic) was used on ceremonial occasions, being part of the insignia of a sixteenth-century guild.

Over fifty pieces of armour survive but there are only a few complete suits. Some of these are quite rare, such as the sixteenth-century breastplate bearing the signature of Pompeo della Chisa of Milan, armourer to Philip III of Spain and the Dukes of Mantua, Milan and Parma (M 4872: pl. xlviiid). Other interesting pieces include an early sixteenth-century brigandine covered with red velvet and a breastplate in plain russet steel, ornamented with brass-headed studs, worn by the French Imperial Guards and taken at Waterloo. Armour was very expensive and much of it was probably reworked, which explains why so little has survived from the Middle Ages. Mayer did originally have a number of early English and German pieces which have since been lost. These included a casque and a coat of mail which Gatty judged to be twelfth-century.[17]

Archaeologically one of the most important pieces of armour, since lost, was the conical casque found, according to an old label, 'on the battle field of Walric'.[18] It is

PLATE XLVI

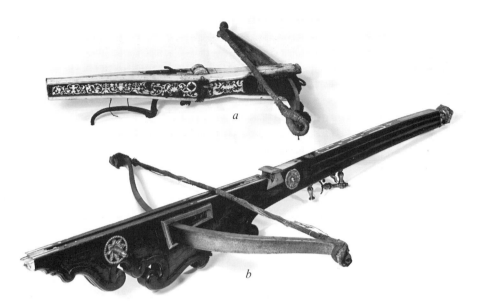

a. German sporting crossbow, sixteenth century (length 600 mm.) (M 4797)
b. Flemish sporting crossbow, late eighteenth century (length 1035 mm.) (M 4796)

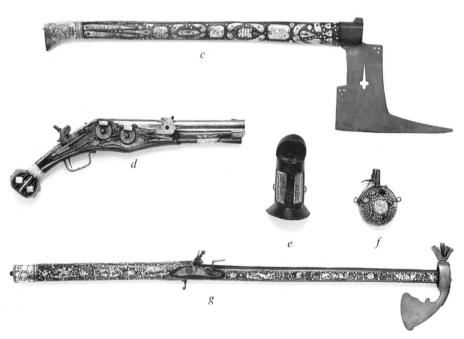

c. Saxon miner's axe, late sixteenth century (length 670 mm.) (M 4930)
d. German double barrel wheel-lock pistol, sixteenth century (length 500 mm.) (M 4708)
e. German cartridge carrier, seventeenth century (height 130 mm.) (M 4730)
f. German hemispherical powder flask, late sixteenth century (diam. 80 mm.) (M 4737)
g. Silesian flintlock musket-cum-axe, *c*. 1700 (length 925 mm.) (M 4766)

Reproduced by courtesy of NMGM

PLATE XLVII

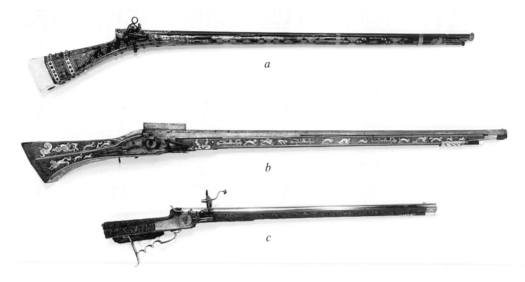

a. Turkish flintlock inlaid with gold, silver, mother of pearl, ivory and coral, late eighteenth century
(length 1500 mm.) (M 4713)
b. Flemish wheel-lock sporting musket, seventeenth century (length 1550 mm.) (M 4762)
c. German wheel-lock musket, seventeenth century (length 1110 mm.) (M 4759)

d. Detail of *b* (M 4762)

Reproduced by courtesy of NMGM

PLATE XLVIII

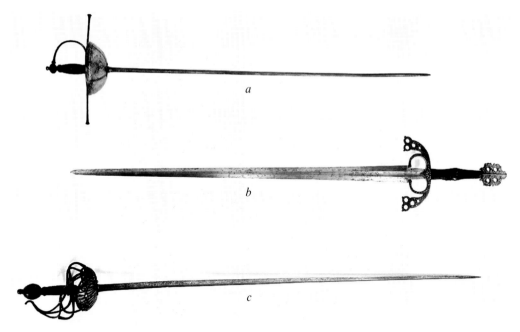

a. Italian cup-hilted tuck sword, seventeenth century (length 1310 mm.) (M 4838)
b. German double-edged sword, sixteenth century (length 1210 mm.) (M XII)
c. English tuck sword, with swept hilt shell guards and curved quillons, late sixteenth century (length 1070 mm.) (M 4822)

d. Italian breast plate from a suit of russet armour, signed 'POMPE', seventeenth century (height 470 mm.) (M 4872)

Reproduced by courtesy of NMGM

PLATE XLIX

a. English armet, sixteenth century (height 320 mm.) (M 4892)

b. Italian cabasset, seventeenth century (height 225 mm.) (M 4896)

Reproduced by courtesy of NMGM

one of three known examples of helmets used in East Prussia between the eleventh and twelfth centuries. Only a few helmets now survive in the collection. Two of these are particularly good examples of their type. One is a sixteenth-century English armet, popular for war and tournament until the close of that century. The helmet completely covers the head, face and neck, has a movable chin piece which revolves on the same pivots as the vizor and is closed by a spring bolt on the side (M 4892: pl. XLIX*a*). The other is a seventeenth-century Italian cabasset, worn by foot soldiers from the late sixteenth to seventeenth centuries. Helmets of this type are easily distinguished by the curious little point projecting from the top. It is supposed to represent the stem of a pear from which the helmet takes its name (M 4896: pl. XLIX*b*).[19]

No discussion of this collection would be complete without mention of those items formerly associated with famous events or people, such as the large wheel-lock gun used at the execution of Mary Queen of Scots and preserved in the family of the soldier who used it until acquired by Mayer.[20] Other intriguing pieces include a highland dirk worn by the Duke of Buckingham, heavy boots supposedly worn by Cromwell, a finger from the left-hand gauntlet of Edward the Black Prince, and a dagger and rifle belonging to Mark Bozzaris, a hero of the Greek War of Independence.[21] How Mayer acquired the gauntlet finger is intriguing. It seems highly unlikely that he was among the many nimble-fingered visitors to Canterbury Cathedral who felt obliged to carry off a souvenir of their visit. The finger is not mentioned in the 1852 Catalogue of the Egyptian Museum and so probably came later as part of a group of medieval metalwork. Had Mayer been aware of its importance he would surely have returned it to Canterbury, where it has since been restored to the Black Prince's tomb.

There can be no doubt that Mayer wanted others to share his enjoyment and enthusiasm for arms and armour. He set aside a whole room to exhibit this material at Colquitt Street and generously contributed to other people's displays. He realized the importance of trying to establish a date and provenance for the material he collected, sometimes writing to friends and colleagues for additional information.[22] A catalogue of Mayer's arms and armour has never been produced. Hopefully this may one day be achieved, together with a new display. Mayer was particularly concerned about securing public funds for collecting and preserving objects of national interest so it is most fitting that his centenary year witnessed the opening of a new purpose-built armoury for the storage and continued preservation of these and other weapons.

NOTES

[1] See above, p. 2.
[2] JM, 'On the arming of levies in the Hundred of Wirral', *THSLC*, xi (1859), 83–96.
[3] R. B. Rose, 'Liverpool Volunteers of 1859', *Liverpool Lib. Mus. and Art Comm. Bull.*, vi (1956), 47–66.
[4] MPB and MPL, correspondence with J. Clarke 1854–73.
[5] JM, *Egyptian Museum*, 39–45.
[6] *Mail*, 8 May 1852.
[7] JM, *Egyptian Museum*, 41.
[8] MPL, Thomas Ryder to JM, 7 July 1838.
[9] JM, *Catalogue of the Grand Polytechnic Exhibition at Liverpool Collegiate Institution* (Liverpool, 1847).

[10] *THSLC*, iii (1851), 105, exhibited by JM, 1 May 1851.

[11] MPL, J. Clarke to JM, 31 Jan. 1861.

[12] Nicholson, *Prehistoric Metalwork*, 8–9.

[13] *THSLC*, vi (1854), 133–4, exhibited by JM, 8 June 1854.

[14] *Ibid.*, xi (1859), 83–96, with 8 plates; JM, *op. cit.* (note 2).

[15] C. R. Beard, 'The Joseph Mayer Collections', *The Connoisseur* (Mar.–Apr. 1935), 135–8, 201–5.

[16] D. S. Hawtrey Gyngell, *Armourers' Marks* (London, 1959), no. 16.

[17] H. Ecroyd Smith, unpubl. inventory in Liverpool Mus. (1870), no. 16 (M 4875).

[18] Beard, *op. cit.* (note 15), 137.

[19] A. C. Stone, *Glossary of the Construction, Decoration and Use of Arms and Armour* (London, 1961), 158.

[20] JM, *Egyptian Museum*, 41.

[21] *Ibid.*, 39–45.

[22] MPL, F. Bööcke to JM, 9 Apr. 1856; MPB and MPL, JM and J. Clarke correspondence 1854–73.

The 'Majolica'

T. H. Wilson*

One of the more curious cultural phenomena of the second half of the nineteenth century in England was the fashion for collecting—and sometimes paying enormous prices for—what we now classify as the applied arts of the Renaissance: Limoges painted enamels, Palissy and so-called 'Saint-Porchaire' (alias 'Henri Deux') pottery, and, above all, sixteenth-century Italian maiolica. *Istoriato* ('story-painted') maiolica had already had a certain attraction for collectors before the nineteenth century from its association with the name of Raphael: up to around 1850 'Raphael ware' was the normal English expression, and the idea continually surfaced in the eighteenth century that Raphael and other artists had actually painted maiolica themselves. The competitive fashion for collecting Renaissance maiolica took off in England in the early 1850s and reached its first crescendo at the sale in 1855 of the astonishingly high-quality collection of Ralph Bernal, M.P. Purchases at the Bernal sale, made with the help of special Treasury grants, provided the basis of the collections of both the British Museum and the Victoria and Albert Museum, and the active interest of the museums was one element in the continuing rise in maiolica prices through the Victorian period.[1]

The two national museums from the 1850s on were the focus of a small group of scholar-collectors—above all, A. W. Franks of the British Museum, J. C. Robinson and C. D. E. Fortnum. Their work, based on studying pieces with marks, dates and signatures, laid the foundation of all subsequent art-historical study of Renaissance maiolica, and it was they who established the English public collections as the richest in the world. The main English dealers and sale-rooms were in London too. Up in Liverpool, Joseph Mayer, who had been collecting ceramics since the 1820s, stood somewhat apart from this booming Victorian fashion.

Llewellyn Jewitt in an article in the *Art Journal* in 1870 wrote of the 'Mayer Museum': 'Of foreign china the museum contains a splendid collection ... The majolica is particularly fine, and of the highest style and value; and there are also excellent examples of Palissy ware, Luca della Robbia, Henri Deux and other wares of great variety, beauty, and interest.'[2] This part of the collection, the continental pottery, was particularly badly hit by the catastrophe that overtook the Liverpool Museum in World War II: of the 150-plus pieces listed as 'Majolica ware' in H. Ecroyd Smith's inventory, compiled in 1869, not enough now remains to fill a single showcase; the range and quality of the collection has to be deduced from the 1869

176

inventory and the sparse references to the collection in the old literature. The latter, however, are of disappointingly little help; for the striking fact is that the Mayer Collection has been consistently ignored in the standard works on Italian maiolica. Joseph Marryat, in the useful account of English collections in the 1857 (London) edition of his *History of Pottery and Porcelain*, makes only passing mention of 'several cabinets of this interesting Italian pottery' in Mayer's collection; no pieces were lent to the great display of documentary masterpieces accumulated in 1862 by J. C. Robinson for the *Special Exhibition of Works of Art* at South Kensington; C. D. E. Fortnum's monumental 1873 catalogue of the South Kensington Collection only makes passing mention of the Mayer Collection; and in Bernard Rackham's voluminous writings on maiolica, beginning in 1903 and stretching over more than fifty years, this writer has not noticed a single reference to a piece in Liverpool.

The reason for this is not to be found in any distaste on the part of London-based scholars to venture north of the Trent, so much as in the character of Mayer's collecting. The 1869 inventory seems to indicate that Mayer did not buy the expensive 'central masterpieces', or the much-sought-after armorial and documentary pieces which were the delight of younger collectors like Franks and Fortnum. There was, for instance, no signed work by the prolific painter Francesco Xanto Avelli, whose work is represented in all the major modern collections of maiolica. Instead Mayer's collection gave a general overview of the various types of European decorative pottery, mainly tin-glazed, from about 1500 to after 1800: the heading 'Majolica ware' in the inventory included things as diverse as 'Della Robbia' reliefs, Palissy, German stonewares, and eighteenth-century faience from several countries. Mayer's wide-ranging taste contrasts sharply, for instance, with Fortnum's collection, begun in the 1850s and now at the Ashmolean, which was largely confined to Italy in the 'best' period, *c.* 1500–60, and included every signed, marked or dated piece that Fortnum could get his hands on.[3] Mayer's taste reflects the generation gap: he was collecting before Victorian taste had settled on the High Renaissance as the focus of collecting fashion.

Little specific information has been discovered about how and where Mayer acquired his pottery, although much of his collection was certainly acquired by gift or exchange through a network of contacts in England and abroad; and in London, by the 1850s particularly through A. W. Franks. The 1869 inventory does not mention any provenances from well-known or prestigious collections, nor does Mayer's name appear as a direct buyer at the great mid-century sales, Strawberry Hill (1842), Stowe (1848) and Bernal (1855). Furthermore, a very high proportion of pieces in the 1869 inventory are described as broken in various degrees. The writer has the impression of a collector aiming to build up a representative collection of the various branches of 'ceramic art', but not able or not prepared to pay the high prices being asked by the 1850s for 'major' pieces.

Despite this, leafing through the 1869 inventory is a funereally melancholy experience. Brief and inadequate though the descriptions are, there are objects listed, now lost, that any specialist museum would covet. There were some unusually large 'Raphael ware' *istoriato* dishes such as a 'Christ healing the sick, after Raffaelle, in colors, with arabesque borders in blue and yellow; 17 in. diam.' (no. 1788); some large lustred dishes, probably made at Deruta, including 'a Female headed sphinx ... supporting the Arms of the Colonna family' (no. 1974). Dishes with portraits included one of the Emperor Charles V inscribed 'Carilo V Imperat.' (no. 1809), interesting because contemporary 'portraits' on Renaissance pottery are rare. The only dated sixteenth-century piece to have been destroyed was a dish inscribed 'Lucretiia Romana' and dated 1543 (no. 1813). A curiosity was a 'Fountain, in form of a building with court, surrounded by children, animals and reptiles, the whole surmounted by a seated Violin Player; white painted in colors. $21\frac{1}{2}$ in $\times$ $12\frac{1}{2}$ in.' (no. 1849) which was marked 'ROMA 1632': maiolica demonstrably made in seventeenth-century Rome is rare and this elaborate item would be of some art-historical importance, had it survived.[4] Interesting, as much for the provenance as for the object, is the description (no. 1848) of a 'Plaque, with square moulded border representing a half length figure of the Madonna and Infant Jesus, crowned, in base relief with festooned arabesque drapery; white, painted with blue and yellow with rich madreperla glaze. 17 in. $\times$ $13\frac{1}{2}$ in.' which is stated to have been 'Presented to Mr. Mayer by . . . Grand Duke of Tuscany, in 1828'; it is described in the 1852 Catalogue (JM, *Egyptian Museum*) as being by 'Luca Della Robbia'.

These descriptions, and the five pieces here illustrated from those few that survived the Second World War, must suffice to give some flavour of the Mayer Collection of 'Majolica ware' in its original state. It was not, in quality, on a par with the great London collections and its loss is not to be compared with the wartime destruction of the collections in Berlin or Faenza, but it was the earliest-formed major museum collection of continental ceramics in Britain as well as the best and most representative collection of its type in the north of England, and its loss to Liverpool can never be made good.

APPENDIX: THE ILLUSTRATED MAIOLICA

M 1747 (pl. L*a*).

Maiolica bowl, moulded in relief, the design painted and picked out in metallic lustre. In the centre a man in pilgrim's clothes turning over a skull with a stick. Made in the workshop of 'Maestro Giorgio' at Gubbio, dated 1531 on the back. Relief-moulded pieces, in distant imitation of metalwork, were made in considerable quantities in Gubbio in the 1530s. Diameter: 250 mm.

M 1757 (pl. L*b*).

Maiolica plate, painted with intertwining monsters and winged heads on a blue ground. On a tablet is the date, 1533. The 'grotesque' decoration has been enhanced by the addition of metallic lustre in a subsequent firing: this technique was a speciality of the workshop of 'Maestro Giorgio' in Gubbio. Some scholars[5] believe that pieces of this kind were made and painted in Casteldurante, near Urbino, then transported over the mountains to be lustred at Gubbio. Although this certainly did happen on occasion, the present writer thinks it more likely that this piece was both made and lustred at Gubbio. Diameter: 240 mm.

M 1799 (pl. LI*a*).

Maiolica plate, decorated in blue with the three Magi on their way to Bethlehem. On the reverse a mark, the arms of Savona. Made at Savona, second half of the seventeenth or beginning of the eighteenth century. In the seventeenth century, reflecting the fashion for Chinese porcelain, tin-glazed pottery painted only in blue became popular in many parts of Europe. In Italy there were major centres for work of this kind at Savona, Albisola and Genoa, on the north-west coast. Diameter: 460 mm.

PLATE L

a. Metallic lustre bowl, a man in pilgrim's clothes turning over a
skull with a stick. Gubbio, 1531 (diam. 250 mm.) (M 1747)

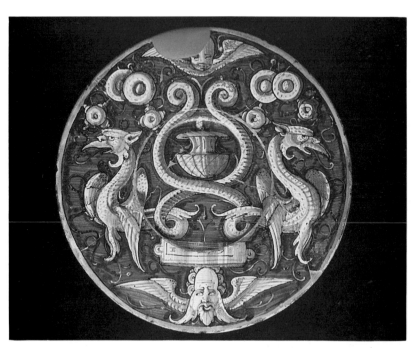

b. Metallic lustre plate, intertwining monsters and winged heads, Gubbio, 1533
(diam. 240 mm.) (M 1757)

Maiolica

Reproduced by courtesy of NMGM

PLATE LI

a. Tin-glazed blue plate, the three Magi, Savona, later seventeenth or early eighteenth century (diam. 460 mm.) (M 1799)

b. Plate, Abraham sending away Hagar and her son Ishmael, made probably at Holitsch, mid-eighteenth century (diam. 250 mm.) (M 1830)

Maiolica

Reproduced by courtesy of NMGM

PLATE LII

Maiolica: drug jar, Adam and Eve, Naples, 1757 (height 170 mm.) (M 1780)
Reproduced by courtesy of NMGM

M 1830 (pl. LI*b*).

Plate painted with Abraham sending away Hagar and her son Ishmael (Gen. 21), in a landscape. The figures are taken from an engraving after Abraham Bloemart.[6] Marked on the reverse 'H.F.'. Probably made at Holitsch, then part of Hungary now in Czechoslovakia, in the mid-eighteenth century in the manner of contemporary Italian maiolica—particularly the work of Bartolomeo Terchi and Ferdinando Maria Campani. Diameter: 250 mm.

M 1780 (pl. LII).

Drug jar, of the shape known as 'albarello'. Painted with Adam and Eve covering their nakedness before God in the Garden of Eden (Gen. 3). Signed 'PC.P. 1757'; probably painted by Pasquale Criscuolo, Naples, 1757.[7] Height: 170 mm.

NOTES

* I am grateful to Margaret Gibson for information on Mayer, to Lionel Burman for making accessible to me the remains of the Mayer Collection, the 1869 inventory, and advice based on his own incomparable knowledge of the collection; and to Martin Royalton-Kisch for advice on the iconography of pl. LI*b*.

[1] For maiolica-collecting in England in the 1850s see T. H. Wilson, 'The origins of the maiolica collections of the British Museum and the Victoria and Albert Museum', *Faenza*, lxxi (1985), 68–80. For some earlier collections see A. V. B. Norman, *Wallace Collection: Catalogue of Ceramics*, I (London, 1976), 19–29; A. Moore, *Norfolk and the Grand Tour* (Norwich, 1985).

[2] *Art J.* (1870), 208.

[3] See J. V. G. Mallet, 'C. D. E. Fortnum and Italian maiolica of the Renaissance', *Apollo*, cviii (1978), 396–404.

[4] This may have been an object resembling the ones in J. Giacomotti, *Les Majoliques des musées nationaux* (Paris, 1974), nos. 1118–19.

[5] cf. *ibid.*, no. 756.

[6] A. Bartsch, *Le Peintre graveur*, new edn. in 21 vols. (Leipzig, 1854–70), III, 147 no. 63.

[7] For other jars from this set, probably made for a monastic pharmacy, see G. Donatone, *La maiolica napoletana del Settecento*, Museo Duca di Martina, Naples, Exhibition Catalogue (Naples, 1980), nos. 15, 16.

The Oriental Collection

Eldon Worrall*

Joseph Mayer's surviving oriental collection, together with Ecroyd Smith's and Gatty's cataloguing of Mayer's oriental material, give a good picture of his tastes, knowledge and connoisseurship in this field. In this area of his collection Mayer has stepped outside his role as just a promoter of the arts and a wealthy collector. He does not appear to be 'buying his way to fame', but seems to be comfortably at home in forming a small but interesting selection of oriental decorative arts, which displays particularly well the technical abilities of the Chinese in potting. The other parts of his oriental collection were probably acquired as a second thought to back up his Chinese ceramics and consist of Chinese and other metalwork, Chinese weapons (pl. LIIIa) and glass, books, Japanese ceramics, etc. What is surprising to me is the lack of truly decorative furnishing ceramics. Mayer's collection consists of mostly small objects of porcelain, not at all 'showy', except perhaps for the fish tank.[1] It would appear that he chose specimens for reasons other than decorative appeal, a fairly unusual approach. During the 1850s and 1860s Liverpool was well endowed with antique dealers and a plethora of auction houses.[2] If this is a dealer's collection, formed for him, it is not a characteristic one, as it is so lacking in decorative types, that is sets of vases, large bowls, etc. Rather, it consists of small items which would add nothing whatsoever to the interior of a room. It is much more probable that Mayer himself was the collecter, being 'on the spot' at one of the major British ports for traffic to and from China. The cost of such Chinese material during the middle of the nineteenth century, obtained *in situ* at the port of Liverpool, was very low, as compared to European porcelain of a decorative nature.[3]

Mayer is a most interesting subject with respect to mid-nineteenth-century British oriental collectors. The possession of oriental artefacts at that time was not so fashionable as it had been earlier. There had been great interest in China during the eighteenth century with the British East India Company shipping in porcelain, silks, tea and other Chinese export materials. Just exactly how much this fashion owed to the cheapness and yet the high quality of the imported goods is not often fully understood. But Mayer fits into neither class: neither as a buyer of oriental goods because they were cheaper than those similar objects available at home, nor as a follower of fashion.[4] He was buying Chinese material after the fashion had well and truly declined; he was, as it were, buying up the results of this earlier 'oriental mania'.

One would expect such a person to belong to a society of like-minded men, and in this respect we must launch a little cheer at him. In the 1850s there was no national society for the promoting of oriental art, but towards the end of Mayer's collecting period there was a very small number of regional societies. One of the earliest was in the port of Liverpool, and it is no surprise to find that Mayer was a prominent member. In 1872 he was on the committee of the Liverpool Art Club for their oriental exhibition.[5]

On examining the remains of his collection, it seems to have been formed to show the great variety of techniques of decoration of which the Chinese potter was capable. Unfortunately, the archaeological wares[6] and classic wares[7] had not yet arrived in this country in any number;[8] otherwise Mayer would no doubt have added, on technical grounds, such specimens to his collection. It is more than likely that he was consciously selecting a museum for the public, rather than merely a private collection to his own personal taste. It does seem most probable that he was systematically forming a representative oriental collection, for public use, of Chinese and Japanese material. Naturally he pursues his own advice given in 1842: 'We shall at the end of this little sketch offer a few general remarks for the guidance of travellers, who may feel inclined to lend their aid in establishing a public museum in Liverpool.' As early as 1842 he wrote, 'Whoever shall have the opportunity of adding either to a private collection or a public museum, will bear in mind how very much is added to the interest of the specimen of a knowledge of the locality where, and the period when it was manufactured and will think no specimens are unworthy mainly for their rudeness of form or ornament.'[9] This is borne out by an analysis of his oriental collection. It is an objective collection of mainly mundane material, apparently selected on a technical basis and showing a good widespread selection of techniques of decoration, etc.

The total number of Mayer's oriental objects runs into many hundreds, comprising Chinese glassware,[10] Chinese ivories,[11] a Chinese printed book,[12] Chinese metalwork, some decorative arts, Chinese ceramics (by far the largest section), seventeenth-century Japanese ceramics, and some Japanese decorative arts (pl. LIII*b*). Apart from the Chinese ivories and glassware,[13] the other oriental collections were probably formed by Mayer by piecemeal addition, rather than by bulk purchase. During the 1850s he was actively engaged in the purchase of Chinese porcelain, evidenced by his correspondence with Franks,[14] and no doubt locally he made known his desires in the direction of oriental art. The records were sold in 1887, but a number of items in his 1867 gift bear inscriptions indicating acquisition locally by Mayer.[15]

One wonders whence Mayer's interest was generated—sadly it is not possible to be certain. His correspondence with Franks indicates that it was Mayer who was the collector of Chinese porcelain. Certainly one good possible cause was Mayer's very strong interest in Liverpool pottery and porcelain. He was the first biographer of this local industry,[16] and there he refers also to oriental subject matter.[17] The Liverpool potters were to a high degree influenced by the Chinese in their productions, and Mayer's sharp eye took this in; perhaps his interest in oriental ceramics and associated arts stems from this overlap, so to speak, with his classification of the local chinoiserie potters. Unfortunately, only a relatively small number of his oriental objects now remain in the Liverpool Museum, but the records of his gifts survive.[18]

Certainly Joseph Mayer was not the first Liverpool collector who owned or displayed oriental material. William Bullock, for one, opened a museum to the public in the first decade of the nineteenth century, containing Chinese textiles, armour, decorative arts, money and so forth,[19] but not Chinese or Japanese porcelain. Mayer, likewise, at first on a somewhat amateurish basis, included a few bits and pieces of oriental in his Colquitt Street museum (1852).[20] William Daniels's portrait of Mayer (pl. I) includes two items of Chinese porcelain: a jardinière in the window and on the mantlepiece a tea caddy.

However, it was after 1852 that he became more interested in Chinese ceramics, albeit as a comparison group to his English chinoiserie ceramic collection and Wedgwood productions. It is certain that between 1852 and 1867 he acquired hundreds of pieces of Chinese and Japanese ceramics. In 1854 Franks sent Mayer, presumably on the latter's instructions, a Chinese dish; in the same letter Franks writes of what is probably the large late Ming oval bowl from Su-Zhou (pl. LIV*a–b*); and as late as 1877 he sent two copies of a Mr Watson's paper on 'the Chinese inscription'.[21] In the following generation, James L. Bowes,[22] who formed a collection of Japanese ceramics between 1867 and 1874, was much influenced by Mayer. He too was a member of the Liverpool Art Club, which in 1872 held its Oriental Exhibition. The following year, Bowes became president of the Art Club. Both men obviously knew each other in the 1860s.

The variety of Chinese material Mayer gave to the Liverpool Museum is of considerable interest: not only the fashionable *famille rose, verte* and *noire*—'export wares', as we know them[23]—but Ming Dynasty wares with underglaze blue decoration, right through to nineteenth-century wares. During the early 1850s, no excavations were being carried out in China, but Mayer does make it clear that it is ornamentation and the techniques thereof that interest him. The Su-Zhou bowl is of perhaps little aesthetic quality; however, it was obviously useful to Mayer in some way or other. It may well have interested him as a comparison to Wedgwood wares which was a name very well known to him and something of a passion of his in collecting. The cockerels and rockwork are sprigged (pl. LIV*b*),[24] this same technique being used by Wedgwood some 150 or 200 years later.

Decorative arts

Amongst the jades, the only surviving piece is an archer's ring superbly carved in low relief and datable to the late Ming Dynasty. The Peking enamels are mostly in the European style, including a teapot on stand, and a large ewer and basin,[25] another rather nice 'Sino-occidental' piece; further large similar dishes are recorded, but all but one were lost in the Second World War. Champlevé enamels are listed, which were no doubt of Ming Dynasty date, and earlier. The only surviving example of this class is a gilt bronze shield boss of Middle Eastern influence and dating from the late Song Dynasty. One later Ming bronze survives, of south Chinese origin, typically badly cast, but still quite decorative. Mayer gave six Qianlong glass bowls in 1867 and four other pieces later, not to mention numerous cased snuff-bottles and a little clothing (in bad condition) of nineteenth-century date, but of little interest in quality. There are opium pipes, spectacles and compasses; and two ivory figures, one of which Mayer counselled against displaying.[26]

PLATE LIII

a

a. Bows with traces of lacquer decoration, seventeenth century (length 1550 mm.) (M 5488)

b. Japanese gilt bronze cup, seventeenth century (height 50 mm.) (M 5360)

Reproduced by courtesy of NMGM

Photographs: M. Krofchak and Lawrence Ma

b

PLATE LIV

a. Su-Zhou glazed pottery footbath, Ming, seventeenth century
(length 750 mm.) (M 2109)

b. Detail of *a* (M 2109)

c. Transitional porcelain dish, with underglaze blue decoration, seventeenth century (diam. 410 mm.) (M 2007)

Reproduced by courtesy of NMGM

Photographs: M. Krofchak and Lawrence Ma

PLATE LV

Photograph: M. Krofchak and Lawrence Ma

b. Vase inscribed Qianlong, eighteenth century (height 230 mm.) (M 1789)

a. Chinese jug, eighteenth century (height 220 mm.) (M 1453)

Reproduced by courtesy of NMGM

PLATE LVI

Photograph: M. Krofchak and Lawrence Ma

a. Toy buffalo, Qianlong, eighteenth century (height 75 mm.) (M 1808)

b. Yixing teapot, early eighteenth century (height 100 mm.) (M1991)

Reproduced by courtesy of NMGM

PLATE LVII

a. Imari jardinière, late seventeenth century (height 175 mm.) (M 1943)

b. Imari tea-kettle, seventeenth century (height 190 mm.) (M 1989)

Reproduced by courtesy of NMGM

Photographs: M. Krofchak and Lawrence Ma

PLATE LVIII

b. Japanese porcelain cup cover and stand, Kutani, nineteenth century (height 100 mm.) (M 1951)

c. Gibson bowl, export ware, early nineteenth century (diam. 250 mm.) (M 2563)

Reproduced by courtesy of NMGM

Photographs: M. Krofchak and Lawrence Ma

a. Arita tankard, late seventeenth century (height 200 mm.) (M 2230)

Chinese ceramics

Mayer's Chinese ceramics in the Liverpool Museum were one of the earliest British collections of Chinese porcelain.[27] He had written in 1867, 'I always had in view to make the Collection as much illustrative of the Arts of the different nations as I could, so as to connect Ancient and Modern Art.'[28] In this case, the illustrations chosen were underglaze blue-painted porcelain, thirty-two items in all: perhaps the finest piece was most probably of fifteenth-century date and painted with trailing vine;[29] of the same date, a dish painted in flower heads;[30] amongst the other pieces of blue and white a large transitional charger is worthy of note (pl. LIVc). Although of south Chinese origin and characteristically poorly made, it serves 'to connect ancient and modern art', in this case the north kiln Ming characteristics and the lesser later south Chinese kilns, absorbing main styles and producing for foreigners.[31] Most of the other pieces in this category are fairly mundane late seventeenth- or early eighteenth-century pieces.

Three pieces of Mayer's blue and white illustrate how easy it must have been then to confuse 'chinoiserie' specimens with Sino-occidental material. Admittedly, Mayer is not necessarily to blame, as the confusion appears in Gatty's records.[32] The first, a silver form jug (pl. LVa), is of a quite common type; but as the Chinese were making copies of European and silver vessels in the time of Emperor Qianlong (jugs being particularly common),[33] it is understandable that Gatty wrote 'of Chinese pattern, but Worcester 1780'. The piece is particularly heavily potted and was probably for this reason confused with English soft paste; so he got it the wrong way round, poor chap! It was not the first nor the last time Sino-occidental art was confused with 'chinoiserie'. The small vase (pl. LVb), painted in underglaze blue, is very mundane; however, the base, which is glazed, is incised by hand, recording the name of J. Wilson, in an eighteenth-century cursive script. This is interesting as it is the only example I know of where an eighteenth-century English collector has permanently identified his property. Indian collectors made a habit of this form of identification,[34] and it may be that J. Wilson also collected in India. The *famille verte* and *famille rose* sections include powder-blue-ground wares of Emperor Kangxi's reign. A rare instance of a 'toy' is the enamelled recumbent buffalo of late Yongzheng or early Qianlong date (pl. LVIa).[35] One *famille verte* dish is particularly good quality,[36] the execution fine and well defined, and the base bearing the six-character mark of Emperor Kangxi and of the period. The largest piece in this category is a fish tank of early Qianlong date;[37] it is described, together with all the *famille rose* wares, as 'decorated in colours of old'. Obviously Ecroyd Smith had not yet read Jacquemart and Le Blant's *Histoire de la Porcelaine*.[38] Some modelled decorated *famille rose* items are represented, a number of which have already been published.[39] Of Mayer's seven listed Yixing stoneware teapots, three survive (pl. LVIb); one is complete with its silver-gilt mounted stand and dates to the early eighteenth century or perhaps a little earlier.

Japanese porcelains

Mayer's Japanese porcelains are quite pleasant and are all correctly ascribed. They are mostly of late seventeenth- or early eighteenth-century date: Imari and Arita. The Imari jardinière (pl. LVIIa) is of European design, with side-handles pierced as mons. The interior is painted with a chrysanthemum, but with a certain artistic licence in that the flower head is combined with a different foliage. The silver-gilt mounted Imari tea-kettle (pl. LVII*b*) is of similar date. A large late seventeenth-century Arita tankard (pl. LVIII*a*) forms an interesting comparison with another of Mayer's selections in the field of Japanese ceramics, a covered porcelain cup or bowl on a stand (pl. LVIII*b*). The latter is described by Ecroyd Smith as 'Japanese Eggshell China—modern'. This Kutani specimen well exemplifies the change in Japanese ceramics from the seventeenth century to the nineteenth: the shift in emphasis from the somewhat sketchy portrayal of figures to the prissy, precise artistry of the mid-nineteenth century. Which pot did Mayer prefer?

Mayer's 'Gibson Bowl' (pl. LVIII*c*), which he obtained from Alexander C. Gibson, F.S.A., of Bebington, is worthy of note as it is a piece of maritime history; it no doubt appealed to Mayer, who had seen many Liverpool soft-paste ship-bowls.[40] It is inscribed in a typically unsure Chinese hand 'Capt. Joseph Gibson the Esther of Harrington'. It is of early nineteenth-century date, datable to the Jiajing Emperor. The *Esther* was a brig of 96 tons, built by H. Millward of Harrington in 1814, the owner noted in Lloyds register for 1820 as being 'J. Gibson' and 'J. Gibson & Co.'. The bowl itself probably dates from 1820. Mayer's interest in Liverpool ceramics led to his interest in Chinese porcelain, and sets him among the founding fathers of British Chinese porcelain collecting: a pursuit no doubt viewed by some as the 'chink in his armour'.

NOTES

* I am particularly indebted to the help of Susan Beby (British Museum); Stuart Munro-Hay (Centre of African Studies, University of Cambridge); Nicholas Pearson (Victoria and Albert Museum); and June Protheroe-Benyon (Whitehaven Museum, Cumbria). Michael Krofchak and Lawrence Ma took the photographs for pls. LIII*a*–LV*a*, LVI*b*–LVIII*c*.

[1] E. E. Worrall, *Precious Vessels* (Liverpool, 1980), pl. 115 (M 2081).

[2] Gore (1856) lists forty-two auctioneers.

[3] Second-hand Chinese porcelain was cheaper than continental and English new porcelain.

[4] The aesthetic and pre-Raphaelite brotherhood had not, as yet, come into being.

[5] *Catalogue of a Collection of Chinese Porcelain*, Liverpool Art Club Exhibition Catalogue (London, 1882).

[6] In this case Han, green lead-glazed wares, Hiao and Tang funeral wares.

[7] The official wares of the court dating to the Song Dynasty.

[8] It was during the very late nineteenth and early twentieth century that such wares started to come out of China, basically due to railway excavations.

[9] JM, *A Synopsis of the History of the Manufacture of Earthenware, with Reference to the Specimens in the Exhibition of the Liverpool Mechanics' Institution* (Liverpool, 1842), 11–12.

[10] Gatty, *Mediaeval and Later*, 45 nos. 195–200: pendant beads, and seven snuff-bottles of the Qianlong Emperor's reign.

[11] F. Pulszky, *Catalogue of the Fejérváry Ivories in the Collection of Joseph Mayer, Esq., F.S.A.* (Liverpool, 1856), 52 nos. 95–102. There are eight in all, one stylistically probably Ming Dynasty, and another of Sino-occidental type, stated to be taken from a Dutch drawing.

[12] M 12080: a printed (woodblock) work of seventeenth-century date, on deposit in the Sydney Jones Library, the University of Liverpool.

[13] Both of these collections came with other extraneous materials and were sold to JM as part and parcel of a major collection.

[14] The correspondence clearly shows Franks's directions and enthusiasm in obtaining Chinese porcelain, including obtaining for Mayer a translation of a Chinese inscription: MPL, A. W. Franks to JM, 24 Nov. 1853, 11 Mar. 1854, 11 Mar. 1877.

[15] One such local acquisition is the 'Gibson Ship-Bowl' (pl. LVIIIc).

[16] JM, *History of the Art of Pottery in Liverpool* (Liverpool, 1855).

[17] *Ibid.*, 19; *id.*, *On the Art of Pottery* (Liverpool, 1871), 40. (a) Mayer states Seth Pennington's (1760s) wares 'have often sold for Oriental china, of which they are a close and admirable imitation', and (b) Mayer describes Liverpool wares, particularly a cup in the East India style, stating that Mr Chaffers, the eighteenth-century Liverpool potter, kept an East India punch bowl 'as a pattern for his workmen to copy'.

[18] Inventory by Ecroyd Smith and Gatty: Liverpool Museum, Departments of Antiquities and Decorative Art (1867 on).

[19] W. Bullock, *A Companion to the Liverpool Museum*, 7th edn. (Bath, 1809), 8, 11, 75, 76, 78. See above, p. 8 note 66.

[20] JM, *Egyptian Museum*, 45: items of Chinese armour, snuff-bottles, a model of a Chinese houseboat and a Mandarin's hat.

[21] MPL, A. W. Franks to JM, 11 Mar. 1854, 11 Mar. 1877.

[22] Bowes, a wealthy wool-broker and connoisseur of Japanese ceramics, opened a museum of Japanese ceramics in Liverpool in 1890. He was the author of *Japanese Marks and Seals* (London, 1882), *Japanese Enamels* (London, 1884), *Japanese Pottery* (London, 1890), and co-author with George A. Audsley of *Keramic Art of Japan* (London, 1875).

[23] The term *famille rose* was first used by A. Jacquemart and E. Le Blant, *Histoire de la Porcelaine* (Paris, Lyon, 1861–62); as would be expected the museum inventory of 1867 (see above, note 18) does not use it.

[24] Produced by the clay being moulded into a regular form by pressing onto a cut-out mould.

[25] The 1867 inventory (see above, note 18) describes it as 'Bason and Jug painted with a European figure'.

[26] Liverpool Museum, Department of Antiquities, JM to J. A. Picton, 1875, where he suggests 'the Chinese carving in ivory of a lady should not go on public display'. It is a medical ivory portraying a reclining naked lady!

[27] Although the South Kensington Museum purchased one item of Chinese porcelain in 1852, they did not acquire any collections of Chinese ceramics until well after Mayer's 1867 gift, whilst the British Museum's earliest collection was received in 1867, by coincidence, from Franks. It was not really until the 1890s and later that collections of Chinese material began to enter into these national collections.

[28] JM to J. A. Picton, 4 Feb. 1867, offering his collection to the town of Liverpool: cf. above p. 20.

[29] No longer surviving but listed in the 1867 inventory (above, note 18), acc. no. 1926.

[30] No longer surviving but listed *ibid.*, acc. no. 1973.

[31] P. Conner, *The China Trade 1600–1860* (Brighton, 1986), 72 no. 94.

[32] C. T. Gatty was responsible for the oriental collection from 1873 to 1884.

[33] M. Vickers, O. Impey and J. Allen, *From Silver to Ceramic* (Oxford, 1986), pl. 59.

[34] M. Green and P. Hardie, *Chinese Ceramics—the Indian Connection* (Bristol, 1982), 15.

[35] Toys or whistles are usually, like this example is, from Fujian but are *blanc-de-chine*, made for export during the eighteenth century. It is unusual to find such an item with enamelled decoration.

[36] Worrall, *op. cit.* (note 1), 76, pl. 109 (M 1885).

[37] *Ibid.*, 78, pl. 115 (M 2081).

[38] Jacquemart and Le Blant, *op. cit.* (note 23).

[39] Worrall, *op. cit.* (note 1), 91, pls. 149 and 150 (M 1972 and 1702).

[40] Mayer gave seven ship-bowls to the Liverpool Museum in 1867. See Philip Nelson, 'Liverpool Delft ship-bowls', *THSLC*, lxxxvii (1936), 113–18.

Joseph Mayer's Wedgwood Collection

Lionel Burman[*]

> Mr Mayer, a most worthy gentleman . . . who honoured Wedgwood in a day when no one cared for his name and few for his works. [Eliza Meteyard][1]

Building the collection

In the course of the century after Joseph Mayer's death the Liverpool Museum has acquired only a modest number of examples of Wedgwood ware; the great majority of specimens in the collection remain the gift of Joseph Mayer. However, the existing collection of Wedgwood is not, to a significant degree, that bequeathed by Mayer, nor indeed was the latter entirely the collection he had formed by 1867. In addition to the items given to the Museum, he had his own extensive personal collection, housed eventually at Pennant House in Bebington, to which he continued to add, and to exchange and sell from, over a long period. It was eventually dispersed by sale after his death. Until 1882 at least, Mayer continued to extend the Museum's holdings of Wedgwood by presenting specimens, and for many years, with Mayer's full approval, the Museum sold or exchanged duplicate specimens, thus further shaping and developing the collection. Therefore, even before the grievous losses, which particularly affected the Wedgwood wares, caused by the bombing of the Museum, the Wedgwood Collection was not entirely in the form of the original gift, but had been in a fairly continuous state of transformation and improvement.

Practically no records survive of the provenance of specimens. Several scattered references by Henry Ecroyd Smith, the first curator, and his successor Charles Gatty, indicate that they had attempted to elicit information from Mayer, but as Joseph Clarke stated in 1875, in a letter to Gatty, 'If you could find Forrest, Mr Mayer's Colquitt Street Curator, he could tell you more where things come from than anybody else, he is an ignorant man with a tenacious memory, who often used to correct Mr Mayer, of whom you will never get much.'[2] Such documentation as Ecroyd Smith and Gatty did secure was seriously depleted by the air-raid of 1941. So far as I can determine, Mayer was one of the few early systematic collectors of Wedgwood, if not the earliest; Thomas de la Rue and Henry Bohn were similarly

;ame time, and other collections may have been in formation
1840s, including possibly the Barlow, Marryat, Brocas and
ompared to Mayer's, how systematic or representative these
)een, however, it is difficult to say. To judge by the published
la Rue Collection was closely comparable to Mayer's; others
ayer was not merely an habitual collector from boyhood: he
benefactor from an early age, his earliest known gift of art
.[3] His first recorded loan of ceramics and other art objects
edgwood) took place ten years later. Further gifts were made
's collection seen on at least two occasions, at loan exhibitions
ie opening of his Egyptian Museum in 1852.[4]

We have three striking pieces of evidence for Mayer's involvement with the study of Wedgwood, and his high esteem for the subject, during the 1840s. The portrait by William Daniels (pl. I) reveals a number of telling details. Not only are there various items of Wedgwood ware prominently in view, including the vase upon which Mayer is casting a collector's proprietorial eye, but the painted cabinet with pictorial centre panel against the left-hand wall is inscribed 'Wedgwood' on a tablet. Clearly, by his fortieth year Mayer had assembled an appreciable group of examples. Another detail worthy of note is the volume of prints in the foreground: this looks remarkably like d'Hancarville's *Antiquités Etrusques, Grecques et Romaines*, or a similar volume, of which there were several, in imitation.[5] D'Hancarville's work, illustrating Sir William Hamilton's collection of Greek vases, was the principal source for many of Wedgwood's neo-classical designs: it indicates Mayer's awareness of the related archival and documentary material. Most of the identifiable Wedgwood pieces in the portrait survive in the Museum's holdings to this day. An encaustic-painted basalte vase stands high above d'Hancarville's book, from which its decoration is derived; it is supported by a jasper candelabrum, which was illustrated by Eliza Meteyard in 1873.[6] She thought this was one of a pair, although only the one was in the Museum's possession; Mayer did, however, own its partner, as it is seen further back along the same wall, supporting a vase which is too vaguely painted to be identified. Further Wedgwood wares are ranged upon the cabinet. The jasper vase with the snake-entwined handles does not appear to have survived (nor the lamp visible upon the table). The two encaustic-painted basalte pieces lurking behind the Sèvres soft-paste porcelain figure group can be identified, one as a vase, the other as an *oinochoe* (pl. LXIa): the jasper plinth beyond them also seems recognizable and the small vase on plinth base in Mayer's hand is unmistakable.[7] Thus, some important examples from the period of Wedgwood's *oeuvre* which in the second half of the nineteenth century was to be the most fashionable had already been acquired by Mayer by the 1840s.

A minor incident in 1844 reveals one of the few pieces of evidence of Mayer's purchases and throws light on the extent of his acquaintance and correspondence. An invoice survives for the purchase of a set of medallions of emperors, during the period of the short-lived partnership of Frederick Wedgwood and John Boyle. At the same time Boyle wrote to Mayer offering to sever this connection and use the capital from his half-share in the business to form a partnership with Mayer. We do not have Mayer's reply to Boyle, who in any case died shortly after.[8] It was, however, through another association that he achieved a remarkable coup in pursuing his self-imposed task. Some thirty years later he described the event to Gatty:

In the year 1845, being in London, I went to take tea with Mr. Chambers, the old friend of Stothard, the artist, and was introduced by Mrs. Chambers to a Mr. and Mrs. Wedderburne. Having previously heard that Mr. Wedderburne had been a traveller in the service of the Wedgwoods for more than forty years, I entered into conversation with him at tea, and he told me many anecdotes relating to the art of pottery ... Amongst other things, he said that after the death of Josiah Wedgwood, in 1795, partly owing to the falling off of orders from the Continent, in consequence of the unsettled state of France, there was little done at Etruria in the finest class of works of art, such as cameos, vases, etc., the sale for them not very encouraging. During a few more years the London warehouse was carried on, and Mr. Wedderburne was chief clerk and adviser; but soon after, the whole of the goods were sold by auction, and the establishment broken up. It was at this time that Mr. Wedderburne purchased a vast quantity of the oldest and best specimens of artistic work, and nearly ruined himself in the transaction. The garrets of his house, he confided to me, were full of them and he would be happy indeed if he could dispose of them at half the price they had cost him. At my request he showed me a few of his specimens and when I saw them my heart beat as I asked him if he had any more, and how much he would want for them. He suggested that I should visit him next day and see the remainder, which I did, and purchased all he had.[9]

In Gatty's words, 'The pieces which Mr. Mayer obtained from Mr. Wedderburne, together with those accumulated at other casual times, form an excellent representative group. The series of portraits is unusually large and the plaques, vases, etc., in jasper, basalt and pottery, contain pieces representing most of the various periods and styles of Wedgwood ware.'[10] It is difficult to guess even what particular pieces may have been included in this selection; I suspect it might possibly have contained some early or trial pieces from the factory, held back from sale—for example, a misfired and blistered example, in blue and white jasper, of the Triton candlestick attributed to William Keeling; even, perhaps, the Museum's copy of the Portland Vase, with its imperfectly fired relief decoration, and quite uniquely separated base.[11]

By 1845, then, Mayer already had assembled an outstanding, and apparently quite varied, collection of Wedgwood wares. Three years later, however, he was to make a discovery of a different kind, which was to render ceramic historians permanently indebted to him and for which alone his contribution to Wedgwood studies deserves to be honoured. Eliza Meteyard's account demands quotation.

Whilst few cared to learn how one of the greatest men of the last half of the eighteenth century lived, and how he wrought, Joseph Mayer was hoarding up every little scrap of information, purchasing old deeds and papers, and seeking amidst the generation fast passing away for vivid glimpses of the man their eyes had looked on and their lips spoken to. Eventually, by a mere accident as strange as it was interesting, a very large portion of the business papers belonging to Mr. Wedgwood's works, both at Burslem and Etruria, passed into his hands ...

While he was in Birmingham ... a sudden thunderstorm forced him to take refuge in a near-by waste and scrap shop. Piles of scrap-iron, copper, brass and junk of every kind littered the floor. While pacing up and down, waiting for the rain to stop, he noticed on the battered oak counter a pile of old ledger books.

Upon closer examination he discovered that the ledgers were from the Etruria factory and related to the wages of the workmen. The scrap dealer informed Mayer that he sold these books to butchers and shopkeepers to wrap up their bacon, butter and green groceries, the big sheets being a convenient size. The scrap dealer who had purchased these from the Wedgwood factory after the death of Josiah II . . . took Mayer up into the loft above his shop where he had many more documents. Mayer purchased all of the material from him and devoted his leisure time to arranging the documents.[12]

Mayer's prowling (in the course of business and collecting) into out-of-the-way establishments and his curiosity and acumen had paid off in a most remarkable coup of archival rescue. He himself was soon to put his find to work, in his paper, 'The History of the Art of Pottery in Liverpool', delivered to the Historic Society of Lancashire and Cheshire in May 1855, in which he quoted a number of extracts from Sadler and Green's correspondence with Wedgwood, from the papers 'now in my possession'.[13]

It was quite in character that Mayer should at this point (1852) inaugurate his Egyptian Museum, in which Room 2 contained a display of British pottery, the emphasis being on Liverpool and Wedgwood wares. He may have been encouraged to present ceramics as a subject of study by the appearance of Joseph Marryat's influential *History of Pottery and Porcelain from the Fifteenth to the Eighteenth Centuries* (London, 1850); this was, in English at least, 'one of the earliest descriptive books on Ceramics'.[14] In the same year James Boardman addressed the Liverpool Literary and Philosophical Society on Thomas Bentley.[15] Although a significant portion of this short paper discussed Bentley's partnership with Wedgwood (quoting Marryat), most of it relates to Bentley's Liverpool connections. Boardman also presented a Wedgwood jasper medallion of Bentley to the Society. Mayer may well have felt that such evidence of curiosity in Liverpool about a local figure who was of outstanding importance in the history of Wedgwood would increase interest in his own collection.

A further stimulus may well have come from his acquaintance with A. W. Franks (1826–97), which, following the latter's appointment to the British Museum in 1851, developed into a close collaboration which continued until Mayer's death; as early as 1853 Mayer presented twenty-four pieces of Wedgwood to the British Museum: the first such gift after the receipt of a copy of the Portland Vase in 1802.[16]

By the time of the Art Treasures Exhibition in Manchester in 1857 there could be little doubt that Wedgwood was news. Waring's sumptuous review volume, to which Owen Jones, Digby Wyatt and A. W. Franks all contributed, illustrated eleven items exhibited by Mayer. Among these was a Wedgwood vase:[17] an early example of Wedgwood's work being regarded as 'an artistic treasure'. J. B. Waring, another leading figure in the exhibition, testifies to the serious scholarly interest in Mayer's collection: 'Wyatt is here and anxious to obtain photographs of a few of your things for his essay in Day's work, especially jewellery. Waagen in his new brochure on the Art Treasures Exhibition draws particular attention to your collection.'[18]

Although we know the origin of almost no single item of Mayer's Wedgwood, some evidence has emerged of his sources and methods. Some items were indeed obtained as gifts or casual purchases, occasionally noted on a label stuck on to the specimen. But it is demonstrable that he used his wide circle of friends and acquaintances, notably A. W. Franks and Joseph Clarke of Saffron Walden (1802–95). Clarke is an intriguing figure, a great deal of whose correspondence with Mayer has survived, covering the years 1852 to 1881, and preserved in the Liverpool City Record Office. He was principally an antiquarian, and his understanding of ceramics seems to have been slight: 'Do you know *Turner* as a potter?', he asks Mayer in the course of announcing a striking find; and on another occasion, 'You are quite aware what little judgment I possess in the matter [of pottery].'[19] Clarke was an assiduous pursuer of antiquities and works of art. On one occasion he wrote to Mayer, 'I have hunted Colchester for delf; if you set me to work, I go to it in earnest, I scour the country round.'[20] He regularly obtained items for Mayer, including a notable bone-china tea service painted with a butterfly pattern and gilded, made between 1812 and 1828, one of only three sets said to have been made.[21]

In 1854 Clarke informed Mayer of the momentous discovery of what he called 'the Old Crockery Shop':

> The owner told me he had not been in the rooms for seven years and only once for fourteen and if you had seen me when I came out you would have laughed, no chimney sweep would have been blacker, three washings, I am not clean yet—he says he took the stock fifty years ago and a great deal of it *too old fashioned* to sell then, there are cartloads.[22]

Unfortunately the details of the wares that Clarke packed up and sent to Mayer are often left unrecorded; he states merely that he is sending white ware or brown ware of no specific origin.[23] Therefore some of the pieces he mentions may be early Wedgwood, Whielden or creamware, which Clarke would not recognize as such, or imitations of Wedgwood such as Turner manufactured, which he could have falsely attributed. In 1855 he wrote to Mayer, 'I have purchased for two guineas a complete Wedgwood dessert service of every imaginable shape, the centre-piece a nautilus—and I have found some curious things besides.'[24] This service survives in the Museum's collection.

The wares purchased from the Old Crockery Shop during the later 1850s seem to have been the last extensive group of Wedgwood which Mayer acquired: although Clarke continued to send him pieces and we have some evidence of exchanges of items with his associates over the next two decades, trafficking appears to have been on a smaller scale. This may have been occasioned by the fact that by about 1860, when a number of active collectors started buying Wedgwood, and particularly after the publication of Eliza Meteyard's *Life of Josiah Wedgwood* in 1865, prices rose dramatically and there was a scarcity of interesting pieces. For example, Sir Joseph Hooker, who started collecting about 1862, was in 1863 buying Wedgwood in Paris as well as London,[25] and by 1894 Professor Church observed that 'not only the shops but the private dwellings of France, Germany, Italy, Holland and Belgium have been ransacked by enthusiastic collectors and eager dealers'.[26] Nevertheless, in his long collaboration with Franks, Mayer continued to exchange specimens of all kinds, including Wedgwood, as well as to arrange purchases and sales, not only from their private collections, but, as Mayer intended, from the Museum collections also. Ecroyd Smith reported in 1870, 'About a hundred pieces (duplicate and triplicate) are now placed in reserve for use in possible exchanges.' Surviving records, both in the Museum and in Franks's letters to Mayer in the Liverpool City Record Office, indicate that such exchanges extended from at least 1853 to 1877.[27]

Documentation and discussion

Complementary to the actual specimens was the hoard of papers and documents, described by Meteyard, mostly retained in Mayer's personal collection at Bebington, which transformed his collecting from a cabinet of *objets d'art* into a resource for study. He himself wrote three papers dealing specifically with pottery. The first appeared as early as 1842 and might be seen as a marker of his future intentions, by a successful businessman and already established collector. Having contributed gifts and loans to the Mechanics' Unions in Liverpool and Newcastle-under-Lyme, he not only lent a number of items again in Liverpool, but prepared the catalogue and wrote a twelve-page *Synopsis of the History of the Manufacture of Earthenware* (1842), an account of the history of the subject, and an explanation of its significance, for the general public.[28] Understandably, an encomium on Wedgwood is a prominent feature of the text. Again, Mayer's pioneering historical essay on 'The History of the Art of Pottery in Liverpool' (1855) remains of fundamental importance and was in its day a model of research and scholarship, and a type of study far in advance of its time.[29] Although encouraged by Clarke,[30] it was not until 1871 that Mayer finally published his reflections on ceramics in general (concentrating on ancient pottery) in *On the Art of Pottery*. This is interesting mostly for Mayer's emphasis on materials and techniques of manufacture and for the way it echoes contemporary ideas and values concerning ceramics. In this context Wedgwood receives little more than a cursory reference.

Mayer saw himself primarily, however, as 'an accumulator of material for other men's use';[31] and it is indeed as a patron of scholarship rather than as an author that he is most deserving of admiration. Here his most enduring achievement was the assistance that he gave to Eliza Meteyard (1816–79). Having, as an established author, turned her attention to ceramics and to Wedgwood in particular and undertaken considerable preparatory studies towards a biography of Josiah Wedgwood, Miss Meteyard was introduced to Mayer by Charles Roach Smith.[32] Mayer, who was himself considering writing a life of Wedgwood, not only put at her disposal his invaluable Wedgwood papers, but assisted her financially and offered her first-hand advice, as well as introducing her to members of the Wedgwood family and to his brother, who helped her further: 'Besides intrusting his literary treasures to my care, Mr Mayer kindly permitted me to work for a fortnight under his personal guidance through the more difficult papers, imparted to me many anecdotes, derived from various sources.'[33] The resulting *Life of Josiah Wedgwood* (London, 1865) still remains a fundamental work of Wedgwood scholarship. It was followed in 1871 by another work deriving from Mayer's Wedgwood papers, *A Group of Englishmen* (London); this provoked hostile criticism from the Wedgwood family, to which Meteyard responded with a vigorous defence of Mayer.[34] Of the four further works on Wedgwood which she published, two gave prominence to Mayer and his collection: *The Wedgwood Handbook* (London, 1875) contained numerous references and *Wedgwood and His Works* (London, 1873), principally consisting of twenty-eight plates, included nineteen items from the Mayer Collection in the Liverpool Museum.[35] The majority of these were plaques, which have not survived, and of the remainder not more than six items can with any assurance be identified in the Museum's collection today. Eliza Meteyard's will stipulated that her personal papers were to be bequeathed to Liverpool Museum but this was not undertaken by her executors.[36]

1867–1941

The collection's subsequent history as a public institution is one mostly of attempts to put it into systematic order and adequately to record it, as well as to improve the arrangements for its display and study. It continued to be developed by exchange, and by the addition of further gifts from Joseph Mayer; among the more notable of these were, in 1868, no less than 2,371 medallions and other small objects, in 1869, a punch bowl of the Etruscan Lodge No. 327, at the Bridge Inn, Etruria, of which only one other similar example is known,[37] and, in 1873, twenty dies for black basalte wares of the Wedgwood and Bentley period.[38] Henry Ecroyd Smith (1823–89), the first curator, it appears now in retrospect carried out a remarkable job between 1867 and 1872, when ill-health and subsequently his resignation brought his work to an end. He listed the entire collection in a series of ledgers, and allocated a number to every specimen. The Wedgwood holdings occupied him from August 1869 until November 1870, when he reported, 'The whole of our large exhibited stock of Wedgwood ware is now inventoried and described for the Public by label.'[39] In the course of his work he was assisted by a number of well-informed visitors who examined the collection, as well as the ever-ready presence of Mayer. Among the helpful visitors were A. W. Franks, Llewellyn Jewitt, Henry Willett and Eliza Meteyard. From this time on, the Wedgwood Collection became increasingly known by references to examples in the growing body of ceramic literature, as well as its display in the Museum and in loan exhibitions. Of the latter, two must be mentioned; in 1869, 470 of the finest pieces, carefully selected under Mayer's supervision, were exhibited at the Wedgwood Institute, Burslem, and in 1879 occurred the Liverpool Art Club's exhibition of the works of Josiah Wedgwood. This was an outstanding event of its kind, and the catalogue remains of lasting significance in the study of the subject. The Liverpool Museum lent a large proportion of the exhibits, and the organization of the exhibition and preparation of the catalogue were the work of Charles Gatty, who had succeeded Henry Ecroyd Smith in 1872–3.

Liverpool Museum owes an enormous debt to Gatty for his contribution to the care of the Mayer Collection. With the advice of A. W. Franks, he rapidly introduced new systems of cataloguing and documentation. His findings appeared between 1879 and 1883 in four valuable catalogues, which covered the greater part of the collection, mostly up to the late middle ages, but no modern ceramics. Gatty did not neglect the Wedgwood Collection nor did he lack interest in the subject. Not only was he largely responsible for the incomparable 1879 exhibition: in the same year major improvements to the display of Wedgwood were carried out, and he was involved in other Wedgwood loan exhibitions. Of one such, in 1875 (presumably the Yorkshire Exhibition of Arts and Manufacture, Leeds), he wrote to Mayer, 'I am not very well being so knocked up with the Wedgwoods.'[40] In 1879 he reported that he was preparing a catalogue of the pottery and porcelain. No evidence of the work has come to light in the Museum's archives: no records seem to exist in Gatty's catalogue format. In 1879 also it was proposed that Gatty should complete the revised edition of Meteyard's *Life of Josiah Wedgwood* left unfinished at her death, but the executors did not proceed with this.[41] Gatty also improved and enlarged the collection, with exchanges and sales of duplicates (sometimes with Franks's help) from 1874, and by personal negotiation: writing to Mayer in 1878, for instance, 'I am so anxious about our sets of intaglios being complete with Wedgwood's Catalogue, that I hope you will not let your *bulk* of small black ones go unless I have seen them', and in the same letter, regarding Godfrey Wedgwood, 'I spent the best part of a day at Wedgwoods and I found all the brothers extremely kind and very useful. They have agreed to provide me with a cast in biscuit of every portrait mould in the factory! and the numbers on them, which will simply enable me to identify most portraits.'[42] Unfortunately, apart from a minute in the reports, no trace or record of these casts can be found in the Museum today. When, in 1884, Gatty resigned, nearly all this work came to an end. Nor was the collection augmented, after Mayer's death, by the Wedgwood in his personal collection, as he himself had hoped: the opportunity to purchase was declined by the City Council.[43]

The collection today

There is one invaluable indirect source of published information about the Wedgwood Collection, the Liverpool Art Club Exhibition Catalogue, *Loan Exhibition of the Works of Josiah Wedgwood* (Liverpool, 1879). The exhibition contained 1,491 exhibits, comprising possibly as many as 2,000 single items, of these a third or more from the Mayer Collection. The catalogue is a model of scholarship. In compiling it, Charles Gatty was one of the first to utilize the early literature of the subject by Meteyard, Jewitt and Chaffers, as well as his own pioneering research. This catalogue is the obvious starting point in putting Mayer's Wedgwood and its documentation in order, since it contains the most important account of a substantial part of the collection. The Museum has the first issue of the catalogue, with extensive annotations that are almost certainly Gatty's own, and the second issue, which has a revised text and many illustrations, again extensively annotated by Gatty. These and Ecroyd Smith's inventory are the best first-hand accounts of the collection.

Of the 1,491 exhibits, 1,112 items relate to cameos and medals. This testifies to the value and esteem they enjoyed in the nineteenth century, and to the pre-eminence of Mayer's collection in this respect; a view Miss Meteyard touched on more than once, also mentioning the hundreds of trial pieces in the Mayer Museum.[44] This is an area in which the Museum is now almost totally deficient: a few items only survive, with no identifiable marks or numbers. The one exception is a group of 542 small classical cameos, in white biscuit, and certainly Wedgwood; these too bear no collection marks or numbers. Coincidentally, the 1879 Exhibition Catalogue, following that of Wedgwood, started with this very class, and all 108 exhibits came from the Mayer Collection. It seems clear that up to about fifty of these, or identical examples, were included in the 1879 exhibition. The Museum's inventory of the plaques, medals and intaglios is concentrated mostly in three ledgers, occupying many pages: its descriptions are inconclusive, with some confusion and discrepancies, with varying amounts of detail. At one point Ecroyd Smith seems to have given up writing entries in full: since he appears to have been transcribing directly from a Wedgwood catalogue (probably the copy printed in Liverpool in 1817), this is understandable. It has therefore not been possible precisely to identify these cameos amongst the thousand or so entries, comprising possibly 15,000 specimens, in the inventory—virtually all now lost. The next group in the 1879 Catalogue is intaglios, and at least a third of the 350 items exhibited was from the Mayer Collection, but none now remain; neither do the 450 or so of the next 636 exhibits, except possibly for a handful of less than a dozen, yet to be identified as Mayer pieces. These are all portrait medallions, and it is to be the more regretted as the Mayer examples appear to have been in some respects unique.

Only a small proportion of the remaining exhibits came from the Mayer Collection: its dominance in representing plaques, medallions and cameos demonstrates how outstanding Mayer's collection was in this field (predictably so, perhaps, in his profession as a jeweller) and how serious its almost total destruction was. These other exhibits comprised decorative and useful wares, mostly what we would call show-pieces. The fifty-four Mayer items included some outstanding surviving examples, such as the Museum's Portland Vase (M 2827), a 'Stella' vase (M 2940), a presentation creamware enamelled cup and saucer (M 2768: pl. LIX*a*), the Nautilus Service (M 3076) and seven encaustic decorated black basalte vases (including M 2984 and M 2989); altogether, about twenty-three items appear to be still extant.[45]

The industrial arts

Mayer's zeal for collecting—in which Wedgwood is one of the steadiest elements throughout his life—accords with his conception of himself: not as a mere tradesman and supplier, but as a cultivator and promoter of the industrial arts, a designer, collector, student and patron. In all his activities one senses a conviction of their artistic and social value, and a patriotic sense of the importance of fostering them to the well-being of his country and his adopted town.

One of Mayer's purposes—if not his principal purpose—in collecting ceramics was to demonstrate the history and development of the art of pottery; underlying it was the concept of progress in the arts. A clear line of descent was seen, in European ceramics, from the pioneering achievements of Palissy, 'The Huguenot Potter' and hero of Samuel Smiles, to Josiah Wedgwood. In Mayer's words, 'Pottery has been a craft steadily progressive from the first', to which he added, 'so might it justly be told of Wedgwood that he found pottery a handicraft in England, and he left it a fine art.'[46] Thus he valued his ceramic collection—not only as an archaeologist, who understood the primacy of pottery wares in studying and judging civilizations—but as a practical craftsman. As Gatty put it, 'Here the traditions of hundreds of years are preserved, and the skilful workman may study the materials, forms, and decorations which have stood the test of time.' In Gatty's words again, 'Here . . . is one of the educational uses of the Mayer Collection; it has assisted modern research, and taken an honourable place in recent art and archaeological literature.'[47] But equal emphasis was given to a more practical educational value: acquiring standards of artistic excellence in manufacture from a study of the past. 'Nine-tenths of the best shapes now used in earthenware, jewellery, and general ornamentation, have been recovered . . . from the ruins of former civilization . . . If a modern school . . . of pure design should ever rise—as all must hope—the boon will be mostly owing to the dissemination, among all classes, of the unrivalled art of Greece and Etruria';[48] and 'Wedgwood applied chemistry to the improvement of the material of his pottery, sought the most beautiful and convenient specimens of antiquity, and caused them to be imitated with scrupulous nicety.'[49] Thus the ceramics collection as a whole, but specifically the Wedgwood, laid emphasis on utility, on the role of classical culture in ornamental design, and the collector's own moral duty to enlighten the ordinary public.

APPENDIX: THE ILLUSTRATED WEDGWOOD

The illustrations have been selected to show as wide a range as possible of the types of wares in Mayer's Wedgwood collection. Most of the ceramic bodies improved or introduced by Josiah Wedgwood are included: Queensware, jasper, black basalte, *antico rosso* and cane-ware, and also an example of painted earthenware, made for the decoration of buildings. There are a few regrettable omissions, for example, Wedgwood's creamware is represented only by an exceptional item, and no variegated wares are shown, in part because there are fewer surviving examples, although some outstanding pieces remain. The early Wedgwood-Whielden earthenwares, little appreciated in the nineteenth century, appear not to have been acquired to any extent by Mayer, nor to have been recorded as such. The 1879 exhibition, compiled on the basis of Wedgwood's published catalogue, included only a small selection of such types, as a supplement. Of the twenty-nine exhibits, four were from the Mayer Collection: one Wedgwood pearlware (the Nautilus Service, M 3076), one of Liverpool-printed delft tiles, and two of creamware—possibly Wedgwood-Whielden.

M 2768: *cup and saucer*; enamel-painted creamware, 1772–80 (pl. LIXa).
Cup 50 mm. high, saucer diameter 120 mm. Cup incised 'C', saucer impressed 'O'.
    The cup and saucer are associated with the Imperial Russian Dinner and Dessert Service executed 1773–4 for the Empress Catherine II: the so-called 'Frog' Service, each piece bearing as a crest a small green frog. Unlike the Frog Service, in which the landscape decoration is painted in a deep mulberry colour, they are decorated throughout in colours, and are part of a small group of such pieces. It is not known what their purpose was: they may possibly have been early trial pieces for the Russian service; alternatively it has been suggested that they were made for presentation to friends of Josiah Wedgwood—we do know that he ordered extra finely decorated examples to be made for display in his London showrooms. G. Woolliscroft Rhead states that a small tea service without the frog was executed, citing the Mayer Collection example, but giving no evidence.
    They were painted at Wedgwood's Chelsea Decorating Studio; the views depict, on the saucer, Stoke Gifford, around the cup a Yorkshire scene and inside the cup the Mausoleum at Castle Howard. (Liverpool Museum also possesses a plate from the 'Frog' Service, numbered 114 (accession number 12–30–24–2).)

M 1169: *clock-case*; jasper, dark blue dip over white, *c.* 1802 (pl. LIXb).
Height 478 mm., width 432 mm. Unmarked.
    The design of the clock symbolizes *Peace Destroying the Accoutrements of War*. It was possibly intended to commemorate the short-lived Peace of Amiens of March 1802, and made to take a clock of French calibre. It was perhaps aimed at the French market, with which its style is consistent. The base portion, however, is incomplete and it is clear that it was never put into production. In 1786 Josiah Wedgwood referred to a design of this character by John Flaxman, but the execution of the clock-case is more consistent with an attribution to Henry Webber.

M 2855–56: *two statuettes, Mars and Venus with Cupid*; white jasper, *c.* 1785 (pl. LXa, b).
Mars 165 mm. high, Venus 160 mm. high. Mars with impressed WEDGWOOD mark, Venus unmarked.
    These small figures appeared amongst Wedgwood's limited output of figure subjects in his 1787 catalogue. They are obviously meant to be companion figures, though differing slightly in concept and execution; moreover, the base of the Venus was built up at the repairing stage, presumably to bring it to the same height as the Mars. They are probably reductions from figures supplied by John Bacon in 1769; he exhibited a Statue of Mars at the 1771 Royal Academy exhibition (no. 3), and a model statue of Venus (no. 7) in 1775.

The Venus is the more distinguished and classical in style and is (apart from the position of the arms) very similar to a seventeenth-century Venetian bronze statuette of Amphitrite (Sotheby Parke Bernet Monaco, 1986, no. 308), although the general treatment is closer to the manner of eighteenth-century terracottas after Duquesnoy's marble statues of female saints. The dating of Wedgwood's catalogue entry precludes its being identified with a plaster modello of Venus and Cupid exhibited at the Royal Academy by John Flaxman in 1787 (no. 655). Both these pieces are crazed in the firing and entered Mayer's collection in a damaged state, suggesting perhaps that they were trial pieces and amongst the items acquired from Wedderburne.

M 2987: *oinochoe (wine jug)*; encaustic-painted black basalte, *c.* 1780–95 (pl. LXI*a*). Height 265 mm. Impressed WEDGWOOD.

Apart from the attractiveness of the medium in itself, the appeal of this jug lies to a large extent in Wedgwood's adaptation of the original Greek shape. It is of the class he described as 'Etruscan Vases', claiming them to have been 'copied from the Antique with the utmost exactness'. The decoration, with a motif of votive figures, was very probably drawn from d'Hancarville's *Antiquités*.

M 3003: *inkstandish*; *antico rosso*, applied with black basalte relief decoration, *c.* 1790–1820 (pl. LXI*b*). Length 300 mm. Impressed WEDGWOOD.

From the 1770s onward Josiah Wedgwood manufactured objects in the Egyptian taste, mostly in jasper and black basalte; with the heightened interest in Egypt following the campaigns of the Napoleonic wars, Josiah II continued and expanded their production. Although much more accurate information was by then available—eminently in Vivant Denon's *Voyage* of 1802—the older type of production continued: often, as here, with a *mélange* of Greek and Egyptian motifs arbitrarily applied.

Josiah Wedgwood had to be persuaded by Bentley, who presumably had in mind classical red-bodied wares, to employ *antico rosso* for other than useful wares, but it was much later that this very satisfying combination of black basalte with the *antico rosso* was adopted.

M 2914: *'broken column' vase*; caneware, *c.* 1786–1800 (pl. LXII*a*). Height 200 mm. Impressed WEDGWOOD.

Wedgwood did not succeed in making a practicable caneware until about 1786. This design (shape no. 566), previously made in blue and white jasper, clearly is ideally suited to the caneware body: its modelling has been attributed to William Keeling (*fl.* 1763–90).

The concept of this seemingly minor piece of decoration touches a deep chord in eighteenth-century sensibilities, evoking ideas about the rediscovery of the classical world, death in Arcadia, the melancholy of ruins and the passage of time; the symbols of decay and the broken column (with its masonic echoes) and the picturesque landscape. Looking back to such works as the engravings of Piranesi, the paintings of Hubert Robert and the buildings of the Désert de Retz, it also foreshadows early nineteenth-century romanticism.

M 2945: *architectural plaque, depicting a bacchanalian figure*; white earthenware, with glazed figure in relief against a painted ground, *c.* 1771–1800 (pl. LXII*b*). Diameter 392 mm. Unmarked.

Josiah Wedgwood, in his 1773 Catalogue, listed more than forty plaques and medallions, in jasper and black basalte and terracotta, intended for wall decoration. This plaque, of the type believed to have been supplied to Robert and James Adam about 1772, is one of a series designed for installing into wall surfaces as part of the scheme of decoration of large halls and staircases. Thirteen of the fourteen subjects in the series are derived from paintings of

PLATE LIX

a. Enamel-painted creamware cup and saucer, 1772–80 (cup: height 50 mm.; saucer: diam. 120 mm.) (M 2768)

b. Jasper clock-case, *c.* 1802 (height 478 mm.) (M 1169)

Wedgwood

PLATE LX

a   *b*

White jasper statuettes of (*a*) Mars and (*b*) Venus, *c.* 1785 (height 165 mm., 160 mm.) (M2855, 2856)

Wedgwood

Reproduced by courtesy of NMGM

PLATE LXI

b. *Antico rosso* inkstandish, *c.* 1790–1820 (length 300 mm.) (M 3003)

Wedgwood

Reproduced by courtesy of NMGM

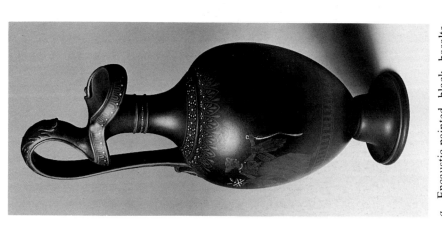

a. Encaustic-painted black basalte *oinochoe*, *c.* 1780–95 (height 265 mm.) (M 2987)

PLATE LXII

b. White earthenware architectural plaque depicting a bacchanalian figure, *c.* 1771–1800 (diam. 392 mm.) (M 2945)

Wedgwood

Reproduced by courtesy of NMGM

a. Caneware broken column vase, *c.* 1786–1800 (height 200 mm.) (M 2914)

dancing figures in the Villa dei Papyri at Herculaneum. These 'Herculaneum Nymphs' were well known from various antiquarian publications in the later eighteenth century. Wedgwood's versions, however, were not made from engravings but cast in 1770 (by Hoskins and Oliver) directly from bas-relief versions made for the Marquis of Lansdowne.

NOTES

* Acknowledgements for advice and help in the preparation of this account are due, amongst others, to Liverpool City Libraries (and especially Mrs N. Evetts, in cataloguing the Mayer papers), to Robin Reilly, J. K. des Fontaines, and Elizabeth Edwards for permission to refer to her undergraduate dissertation, prepared on the basis of study in the Decorative Art Department of Liverpool Museum.

[1] B. and H. Wedgwood, *The Wedgwood Circle 1730–1897* (London, 1980), 300, Eliza Meteyard to Emma Darwin, 3 May 1871.

[2] Liverpool Museum, Department of Decorative Art, J. Clarke to C. T. Gatty, 3 Feb. 1875.

[3] Nicholson and Warhurst, 2.

[4] *Ibid.*, 3, 6 and 8.

[5] P. F. Hugues, called d'Hancarville, *Antiquités Etrusques, Grecques et Romaines*, 5 vols. (Paris, 1785).

[6] E. Meteyard, *Wedgwood and his Works: a Selection of his Plaques, Cameos, Medallions, Vases etc. from the Designs of Flaxman and Others* (London, 1873), pl. XXIII.i.

[7] The surviving identifiable specimens bear the following Mayer collection numbers: on the right the encaustic-painted basalte vase is probably M 2989 and the candelabrum M 2854. Upon the cabinet, the vase seems to be either M 2985 or 2986 and the *oinochoe* M 2987 (pl. LXIa), the plinth probably M 2849, and the vase in Mayer's hand M 2763.

[8] E. Edwards, 'Joseph Mayer's collection of Wedgwood' (University of Liverpool unpubl. B. A. diss., 1985), 19 sqq.; Wedgwood, *op. cit.* (note 1), 242–3. John Boyle (*ob.* 1845), son of Zachariah Boyle of Stoke-on-Trent, had taken out a partnership in Josiah Wedgwood & Sons in 1843.

[9] C. T. Gatty, *The Mayer Collection in the Liverpool Museum considered as an Educational Possession*, Liverpool Art Club (Liverpool, 1878), 20–1.

[10] *Ibid.*, 21.

[11] M 2851 (Triton candlestick) and M 2827 (Portland Vase). For an account of the varying states of the Portland Vase see A. Dawson, *Masterpieces of Wedgwood in the British Museum* (London, 1984), 119–25.

[12] E. Meteyard, *The Life of Josiah Wedgwood*, 2 vols. (London, 1865), I, x; Wedgwood, *op. cit.* (note 1), 272, summarizing E. Meteyard, *A Group of Englishmen* (London, 1871), x–xiii.

[13] JM, 'The history of the art of pottery in Liverpool', *THSLC*, vii (1855), 178–210 (revised edn., Liverpool, 1873). These manuscripts never entered the Museum's collection, but remained with Mayer, to be sold after his death. They were purchased by Godfrey Wedgwood and eventually found their way to their present home, at Keele University.

[14] U. des Fontaines, 'The Wedgwood collection of Sir Joseph Dalton Hooker', *Proc. Wedgwood Soc.*, vii (1968), 179–80.

[15] J. Boardman, *Bentleyana: or, A Memoir of Thomas Bentley, sometime of Liverpool, with Extracts from his Correspondence* (Liverpool, 1851).

[16] Dawson, *op. cit.* (note 11), 7; H. Tait, 'The Wedgwood Collection in the British Museum II', *Proc. Wedgwood Soc.*, v (1963), 32–3. However, R. L. Hobson, *Catalogue of the English Pottery in the British Museum* (London, 1903), lists only twenty-one such pieces.

[17] J. B. Waring, *Art Treasures of the United Kingdom from the Art Treasures Exhibition, Manchester* (London, 1858), 'Ceramic Art', 31.

[18] Liverpool Museum, Waring to JM, 5 Aug. 1857. Waagen observed to Mayer on 18 August 1856 (MPL): 'I am telling to all my people of the importance of your great collection.' His complimentary tone may have been conditioned by his seeking, in the same letter, to obtain a substantial loan from Mayer. Mayer's collection is not referred to at all in G. F. Waagen's *Treasures of Art in Great Britain*, 3 vols. and suppl. (London, 1854–7), III, 229–42 (visit to Liverpool).

[19] MPL, Clarke to JM, 19 Oct. and 4 Nov. 1854.

[20] MPL, Clarke to JM, Oct, 1854.

[21] M 3110, probably pattern no. 591; cf. Edwards, *op. cit.* (note 8), 18.

[22] MPL, Clarke to JM, 19 Oct. 1854.

23 Edwards, *op. cit.* (note 8), 17.
24 MPL, Clarke to JM, 7 July 1855. The Nautilus Dessert Service is M 3076; cf. Edwards, *op. cit.* (note 8), 18.
25 des Fontaines, *op. cit.* (note 14), 165.
26 A. H. Church, 'Josiah Wedgwood, Master Potter', *The Portfolio*, iii (Mar. 1894), 100.
27 Liverpool Museum, Department of Antiquities, Guard Book I, 80; cf. *ibid.*, 87.
28 JM, *A Synopsis of the History of the Manufacture of Earthenware; with Reference to the Specimens in the Exhibition of the Liverpool Mechanics' Institution, 1842* (Liverpool, 1842) (text only, no catalogue entries).
29 JM, *op. cit.* (note 13), 178–210.
30 MPL, Clarke to JM, 31 July 1855.
31 MPL, JM to J. A. Picton, 4 Feb. 1867.
32 J. B. Smith, 'The early biographers of Josiah Wedgwood', *Proc. Wedgwood Soc.*, iv (1961), 232–44.
33 Meteyard, *op. cit.* (note 12), I, xiv.
34 Letter to Emma Darwin, 1871, *op. cit.* (note 1).
35 Meteyard, *op. cit.* (note 6), pls. III, V, VI, IX-XI, XIII, XX, XXII-XXIII, XXV, XXVII.
36 Some are deposited at Swiss Cottage Library, London Borough of Camden.
37 Liverpool Museum 11.9.68.5. The comparable piece is in a private collection in the U.S.A.
38 Liverpool Museum, *Annual Rep.* (Liverpool, 1868, 1869 and 1873).
39 Liverpool Museum, MS, H. Ecroyd Smith, 'Report of Progress'.
40 MPL, C. T. Gatty to JM, 25 Feb. 1875.
41 The idea was revived by Godfrey Wedgwood *c.* 1890, but eventually taken up by Samuel Smiles: Smith, *op. cit.* (note 32), 241.
42 MPL, C. T. Gatty to JM, 2 Mar. 1878.
43 Nicholson and Warhurst, 10; Liverpool Museum, *Annual Rep.* (1886); Edwards, *op. cit.* (note 8), 28.
44 E. Meteyard, *The Wedgwood Handbook* (London, 1875), 69.
45 It requires more detailed study to be certain, rendered more difficult because only three are illustrated, although references are given to nine other illustrations elsewhere; the investigation is still in progress.
46 JM, *On the Art of Pottery* (Liverpool, 1871), 3 and 39.
47 Gatty, *op. cit.* (note 9), 23.
48 JM, 'Presidential Address 9 May 1867', *THSLC*, new ser. vii (1868–9), 3.
49 Gatty, *op. cit.* (note 9), 30–1.
50 P. F. Hugues, *op. cit.* (note 5).

Napoleonic Memorabilia

Irene Collins

There is a good deal of mystery as to when and where Joseph Mayer acquired the collection of Napoleonic memorabilia which he subsequently sold to John Mather, merchant, of 58 Mount Pleasant.[1] The *Liverpool Chronicle*, reporting on an exhibition of the objects in 1854, described the whole collection as having 'previously belonged to the Bonaparte family'.[2] Mayer himself claimed that some of the items (a set of jewellery, a snuff-box lined with gold) had previously belonged to the Empress Josephine, and that others (a signet ring, a snuff-box set with precious stones) had once belonged to Napoleon; but he never said by what route they had reached him.[3] He claimed that one of the miniatures (a portrait of Napoleon's father) had belonged to Louis Napoleon in the days before the latter became Emperor Napoleon III, and that another (of Napoleon in robes of state) had come from the collection of the Emperor's uncle, Cardinal Fesch; but his friend Joseph Clarke told Charles Gatty, in a letter dated 3 February 1875, that all the miniatures had been bought from Louis Napoleon. Clarke remembered seeing them shortly after they were purchased, looking 'resplendent'; Louis Napoleon, he wrote, would have liked to have bought them back again, but they had been 're-sold to Mr Mather for £3,000'.[4]

The first exhibition of Mayer's 'drawings, miniatures, cameos and other objects of art illustrative of the Bonaparte family and the principal persons connected with the Republic and Empire of France' was held at the Philharmonic Hall, Liverpool, on 27 September 1854 as one of the attractions at a soirée given by the Historic Society of Lancashire and Cheshire to the British Association.[5] The collection had by then been sold to Mather, but Mayer retained sufficient interest in it to draw up a catalogue with an accompanying essay on the events of the period. 1,500 copies of the publication were placed on chairs for the visitors.[6] Eighty-nine items were listed, though no more than sixty-eight could truly be said to have illustrated the period of the French Revolution and Empire (the rest included such gems as miniatures of Henrietta Stuart, by Petitot; Georgiana Duchess of Devonshire, by Hone; and Mrs Jordan the actress, by Cosway). The inaccuracy of the title to the exhibition seems to have passed unnoticed in the general acclaim accorded to the exhibits themselves.[7]

A similar exhibition was mounted during the following year at a soirée given in the Town Hall by the Mayor of Liverpool, James Aspinall Tobin, in honour of the victories gained by Britain, France and Sardinia in the Crimean War. A new catalogue was drawn up, listing 104 items, of which about eighty could be described as relevant to the title.[8] They included a number of dazzling objects which had not been mentioned before, notably a Pistrucci cameo and a brooch and breast-pin containing locks of Napoleon's hair. Another acquisition not mentioned before was 'a series of gold, silver and bronze medals illustrative of the principal events of the life of Napoleon the Great'.

Nothing more was heard of the collection until it arrived in the Liverpool Museum in November 1872. John Mather had stated in his will, made in 1863, that the collection was to remain in the possession of his sister during her lifetime, and upon her death was to pass to the Mayor and Corporation of Liverpool for the benefit of the public. The inventory drawn up by the executors was a curious document, listing thirty-five items (all miniatures), but with gaps in the numbering so that the final figure was eighty-one.[9] A catalogue published by the Museum in 1874 was soon out of print.[10] When Gatty made a definitive catalogue in 1883 the collection consisted of thirty-seven miniatures, six snuff-boxes (four of which were mounted with miniatures), eleven miscellaneous objects and 147 medals, all genuinely relating to Napoleon and his family.[11] Gatty also listed a further eight Napoleonic keepsakes, none of which had come from Mather but some of which are known to have belonged at one time or another to Mayer. They included a chair, said to have been used by Napoleon at St Helena and given to Mayer in 1860 by Miss H. W. Barber, a friend of W. H. Rolfe, whose Anglo-Saxon antiquities Mayer had bought three years earlier. It had been given to her by a much-loved cousin who had served in the Royal Navy, and she hoped that by placing it in Mayer's Museum alongside Rolfe's collection she would secure a mention of it in Mayer's projected publication.[12] Unhappily, the chair has gone missing, as have several Mayer items bequeathed by Mather, including a gold ring set with a sardonyx cameo of Napoleon, and a gold snuff-box ornamented with diamonds and lapis lazuli and set with a cameo carved by the great Italian craftsman Morelli. The box and the ring are said to have been gifts from Napoleon and Marie-Louise to Marshal Ney and his wife. Public attention was drawn to them when they were exhibited at the Town Hall during a visit by King Edward VII and Queen Alexandra to Liverpool in July 1904, and they were stolen from the Liverpool Museum shortly afterwards.[13]

Miniatures

Mayer confidently identified all but one of the miniatures in his collection—a delightful portrait of a lady with brown eyes and brown hair curling on to her right shoulder. She is seated, with forearms resting one on top of the other, and wearing a white muslin high-waisted dress and a white lace-trimmed turban with the folds falling on to her left shoulder (4.9.73.41; ivory, 66 mm. diameter, signed and dated 'J. Isabey 1804' on the right: pl. LXIIIa). Some of the identifications now seem dubious, but they were obviously made in good faith. No-one questioned them in 1854 when the miniatures were viewed by several hundred members of the British Association, and the details given by Mayer on that occasion were repeated by Gatty when he catalogued the Mather bequest in 1883.

No self-respecting collector of Napoleonic miniatures could have afforded to be without examples of the work of the three most fashionable artists of the period: Jean-Baptiste Isabey, Jean-Baptiste-Jacques Augustin and Daniel Saint. Mayer acquired no fewer than five miniatures signed by Isabey, two signed by Augustin and one by Saint. In addition to the portrait of the unknown lady, the Isabeys include two portraits of Napoleon: a handsome picture of him as Emperor, in state robes and an ermine cape with the grand collar of the Legion of Honour, and on his head an elegant version of the crown of golden laurels (4.9.73.18; ivory, 57 × 37 mm., signed 'Isabey' vertically on the right: pl. LXIIIb) and another done some years later when his features were flabbier and his hair thinner, in which he wears the blue and white uniform of a colonel of the *grenadiers à pied* of the Guard, with the cross, badge and ribbon of the Legion of Honour and the cross of the Order of the Iron Crown (4.9.73.27; ivory, 53 × 38 mm., signed 'Isabey' vertically on the right). Mayer said that this last miniature was 'painted by Isaby [*sic*] at Elba', but this cannot have been the case, since Isabey was occupied at the Congress of Vienna during the nine months Napoleon spent in exile on the island. The remaining two miniatures signed by the great artist are less easily identified. Mayer believed the young lady in a white gown embroidered with golden bees and with a coronet of roses on her head (4.9.73.21; ivory, 88 × 72 mm., signed 'J. Isabey' horizontally on the right) to be Marie-Louise, and the middle-aged gentleman in a blue uniform with a high collar (4.9.73.9; ivory, 70 × 54 mm., signed 'Isabey' vertically on the right) to be Napoleon's stepson Eugène Beauharnais, painted some years after the fall of the Empire; but the first bears more resemblance to Napoleon's step-daughter Hortense, Queen of Holland, than to Marie-Louise and the second, though not unlike Eugène as to features, is puzzling in that the uniform carries no decorations.[14]

Mayer believed that three other miniatures in his collection were also painted by Isabey, though they are not signed. He named the sitters as Murat, King of Naples, Napoleon's brother-in-law (4.9.73.36; ivory, 38 × 28 mm.), Lucien Bonaparte, Napoleon's younger brother (4.9.73.29; ivory, 63 × 54 mm.), and François-Charles, King of Rome, Napoleon's little son (4.9.73.25; ivory, 40 × 32 mm.). The first is undoubtedly Murat, whose swashbuckling appearance, with or without moustachios, attracted many artists.[15] The young man in a blue jacket and white stock is not Lucien, and the cheeky urchin with light brown hair, white blouse and blue girdle is probably not the King of Rome, but both miniatures are of good quality and altogether charming. It is a pity that a miniature of the King of Rome by the excellent Swiss artist Constantin has gone missing.[16]

The work of Isabey's chief rival, Augustin, is represented by two miniatures: one of Princess Catherine of Würtemberg at the time of her marriage with Napoleon's youngest brother Jerome (4.9.73.83; ivory, 50 × 40 mm., mounted in gold on the lid of a snuff-box, signed and dated 'Augustin 1808' on the left: pl. LXIIIc),[17] and the other of a young lady in a white dress with a white band in her brown hair (4.9.73.22; ivory, 58 mm. diameter, signed 'Augustin' vertically on the left) believed by Mayer to be Marie-Louise.[18] Both ladies have the cheerful expression which Augustin was noted for giving his female sitters. The second is again not very like known portraits of Marie-Louise and should perhaps be considered that of a more attractive lady. A third miniature in the collection may also have been the work of Augustin, or at least have emanated from his studio. It shows Jerome Bonaparte, King of Westphalia, wearing the white dress uniform of the Westphalian infantry and the red ribbon, star and badge of the Grand Eagle of the Legion of Honour (4.9.73.31; ivory, 54 × 40 mm.) and was probably painted at the time of his marriage.[19]

The only work by Saint is a portrait of Josephine, wearing a white dress and an elaborate coronet of pearls (4.9.73.12; ivory, 38 × 28 mm., signed *Saint* on the left). Saint usually produced several versions of his paintings, to the infinite confusion of collectors. Replicas of his work were also made by other artists: a portrait of Josephine against a dark red curtain (4.9.73.17; ivory, mounted on the lid of a snuff-box, signed and dated 'I.P. 1813') which we find in Mayer's collection is an adaptation of a popular portrait by Saint in which the curtain is dark green. The signature 'I.P.' probably stands for J. Parent, a competent but humdrum artist who worked prolifically in Paris during the last years of the Empire.

There were several other miniature painters of the period whose work sometimes equalled that of the established favourites. Two such artists were Giovanni Battista Gigola and Nicolas-François Dun. The Italian Gigola, after working for some years in Paris with Isabey, settled in Milan and developed a pleasing style of his own. His portrait of his patron, the twenty-four-year-old Eugène Beauharnais, Viceroy of Italy (4.9.73.8; ivory, 48 × 30 mm., signed 'Gigola': pl. LXIIId) is one of the gems of Mayer's collection. It shows the young man wearing a turquoise jacket, white ruff and cravat, with a broad orange ribbon and the grand collar of the Legion of Honour (second type). The lips are slightly parted, but they do not smile, and the expression is one of slight wonderment. Nicolas Dun was born in France but worked for most of his life in Naples. His painting of a mature lady in a highly picturesque costume— white dress with bronze ribbon, pink shawl, and yellow and blue fringed scarf worn like a turban round the head (4.9.73.2; ivory, 64 × 50 mm., signed 'Dun')—stands out from the rest of the collection because of its clear, almost luminous pastel shades and the carmine colouring of the face. Mayer believed it to be a portrait of Napoleon's mother, 'Madame Mère'. The strong, handsome features here represented would have done justice to that formidable lady, but they are not very much like those of other portraits of her, and the identification must be considered doubtful. The painting probably dates from the late eighteenth century when this artist was producing his best work.

Other miniatures in the collection are not without merit. A portrait of Josephine wearing an unusual dress, royal blue with a large white stand-up frill (4.9.73.11; ivory, 58 × 40 mm.) and one of Caroline, Queen of Naples (Napoleon's sister and the wife of Murat), wearing a pale blue dress and an extravagant suite of sapphires and diamonds (4.9.73.33; ivory, mounted in gold on the lid of a snuff-box) are probably by (or after) Louis-François Aubry, an assistant of Isabey and a well-known teacher of art.[20] Felicity Varlet, whose large miniatures were exhibited in the salons of the Restoration, was noted for the soft outlines she gave to the face and for her skilful treatment of hair; an attractive water-colour of a young lady in a pale blue chiffon dress with cornflowers in her hair (4.9.73.30; 136 × 70 mm., signed and dated 'Felicia Varlet, 1822') was identified by Mayer as Hortense Beauharnais, sometime Queen of Holland, Napoleon's stepdaughter and the wife of his brother Louis. A portrait of Napoleon's scandalous niece Letitia, daughter of Lucien, in a dark blue off-the-shoulder dress and wearing a high tortoiseshell comb in her hair (4.9.73.30; 133 × 111 mm., signed 'Herman 1832') is almost certainly the one which her father-in-law, Sir Thomas Wyse, saw exhibited in the window of an artist's shop in Boulogne in 1832 and tried to buy for propriety's sake.[21] It has been suggested that Herman was an Englishman, but little is known about him; he was described by Schidlof as 'a good artist of the second order'.[22] Sophie Lienard was recognized in Paris in the 1840s as a skilful painter on porcelain; her portraits of Josephine and of

Napoleon's son in early manhood (4.9.73.16 and 26) are both in this medium and are probably based on originals by Isabey.

The miniature which Mayer apparently regarded as the prize of his collection creates something of a problem (4.9.73.1). Mayer said that it had once belonged to Louis-Napoleon and that it was the only known portrait of Charles Bonaparte, Napoleon's father. It has a handsome gilt frame with the name 'Charles Bonaparte' inscribed on the mount. Carlo Buonaparte, a lawyer at Ajaccio, died at the age of thirty-nine, many years before his son became famous. It stands to reason that there were few portraits of him. By the time Mayer composed his catalogue, however, there was a retrospective portrait by Girodet which had been accepted as a good likeness and which Mayer's miniature does not resemble. It is nonetheless a work of quality, though the identification of the sitter cannot be established without further evidence.[23] If there had been proof of Louis-Napoleon's ownership of the miniature it might have clinched the matter, since he could have been expected to know whether it was or was not a portrait of his grandfather.

In 1887 Dr John Lumsden Propert, in the first comprehensive history of the art of the miniature, issued a warning to collectors interested in French portraits. 'I am sorry to say the French hold an unenviable pre-eminence for the production of spurious enamels and miniatures', he wrote. 'It is really a matter of some danger to attempt a collection of French specimens; many at once no doubt display the cloven hoof clearly enough to warn off even a novice, but I have seen some which would puzzle an expert.'[24] The warning came too late for Mayer, who would probably not have heeded it anyway. He was sometimes taken in, but not ludicrously so. At a time when 'Young Napoleons' and 'Early Josephines' were rife on the market, he bought only one of each. The remarkable portrait (4.9.73.5; ivory, 55 mm. diameter) of a young man with a wasp-waist and light brown hair *en queue*, wearing a caped greatcoat in blue and red with two rows of large brass buttons, is unlikely to have been a contemporary painting of Napoleon as a military student at Brienne, but it has its charm; and the portrait of Josephine (4.9.73.7) in the type of dress she would have worn at Martinique in the days of her youth does not even pretend to be other than make-believe: it is signed on the right-hand edge by Robert Hollier, a miniaturist of some distinction during the Empire, and it was based on a painting by Robert Lefevre. Mayer, in other words, acquitted himself well on his excursion into the French minefields; his collection contains a fair number of items which are creditable as works of art, and the whole forms an interesting example of the fascination of Napoleonic memorabilia for Englishmen of his time.

Miscellaneous objects

The French Revolution put an end to many courtly customs, including that of taking snuff. With Napoleon's coronation as Emperor the noxious habit revived, and snuff-boxes became once more the ideal gift for favoured visitors at court: Napoleon had them made for the purpose at the rate of something like a hundred a year. The opulence of the boxes varied, presumably according to the status of the intended recipient: not all were jewelled, like the one given to Marshal Ney. A more typical example would be the tortoiseshell box, oblong with concave sides, edged with gold and set with a miniature portrait of Napoleon mounted in gold on the lid (4.9.73.6: pl. LXIVa);[25] or the round tortoiseshell box set with a miniature of Princess

Catherine of Würtemberg, mounted in gold and surrounded by a narrow band of the newly-discovered Prussian blue enamel (4.9.73.38: pl. LXIIIc). The cheaper wooden box, carved with a Napoleonic medallion (M 195), is of the type used by lesser mortals: large numbers of them were manufactured in France and put on sale in Paris at the time of 'the second funeral' (the transference of Napoleon's remains from St Helena to the Invalides in 1840) and it is likely that Mayer bought this item then. Portrait rings and brooches of the type found in Mayer's collection—a ring with an oval bezel set with a crystal enclosing a miniature of Napoleon (4.9.73.15) and a brooch to match, set with a miniature of Josephine (4.9.73.14)—were also produced in quantity, to meet public demand.

The wearing of jewellery was frowned upon during the Revolution, and jewellers had reason to be grateful to Napoleon, whose vision of glory demanded that the female members of his family should be arrayed in precious stones; they are indebted also to Josephine, whose extravagance in matters of dress and ornament equalled that of Marie Antoinette. Sets of jewellery, or *parures*, came once more into fashion, with tiara, necklace, earrings, brooch, waist-buckle, ring and bracelets for each arm made to match. The set obtained by Mayer (4.9.73.48) was not composed of dazzling gems but of cameos, forty-three in all, depicting classical subjects and carved in high relief from onyxes with four layers of colour. They are said to be the work of Girometti of Rome, though they do not carry his signature; and Mayer believed that they had been given by Napoleon to Josephine, though this is unlikely to have been true. Napoleon was fascinated by cameos, which he first encountered during his Italian campaign in 1796. Mayer's large onyx (4.9.73.42; 40 × 35 mm.), carved with a laureated head of Napoleon in cameo, is a good example of the type which became fashionable in both France and Italy under the Empire.

The use of hair as a memento became increasingly popular as classicism gave way to romanticism, and it was to be expected that there would be several examples in Mayer's collection—a gold breast-pin (4.9.73.51) and an enamelled brooch (4.9.73.52), both containing locks of Napoleon's hair, and a snuff-box (4.9.73.17) mounted with strands of Josephine's hair. Mayer believed that the breast-pin and brooch had been given by Napoleon himself to two of his British visitors at St Helena, and that the snuff-box was bequeathed by Josephine to Madame Ney, but it seems more likely that all three items were products of the Napoleonic legend. The same is probably true of the tiny trinket, 31 mm. high and 23 mm. wide, set with a cornelian engraved with the Imperial eagle and the initial 'N' in intaglio, and surmounted by military accoutrements in gilt-copper (4.9.73.50: pl. LXIVb). Mayer described the object as Napoleon's private seal, pointing out 'the concealed recess alluded to in the Life of Napoleon'. No such seal is known to have been used by Napoleon, however, and Mayer neglected to mention to which 'Life' of Napoleon he referred. The artistic style is not reminiscent of the First Empire, and most of the military accoutrements represented in minuscule are not French. The engraving of the cornelian has been attributed by more than one writer to Nicola Morelli, but this could be due to a confusion arising from police notices issued in 1905, when the so-called seal was stolen from the Liverpool Museum at the same time as two known Morelli items (happily the seal was later recovered from a pawnbroker's). The work is, nevertheless, beautifully executed and the trinket forms an unusual and intriguing item to set beside the thousands of rings, brooches and boxes which evoked the myth of Napoleon.[26]

PLATE LXIII

a. Unknown lady, by Isabey

b. Napoleon, by Isabey

c. Catherine of Würtemberg, by Augustin

d. Eugène Beauharnais, by Gigola

Reproduced by courtesy of NMGM

Photographs: Margaret Gibson

PLATE LXIV

a

a. Napoleon (snuffbox) (anonymous)

b. Napoleonic seal (height 30 mm.)

c. Napoleon, by Pistrucci after Canova's statue in Apsley House

Reproduced by courtesy of NMGM

b

c

PLATE LXV

Photograph: Margaret Gibson

a

b

c

d

a. Napoleon as conqueror of Egypt, 1798

b. Napoleon, by Andrieu

c. The Peace of Amiens

d. Napoleon as Jupiter

Reproduced by courtesy of NMGM

PLATE LXVI

Photograph: Margaret Gibson

a

b

c

d

a. Napoleon's wedding to Marie Louise

b. Napoleon as Charlemagne

c. Eagle standards on the banks of the Volga

d. Mars offers an olive branch to Britain

Reproduced by courtesy of NMGM

One of the most valuable items from Mayer's collection remaining in the Liverpool Museum is a tiny figure of Napoleon, modelled on the famous statue of the Emperor at Apsley House, very skilfully cut in cameo on a sardonyx, signed 'Pistrucci' and mounted in gold on the lid of a tortoiseshell snuff-box (4.9.73.49: pl. LXIV*c*). Mayer said that the cameo had been cut to the order of George IV, but unfortunately no evidence has been found of any such order placed by George IV either as Prince Regent or as King. Pistrucci could have produced this minuscule replica of Canova's statue either when he and Canova were in Tuscany, working for Napoleon's sister Elisa, or sometime after 1816 when he was in London, working for the Royal Mint, and Canova's statue had been brought to England for presentation to the Duke of Wellington. As an engraver and carver of hard stone Pistrucci was undoubtedly the greatest technician of his time. Mayer obviously admired his work, for he wrote to him in 1843 with the possibility of commissioning him to make either a portrait-medal or a marble bust; but the negotiation seems not to have progressed, possibly because Pistrucci, as usual, quoted a very high price.[27] There is no record of how Mayer came to purchase the 'Canova' cameo, or of when precisely he did so: the fact that he listed the item in 1855 and not in 1854 is inconclusive, as he may simply have forgotten it earlier. Pistrucci died in 1855 but there was no sale of his effects; they were left to his daughter, who took them back with her to Italy. The original wax model of the cameo is to be found in the Pistrucci Wax Collection in the Museo de la Zecca in Rome.[28]

Medals

The collection of medals which Mather bequeathed to the Museum (4.9.73.58–204) does not quite measure up to the title given it by Mayer in 1855: 'a series of gold, silver and bronze medals'. If there had ever been any quantity of gold and silver medals, they had been disposed of by 1872, leaving only one gold piece among the bronze. The rest of the collection could never have been considered rare.[29] All but one of the medals were struck at the Medal Mint in Paris, where they were put on sale to individual purchasers to make money for the Mint. Mayer could either have bought them second-hand from a French collector or bought a set direct from the Medal Mint at any time during the 1830s and 1840s, as many English collectors did. This does not make them any the less interesting: indeed, they are a tribute to Mayer's good sense in never neglecting to purchase objects simply because they were easily available.

The medals celebrate Napoleon's achievements from 1796, when he became a general in the armies of the Directorate, through 1800 when he became First Consul and 1804 when he became Emperor, to March 1814 when he escaped from his first exile on the island of Elba and returned to France for the Hundred Days. At first sight, they seem to provide evidence for the old textbook cliché that France worshipped Napoleon from the day of his first victory at Montenotte. On closer inspection, however, it is clear that most of the medals celebrating Napoleon's exploits under the Directory were inserted into the collection at the Medal Mint at a later date. Seven of them, including the stunning representation of Napoleon as conqueror of Egypt, driving between Cleopatra's needle and Pompey's pillar in a triumphal chariot drawn by two camels (pl. LXV*a*),[30] are inscribed with the name of Vivant Denon, who was not appointed Director of the Medal Mint until 1803. A further four, celebrating episodes in the first Italian campaign, were originally struck in Italy; the dies were then sent to Paris where they were re-struck at the Medal Mint some time later.[31]

Napoleon was fully conscious of the use which could be made of medals to connect his personal career with a variety of praiseworthy events. During the Life Consulship he took a keen interest in plans formed by the Ancient History and Literature section of the Institut de France to produce a Medallic History on the lines of those provided by the 'Little Academy' for Louis XIV. For some reason these plans came to nothing, but from 1803 Vivant Denon took it upon himself to produce the semi-official series which forms a large part of the collection purchased by Mayer. Denon always discussed with Napoleon his ideas for subjects to be treated,[32] and the series therefore gives some indication of those aspects of the regime which Napoleon himself thought were capable of enhancing his glory. Domestic measures such as the establishment of Schools of Pharmacy, the founding of an orphanage, the opening of a canal and the formation of a society for the encouragement of vaccination found a place in the Medallic History along with major battles like Austerlitz and Wagram. The creation of new states (the Grand Duchy of Warsaw, the Kingdom of Westphalia) was celebrated equally with annexations of further territory (Liguria, the Papal States). Entry by French armies into foreign capitals was always marked (even Moscow). An incident which occurred in the early days of the Consulate (the death of General Desaix at Marengo) was turned into a legend for which no fewer than four medals were struck, the last as much as ten years after the event.[33] The two most splendid ceremonial occasions (the coronation of Napoleon and the marriage of Napoleon with Marie-Louise) were given special treatment: medals of four different sizes were struck for both events, the smallest (15 mm.) designed to be thrown in large numbers by heralds at arms to the crowds.

The Medallic History of Napoleon, though perhaps not quite so prestigious as that of Louis XIV, is nevertheless highly regarded by experts.[34] Denon employed a variety of artists, and, whilst allowing them more individual scope than their predecessors of the seventeenth century had enjoyed, he kept a tight enough rein on them to make the years of the Napoleonic Empire into an homogeneous whole as far as medallic art was concerned. The medals were almost all 40 mm. in diameter.[35] Unity was emphasized by the use of Andrieu's portrait of Napoleon, calm and depersonalized and crowned with laurel leaves like Caesar Augustus, as the standard obverse (pl. LXV*b*). The neo-classical style which predominated was not original— signs of it had appeared on medals designed during the Revolution, and it had received its purest expression during the Consulate in medals commemorating the Peace of Amiens (pl. LXV*c*) and Napoleon's fourth year in office[36]—but the Empire demonstrated its versatility to the full. It often demanded a high standard of expertise which was fully met by engravers.

Neo-classicism in its most extreme form resulted in unpleasant representations of Napoleon as Jupiter, hurling thunderbolts indiscriminately on young and old (the Battle of Jena, by Galle; pl. LXV*d*), and as Hercules, battering a fallen giant with his club (the Battle of Wagram, also by Galle). On other occasions, artists were content to clothe Napoleon in classical costume: he frequently appeared in a Roman toga, as on Brenet's medal for the promulgation of the *Code Napoléon*. More absurdly, Jouannin represented him in Roman costume at his wedding with Marie-Louise, conducting to the altar a bride so transparently clad as almost to appear naked (pl. LXVI*a*). Napoleon preferred artists to allude to medieval times, though this also could lead to incongruities, as when Brenet depicted fourteen German princes in medieval costume swearing allegiance in the presence of Archbishop Dalberg, newly created Prince Primate of the Confederation of the Rhine.[37] More successful was Andrieu's medal celebrating the alliance between France and Saxony in 1806, on which the usual bust of Napoleon is coupled with the head of Charlemagne, bearded and crowned (pl. LXVI*b*).

Napoleon's chosen symbol, the eagle, appears on numerous medals, either perched on the thunderbolt of Jupiter or surmounting the standards which Napoleon distributed to the army in 1804. Eagles were seen hovering over the battlefield of Jena and resting on the Tarpeian Rock; eagle standards were planted on the banks of the Volga (pl. LXVI*c*) and on the highest tower of the Kremlin; Napoleon was even shown flying on an eagle's back, threatening vengeance upon four German fortresses which had stood out against him. Usually the Roman eagle was used, but by an unintended irony the Ptolemaic eagle, less plump and prosperous, was chosen to advertise Napoleon's victories at the beginning of the otherwise disastrous campaign of 1814.

Medals illustrated more clearly than any other art form Napoleon's faith in war as a means of obtaining peace. As early as 1802, Dumarest represented him as Mars offering Britain an olive branch of peace. In 1803, when his relationship with Britain was breaking down, Denon presented him with a medal which again showed an armed figure with an olive branch, and bore the legend '*Armé pour la paix*'. After the defeat of Austria at Austerlitz, Galle pictured Napoleon with a sword in one hand and an olive branch in the other, and, when Austria had been defeated once more in 1809, Andrieu depicted him as Mars setting fire with the left hand to a pile of ammunition and with the right hand holding out an olive branch over the altar of peace (pl. LXVI*d*).

Napoleon shared with the ancient world a strong belief in Fortune, usually seen as a goddess who could be courted with brave deeds but whose favours were fickle. He attributed to good fortune his escape from Egypt and successful landing at Fréjus, an event celebrated by Galle with a medal bearing the legend '*Bonus Eventus*'.[38] Four years later, Brenet dedicated a medal to '*La Fortune Conservatrice*', an allegorical female steering a boat guided by the star of destiny;[39] and ten years later still he designed a medal showing the same female, again in a boat, but with the wind spilled from the sail and the star of destiny replaced by a broken wheel.[40] None of this prevented Napoleon from priding himself on having re-established public worship, though Andrieu's medal on the occasion of the Concordat displayed a welter of pagan and religious symbols; not did it prevent him from inviting the Pope to consecrate him as Emperor at Notre Dame. The medals designed for public distribution on the day of the coronation bore no sign of religion, since Napoleon thought it more important to emphasize the role of Senate and People, but a special medal bearing a portrait of Pius VII and a view of the Cathedral of Notre Dame was designed by Andrieu and Jaley to present to the Pope.

Contemporary detail occasionally found a place among the symbols and allegories. Architectural verisimilitude was particularly valued—the medals provide fine views of the Arc du Carrousel, Notre Dame, the Cathedral Church of St Stephen at Vienna, the Brandenburg Gate at Berlin, the Rialto Bridge at Venice and the Alcala Gate at Madrid. Realism was carried furthest, however, in Galle's portrayal of the retreat of the Grand Army from Moscow. Galle had never been afraid of depicting the horrors of war, as can be seen in his medals commemorating the battles of Jena, Freidland and Wagram. In his *Retraite de l'Armée* a horse lies dead and gun carriages burn, in a dreary landscape marked by a solitary tree. Symbolism, nevertheless, plays an important part: in the foreground a dismounted warrior, perhaps Mars himself, flees before the icy winds directed at him by Boreas from a stormy sky.

NOTES

[1] Apart from these few biographical details from Gore (1853), 392, nothing is known of John Mather.

[2] *Liverpool Chronicle*, Suppl., 30 Sept. 1854.

[3] JM, *A Catalogue of the Drawings, Miniatures, Cameos ... Illustrative of the Bonaparte Family* (Liverpool, 1854), 6–7.

[4] Liverpool Museum, Department of Antiquities, Guard Book I, 200.

[5] JM, *op. cit.* (note 3); *THSLC*, vii (1855), 4*–6*.

[6] *THSLC*, vii (1855), 4* app.

[7] See, e.g., *The Times*, 30 Sept. 1854.

[8] JM, *A Catalogue of the Drawings, Miniatures, Cameos ... Illustrative of the Bonaparte Family* (Liverpool, 1855).

[9] Liverpool City Record Office, Liverpool Council Papers, 9 Nov. 1872.

[10] *A Catalogue of the Mather Collection of Miniatures, Medals etc. relating to the Bonaparte Family* (Liverpool Free Public Library, Museum and Gallery of Arts, 1874).

[11] Gatty, *Mediaeval and Later*, 92–108.

[12] MPL, H. W. Barber to JM, 30 Mar. 1860, with memo by JM.

[13] *Liverpool Echo*, 27 Apr. and 1, 9, 16 May 1905.

[14] Illustrations of other miniature portraits of Hortense and Eugène by Isabey are to be found in M. de Basily-Callimaki, *J. B. Isabey, sa vie, son temps* (Paris, 1909), 152, 322.

[15] In this portrait he has curling moustachios, but there is another miniature in the collection which shows him in the same costume but without moustachios.

[16] It obviously arrived in Liverpool Museum, since it was catalogued by Gatty.

[17] Gatty confused this miniature with one of Caroline, Queen of Naples, and reversed the names of the two ladies. The Wallace Collection contains an identical miniature, not signed, considered to be 'in the manner of Augustin': see G. Reynolds, *Catalogue of Miniatures* (London, 1980), no. 177.

[18] The background to this miniature is discoloured, probably due to 'weeping'.

[19] There is a very similar miniature in the Wallace Collection, signed 'Augustin'. See Reynolds, *op. cit.* (note 17), no. 171.

[20] The Wallace Collection has the same miniature, signed 'Aubry', considered to be Pauline Bonaparte, Princess Borghese; *ibid.*, no. 226.

[21] Correspondence between W. Bonaparte-Wyse and Liverpool Museum, Department of Decorative Art, 1968. This miniature has a crack at the bottom right-hand edge, running to about half-way up.

[22] L. R. Schidlof, *The Miniature in Europe* (Graz, 1964), is an authoritative work.

[23] M. J. Samoyault, Director of the Musée national du Château de Fontainebleau, to whom I am indebted for comments on the iconography of all the miniatures in the collection, has pointed out that this miniature does not resemble the one in the Museo Napoleonico in Rome either.

[24] J. L. Propert, *A History of Miniature Art, with Notes on Collectors and Collections* (London, 1887), 96.

[25] The miniature (enamel) in which Napoleon is seen wearing the green uniform of a colonel of the *chasseurs à cheval* of the Guard is of inferior quality to the box.

[26] I am grateful to M. Gérard Hubert, Inspecteur Général des Musées chargé de la Conservation du Musée national des Châteaux de Malmaison et de Bois-Préau, for giving me an opinion on the seal. The engraving was first attributed to Morelli by R. Forrer, *Biographical Dictionary of Medallists* (London, 1909), IV, 147. Forrer described the seal as made of gold. He had obviously not seen it, since he believed it to be still missing from Liverpool Museum.

[27] Mayer's letter to Pistrucci has not been preserved, but its contents can be deduced from Pistrucci's reply, dated 8 Feb. 1843: Fitzwilliam Museum, Cambridge, Department of Manuscripts, MS 9.1985.

[28] The wax is illustrated in anon., 'Cenni sulla vita e sulle opere di Benedetto Pistrucci', *Relazione della R. Zecca* (Rome, 1940), 227. I am grateful to Dr J. G. Pollard for referring me to this work and for many other helpful suggestions on this topic.

[29] Mayer's medal collection corresponds almost exactly with the collection described in J. C. Laskey, *A Description of a Series of Medals Struck at the National Medal Mint by Order of Napoleon Bonaparte, Commemorating the Most Remarkable Battles and Events during his Dynasty* (London, 1818). The only difference is the addition by Mayer of the medal struck at Milan to commemorate the French victory at Marengo (1800) and four medals struck at Paris in 1814 to commemorate visits by Princess Elisa Bonaparte in 1811 and by the rulers of Austria, Prussia and Russia in 1814 to the Medal Mint. Mayer's total of 147 medals is a small number compared with the 1,276 described by C. Lenormant, *Trésor de numismatique et de glyptique*, 20 vols. (Paris, 1834–46), I, *Médailles de la Révolution française* (1836) and II, *Médailles de l'Empire français* (1840); and a drop in the ocean compared with the 1,888 listed by L. Bramsen, *Médailleur Napoléon le Grand*, 3 vols. (Copenhagen, 1904). Both these authors included Napoleonic medals struck in European countries other than France, however.

[30] Three medals commemorate the Egyptian Campaign, which Napoleon always pretended was a triumph even though the British destroyed his fleet in the course of the campaign and his army shortly afterwards. The medals commemorate the conquest of Lower Egypt with a view of the Pyramids on the reverse by Brenet; the conquest of Upper Egypt, showing on the reverse a crocodile tied to a palm tree, by Galle; and the conquest of the whole of Egypt, referred to here, which was also designed by Brenet.

[31] They were designed by Lavy to commemorate the battles of Millesimo and Castiglione, the crossing of the river Tagliamento and the surrender of Mantua. Specimens from the first issue were referred to by Latta as rare: see *The Unequalled Collection relating to Napoleon and the French Revolution of William J. Latta*, Anderson Galleries, New York Metropolitan Art Association, Sale Catalogue (New York, 1913), 201, 489–91.

[32] F. Benoit, *L'Art français sous la Révolution et l'Empire* (Paris, 1897), 175, 411.

[33] Desaix, whose cavalry charge contributed a great deal to Napoleon's victory, was reputed to have said as he was dying, 'Tell the First Consul that my only regret is that I have not done enough to be remembered by posterity.'

[34] M. Jones, *The Art of the Medal* (London, 1979), 83–9, 99–102.

[35] Larger medals, more than 60 mm. in diameter, were produced at the request of the Paris authorities (1) in honour of the banquet given for Napoleon at the time of the coronation and (2) to mark the occasion when they formed a deputation to congratulate Napoleon on his victory over Germany, 1805. These two medals were not included by Denon in his Medallic History.

[36] For an appreciation of these medals see Jones, *op. cit.* (note 34), 100–5.

[37] The figure in the centre of the group is wrongly identified by Laskey, *op. cit.* (note 29), 123, as Napoleon's uncle, Cardinal Fesch.

[38] On this medal, Fortune is represented, unusually, by a young male figure.

[39] This medal is sometimes said to have referred to Napoleon's preparations for the invasion of England, but comparison with Brenet's medal *Fortune Adverse* makes it seem more likely that the artist was referring to the good fortune which had attended Napoleon during his four years as First Consul.

[40] This medal does not form part of the collection described by Laskey or of the collection bought by Mayer. It was first struck in England, where Brenet worked after the fall of the Empire, and did not find its way to the Medal Mint in Paris until later.

Appendices

Catalogues

1852	*Catalogue of the Egyptian Museum, No. VIII, Colquitt Street* (Liverpool)
1856	F. Pulszky, *Catalogue of the Fejérváry Ivories in the Museum of Joseph Mayer* (Liverpool)
1856	C. Roach Smith, *Inventorium Sepulchrale* (London) (= the Faussett Collection)
1857	*Catalogue of the Collection of Assyrian, Babylonian, Egyptian, Greek, Etruscan, Roman, Indian, Peruvian and Mexican Antiquities formed by B. Hertz and now in the Possession of Joseph Mayer* (London)

Public Sales in which Joseph Mayer was a vendor

1857	Mar. 24–6 Lugt 23471	Phillips: Hertz Collection
1859	Feb. 7–24 Lugt 24633	Sotheby's: Hertz Collection
1873	Oct. 20 Lugt omits	Branch and Leete: household furniture (68–70 Lord Street)
1875	Feb. 12–13 Lugt 35348	Sotheby's: ceramics
1878	June 21, 24 Lugt 38537	Sotheby's: ceramics and *objets d'art*
1886	July 8–10	Branch and Leete: household furniture (Pennant House)
1887	May 23–6 Lugt 46620	Sotheby's: coins, medals and jewels
1887	July 19–21 Lugt omits	Sotheby's: books and MSS, including Nelson papers
1887	July 21–4 Lugt 46763	Sotheby's: prints and drawings; Wedgwood papers
1887	Dec. 15–16 Lugt omits	Branch and Leete, Liverpool: pictures and documents of local interest; two diamonds from the Hope Collection

Liverpool Museum Catalogues

In 1867 JM presented his collection to Liverpool Museum, apparently retaining the documentation in his own hands. Henry Ecroyd Smith, the first Keeper of 'the Mayer Museum' (as it was still called), entered approximately 5,000 items, mainly ceramics, with some glass and metalwork, in 'Registers'. Most of this material relates to the Department of Decorative Art. Charles Tindall Gatty, Assistant Keeper and, from 1875, Keeper, compiled a slip-catalogue of 10,000 items, mainly relating to the Departments of Antiquities and Ethnology. Gatty at least (if not Ecroyd Smith) had sound practical advice from A. W. Franks on the principles of cataloguing. But he had to reconstruct the documentation with very little help from Mayer.

Gatty published the following catalogues (all in Liverpool):

1877   *On some Ancient Glass in the Mayer Collection*
1877   *Catalogue of the Mayer Collection*, i: *The Egyptian Antiquities*
1879   *Catalogue of the Mayer Collection*, i: *The Egyptian, Babylonian and Assyrian Antiquities*, 2nd edn.
1879   *Catalogue of the Engraved Gems and Rings in the Collection of J. Mayer*
1882   *Catalogue of the Mayer Museum*, ii: *Prehistoric Antiquities and Ethnography*
1883   *Catalogue of the Mayer Museum*, iii: *Mediaeval and Later Antiquities*
1883   *Catalogue of the Mayer Museum*, iv: *Greek, Roman and Etruscan*

Gatty's slip-catalogue was maintained and improved by Miss Elaine Tankard, Keeper of Antiquities 1931–66 but the only further publication was C. R. Beard, 'The Joseph Mayer Collections', *The Connoisseur*, xcv (1935), 135–8, 201–4. The Mayer Collection—particularly the Wedgwood—suffered in the fire of May 1941, and in the difficult conditions of the late 1940s and early 1950s. It is only in the last few years that catalogues have appeared again, now of the Museum's collections as a whole:

1979   I. G. Wolfenden, *Historic Glass from Collections in North-west England*, Exhibition Catalogue
1980   S. M. Nicholson, *Catalogue of the Prehistoric Metalwork in Merseyside County Museums*
1980   E. E. Worrall, *Precious Vessels: 2,000 Years of Chinese Pottery*, Exhibition Catalogue
1982   M. Warhurst, *Merseyside County Museums: Ancient British and Later Coins to 1279*, Sylloge of Coins of the British Isles 29

Catalogues currently in preparation and containing a significant amount of Mayer material are:

J. Turfa, *The Etruscan Collection*
M. Gibson, *Late Antique and Medieval Ivories*
M. Henig, *Classical Gems*
A. de Joia, *Egyptian Stelae*
A. R. Millard, *Cylinder Seals*

APPENDIX II: JOSEPH MAYER'S PERSONAL PAPERS

Although no systematic search has been made for letters from or to JM, enough has come to light to justify a checklist. We are especially indebted to Michael Rhodes of the Museum of London, who has supplied details of letters of JM to Charles Roach Smith (hereafter CRS), and to Naomi Evetts, Assistant Archivist in the Liverpool Record Office, whose analysis of the Mayer papers there deposited we print in full.

Aberystwyth
National Library of Wales. MSS 4914–15 D. Material relating to the life and work of John Gibson, sculptor (1790–1886), collected by JM and including letters from Gibson to JM.

Bebington (Wirral)
Public Library. Two files of letters, press-cuttings and photographs. JM's 'Autograph Book' (i.e. visitors' book) for 1843–85.

Cambridge
Fitzwilliam Museum. MS 9.1985. Letter to JM from B. Pistrucci quoting prices for a medal or a portrait bust (8 Feb. 1843).

Dorchester
Dorset County Museum. Bound volume of letters relating to C. Warne's *Ancient Dorset* (1872), including JM to C. Warne.

Durham
University Library. MSS Add. 282 and 287 (CRS to JM), 293 (JM to CRS); MS 913.42 B8 (CRS to JM and J. O. Halliwell to JM).

Keele
University Library. MSS 27823.36–27825.36 (JM's notes on pottery). 27826.36 (A. W. Franks to JM). Deposited by the Trustees of the Wedgwood Museum, Barlaston, Stoke-on-Trent.

Liverpool
City Record Office. The papers fall into two categories—(a) those received in 1972 and (b) those purchased or acquired by Liverpool City Libraries from the 1860s to date.

(a) In November 1972 a number of boxes of JM's papers were received as a donation from the then Borough Librarian of Bebington. Much of the material appears to be part of JM's 'general correspondence'. In November 1886 Peter Cowell, Chief Librarian of Liverpool, submitted a report . . . *on the Books and Manuscripts belonging to the late Mr. Joseph Mayer in Pennant House, Bebington* to Liverpool's Library, Museum and Arts Committee. Cowell's signed copy of his report has survived. After listing some of the outstanding items in the collection he continues (p. 3) 'there is an immense quantity of Mr. Mayer's general correspondence, also of the correspondence of Mr. C. Roach Smith with various antiquaries'. The correspondence donated in 1972 is made up of over 2,500 letters written between the 1840s and the early 1880s. A number of the letters are addressed to CRS, and some to other of Mayer's friends (some of these being dated earlier than the 1840s); but most of the letters are JM's personal correspondence, that is to say letters *received* by him rather than 'collected' by him. There are many letters from Mayer's antiquarian friends and acquaintances—over 500 of them from Joseph Clarke of Saffron Walden and CRS alone—but the full range of his correspondents was wide. Besides letters the papers include water-colour sketches, drawings, photographs, newspaper cuttings, invitations, menu cards, notices, prospectuses and other printed material. The Record Office reference for all these papers is now 920 MAY.

JM himself attempted some arrangement of these papers. Many documents are in paper folders or on mounts on which he has added his own pencilled comments, biographical notes on the writer and often a heading: e.g. 'JM Private', 'JM Literary', 'Pottery', 'Geography', 'JM Antiquarian'. Dates on some of these notes indicate that Mayer was working on his papers as late as 1882. By the time of their arrival in the Record Office many of the mounts and folders had become separated from their contents. Mayer put with his letters relevant printed material, drawings, etc., and much work remains to be done in re-assembling the papers as nearly as possible to their intended arrangement. At least some of the papers were kept in portfolios, some disintegrating examples of which have survived. Bound by Stephen Amer Junior of Birkenhead (in business as such c. 1867–91) their leather spines were stamped 'MAYER CORRESPONDENCE' with a number. Mayer's hand-printed labels remain on five of the front boards—'ANGLO-SAXON SCHOLARS. THE REV. D. H. HAIGH, D.D.', 'GIOVAN FONTANA', 'JOSEPH MAYER. PERSONAL', 'JOSH CLARKE F.S.A. VARIOUS CORRESPONDENCE' and 'MAYER. PERSONAL. ART. ARTISTS ETC.'

(b) The second category of Mayer's papers does not form a coherent group. The only common factor is that every item was once in JM's possession or had formed part of his collections. A local (Liverpool, Lancashire, Cheshire) connection was usually the reason for the Library's acquisition of Mayer material. It is very varied in content, with possibly a greater number of papers relating to artists with local connections, and has been acquired piecemeal over a period of nearly 120 years as illustrated by the following examples. In March 1868 Mayer himself gave to the Library the 'Underhill Papers', MSS towards a history of Liverpool by John Green Underhill (1814–35). In December 1887 the Library purchased a number of lots 'per Henry Young and Sons' (Liverpool booksellers) from the Branch and Leete sale of 'The Local Portion of the Mayer Collection' in Liverpool. These included such varied items as Ozias Humphry's MS 'Memoir of George Stubbs' (1724–1806), a Liverpool 'Provisional Cavalry List', 1797–99, and a collection of material relating to William Roscoe (1753–1831). In 1893 the Liverpool bookdealer Edward Howell presented the Library with the 'Memorandum Book (1766–88) of John Sadler', pottery printer, which had appeared as Lot 147 in the Branch and Leete catalogue. In 1912 Howell printed a transcript of the minute book of Liverpool's 'facetious Society of Ugly Faces', the original MS of which he describes as having been in JM's collection. The MS itself was eventually acquired for the Liverpool Record Office in February 1959. In 1945 Revd C. H. Steel of Middlesborough presented the Library with eight letters from JM to John Gibson of Whitehaven. As recently as 1982 some of Mayer's papers relating to Henry Hole (*ob.* 1820), wood engraver, were purchased from an Oxford bookseller, complementing a collection of Mayer's Henry Hole drawings and letters given to the Library in 1928 by Robert Gladstone of Liverpool (1866–1940).

By the first decade of this century the Library had acquired a considerable number of Mayer items. In the interleaved and annotated copy of the Library's *Liverpool Prints and Documents Catalogue* (1908) many of the entries for volumes, drawings, prints, collections of manuscript material, etc., are followed by the bracketed entry 'Mayer . . .' or 'Joseph Mayer Papers'. The Library's old stock books record further purchases of Mayer material in the 1930s and 1940s. Inevitably, the intermittent acquisition of Mayer material over a long period by a large institution has meant that, in terms of location, it is scattered. Some it has been possible to re-assemble as a group in the Record Office. Other items, some autograph letters or material of slighter local association, are amongst the Library's general manuscript collections in the Hornby Library. There is still Mayer material to be identified and its provenance traced, but it is hoped to produce one list of all the acquired Mayer items in this second category.

(a) and (b) Examination of both groups of papers raises the question of their interrelation. How much of Mayer's personal correspondence was sold after his death? A portfolio, labelled by Mayer, of papers relating to William Daniels (1813–80), the Liverpool artist, was purchased by the Library from a private individual in 1968. It includes a number of letters from Daniels to Mayer and in all respects appears to belong to the first group of papers. In many cases the difference between the two groups must only be one of accession.

Liverpool Museum, Archive Department. Acc. no. 38.48. Twenty-one letters, of which ten are CRS to JM. Acc. no. 50151. Sundry letters, including CRS and J. Clarke to JM, and JM to CRS.
University of Liverpool, Sydney Jones Library. MS 25.66. Forty-three letters from W. Bell to JM, *re* his facsimile and translation of *Sprott's Chronicle*; fo. 65 sq., twenty-five letters to JM acknowledging the gift of *Sprott's Chronicle*; fo. 90 CRS to JM.

London
British Library. MSS Add. 33346–7, 33963, fos. 76–83 (Thomas Wright to JM), 34098 (JM's correspondence *re* the Simonides papyri).

British Museum, Dept. of Medieval and Later Antiquities. Two letters JM to A. W. Franks, and two others CRS to JM.

British Museum, Dept. of Prehistoric and Romano-British Antiquities. One letter JM to CRS.

Society of Antiquaries of London. MS 857. Letter from JM to W. H. Rolfe.

Swiss Cottage Library, London Borough of Camden. Twenty-three letters from Eliza Meteyard to JM.

Sheffield

City Museum. Bateman Papers include two letters from JM to CRS.

Stafford

William Salt Library. MS 70/45. Two letters from William Salt to JM.

Washington D.C.

Folger Library. MSS C.b. 16–20, W.a. 81–2, W.b. 67–9 (CRS to JM and J. O. Halliwell-Phillipps to JM).

Index

Compiled by Isobel Thompson

232

Darlington (Co. Durham), Sams Collection of Egyptian antiquities exhibited at, 49

d'Athanasi, Giovanni, collector of Egyptian antiquities, 47; sale of collections of, 48

della Chisa, Pompeo, armourer, 169

de la Rue, Thomas, early collector of Wedgwood ware, 195–6

Dennis, George, *Cities and Cemeteries of Etruria* by, 77–8, 84

Denon, Vivant, Director of Paris Medal Mint, 222, 223, 224; Napoleon's 'Medallic History' organized by, 223

Derby, Earl of, his natural history collection at Liverpool, 20

Desborough (Northants), Iron Age mirror from, 132

Description de l'Egypte, 66

d'Hancarville, *Antiquités Etrusques, Grecques et Romaines,* by, source of Wedgwood designs, 196

Dickens, Charles, bust of, commissioned by JM, 39; visits to Liverpool, 30, 39

Dijon (France), museum at, 4

Dodd, Thomas, auctioneer and printseller, memorial relief of, 38; sculpted for 'Gallery of Friends', 39

Douglas, Revd James, Faussett's Anglo-Saxon finds published by, 118

Douglas and Lockwood, architects of 'black and white' revival, 38

Drovetti, Italian collector of Egyptian antiquities, 49

Dumarest, Napoleonic medal by, 224

Dun, Nicolas-François, miniature by, 215

Eastwood, dealer in Billies and Charleys, 131

Ecroyd-Smith, Henry, first keeper of Mayer Museum, 20; antiquities from Meols collected by, 123; recording of Mayer collections by, 20, 43: Chinese and Japanese porcelains, 192, 193; continental pottery, 176–7; Wedgwood ware, 195, 199, 201, 202

Edinburgh: Royal Museum of Scotland, Egyptological collections, 48

Edwards, Amelia B., on JM's Egyptian collections, quoted, 45, 56; on Thebes, quoted, 46; Theban toilet objects noted by, 59

Egerton, Sir Philip de Malpas Grey, Birkenhead Docks foundation stone laid by, 5

Egypt Exploration Fund, 45, 67

Egyptian antiquities in JM's collection, 45–70; described, 49–61; awakening of European interest in, 46–8; powdered mummy as medicine, 46–7

Late Period coffins, 50–1; mummies, 49–51; Neferronpet pyramidion and tomb,

56; ebony figure of Nubian servant, 58; stelae, 55–6; stone statues, 56–8; wooden figures, 58.

Objects of daily life, 58–60; alabaster vessel, 60; cosmetic box and spoons, 59; earrings, 60; engraved gems, 98; forged gold diadem and silver figures, 60; faience playing-piece, 60; 'girdle of Ramesses III', 60; glass vessels of Roman period, 87; gold rings, 51, 59; Graeco-Egyptian amulets, 97, 102; jewellery, 59, 60; wooden objects, 60; writing tablets, 54

Religious and cult objects, 60–1, 66; Amun-Re figure, 61, 66; bronze deity figures, 60–1, 66.

See also Hertz collection; Papyri; Salt Collections; Sams Collection; Stobart Collection; Stürmer Collection; Valentia Collection

Egyptian Antiquities Service, 48

Egyptian Museum, 8, 10, 11, 20, 46, 48, 66; documentation of, 20, 43; in Harris portrait, 8, 11, 45; transferral to town of Liverpool, 20, 29, 67

Arms and armour, 167, 174; Assyrian and Babylonian antiquities, 71–5; Chinese porcelain, 185; Egyptian antiquities, described, 49–61; 'Jewellery, Vase and Idol Room', 57, 59, 60, 66; 'Mummy Room', 50–1, 55, 57, 66; 'Stele and Monumental Room', 55, 56, 57; engraved gems, 94; Etruscan, 84; Fejérváry ivories, 106; Greek vases and terracottas, 87; Library, 66–7; Liverpool and Wedgwood wares, 198; manuscripts, 137; Roman glass, 92; *see also* Mayer Museum

Elkington's of Birmingham, 6

Elsby, Miles Pilling, Bebington schoolmaster and librarian, 30, 31

Emery, Walter Bryan, influence of Mayer Collection and John Garstang on, 67

Enamels, medieval: bibliography, 114; catalogue, 114, 117; in Pennant House collection, 21

Esterhazy, Prince, Roman glass vessels from collection of, 87

Esther, brig, of Harrington, 193

Etruria (Staffs.), Wedgwood punch bowl from Bridge Inn at, 201

Etruscan antiquities, in JM's collection, 77–85; background to their collection of, in eighteenth and nineteenth centuries, 77–8, 84; amber object, 83; amulets, 78, 83; bronzes, 83, 84; ceramics, 83; cinerary urn, 78; cornelian scarabs, 83; engraved

commemorative medals, 10, 213, 222–5; cameos, 213, 217, 222; jewellery, 217; miniatures, 213–16, 217; snuff-boxes, 213, 214, 216–17, 222; occupation of Egypt by, 47

Nelson, Philip, owner of medieval silver seal, 94; Gothic ivory panels added to Mayer Collection by, 112

Newcastle-under-Lyme (Staffs.), ix; JM's generosity to, 21, 168, 200; Pottery Mechanics' Institute, 4, 86, 200; Theatre Royal, 1; Thistlebury House, 1, 11

New South Wales (Australia), Fontana sculptures sold to government of, 38, 39

New York (USA): Metropolitan Museum, Etruscan engraved mirror in, 83; gem collection of, 96; Magdeburg ivory panel in, 108

Ney, Marshall, jewelled snuff-box given by Napoleon to, 213, 216

Nicholson, Susan, JM's prehistoric metalwork described by, cited, 43

Nineveh (Iraq), antiquities from, 75

Niẓāmī, Persian works of literature by, 158

Northumberland, 4th Duke of, Egyptian antiquities collected by, 58

Nuremberg (Germany), wheel-lock pistol from, 169

Ochsenhausen (Germany), association of psalters with monastery of, 146–7

Oxford: Ashmolean Museum, Fortnum Collection of Italian maiolica in, 177; gravegoods from Anglo-Saxon cemetery at Fairford in, 122

Manuscript pledged in loan-chest at, 142

Paintings in JM's collection, 8, 21, 165; at Mayer Hall, Bebington, 34; miniatures with Napoleonic associations, 213–16; 217; Persian miniatures, 160

Works by JM, 123, 165; *see also* Prints and drawings

Palmer, Nigel F., on *Parzival* fragments from binding of Latin psalter, 145–51

Papyri, in Egyptian Museum, 49, 51–4; European interest in collecting, 51–2; *Book of the Dead*, 52; forged rolls, native, 52; Hyperides papyri, 53; investigative texts into robberies at Thebes, 53; Papyri Mayer A and B, 52–3, 54; Simonides papyri, 12, 54

Parent, J., 215

Paris, Matthew, 139

Paris (France): Bibliothèque Nationale, 'Master Alexander' illuminated bible in, 139; Ochsenhausen psalter in, 146, 147; Institut de France, Medallic History plans of, 223; Musée Cluny, late antique ivory panel in, 107–8; St Denis, eighth-century ivory and silver doors of, 108

Fifteenth-century artists in, 139; Napoleonic medals from Medal Mint at, 222–3

Parkes, Sir Henry, Premier of New South Wales, 39

Passau (Germany), sixteenth-century blades from, 168

Paton, Fiona, on JM's collection of arms and armour, 167–75

Pennant, Thomas, traveller and naturalist, 29

Pennant House collection, 20, 21, 29; gems in, 96, 97; inaccessibility of, 98, 102; sale of, 96, 97; Wedgwood ware in, 195, 202

Pepper, John, builder and bridge designer, 1; on memorial tablet, 21

Pepys, Samuel, on visit to see a mummy, quoted, 47

Peraldus, Gulielmus, *Summa de vitiis* by, 142

Perkin, Michael, on JM's western manuscripts, Latin and vernacular, 138–44

Persia, manuscripts of, 158–60, 162

Peter of Poitiers, *Compendium genealogiae Christi* by, 139

Pigeon, Henry, joint founder of Historic Society of Lancashire and Cheshire, 6

Pistrucci, Benedetto, cameo after Canova's statue of Napoleon by, 213, 222

Plate, gold and silver; commercial development of electroplate, 5–6; designed by JM, 5, 6, 22, 165; paper on gold plate in JM's collection read by forger Simonides, 53

Pompeii (Italy), JM drawings of 'House of Pansa' at, 86

Poole (Cheshire), medieval silver seal associated with, 94

Porteous, Beilby, Bishop of Chester, commonplace book item by, 143

Possenti Collection, Magdeburg panels possibly from, 108

Post-medieval: *see* Arms and armour; Pottery, post-medieval

Pottery, history of, as a theme in JM's museum, 8, 123, 203; papers and specimens relating to, 20, 200

Classical: Etruscan, 83; Greek vases and figurines, 87; Hellenistic dish repurchased from Hertz Collection, 92; Mexican, 11

Post-medieval, 8, 118, 131; Liverpool Herculaneum wares in JM's collection, 8, 20, 123; JM's study of, 122–3; JM's papers on Liverpool pottery, 123, 184, 198, 199, 200; Liverpool potters influenced by Chinese imports, 184; soft-paste